T0226244

Lecture Notes in Computer Science   11001

Commenced Publication in 1973
Founding and Former Series Editors:
Gerhard Goos, Juris Hartmanis, and Jan van Leeuwen

More information about this series at http://www.springer.com/series/7409

Armanda Rodrigues · Benjamim Fonseca
Nuno Preguiça (Eds.)

Collaboration and Technology

24th International Conference, CRIWG 2018
Costa de Caparica, Portugal, September 5–7, 2018
Proceedings

 Springer

Editors
Armanda Rodrigues ⓘ
Department of Computer Science,
  Faculty of Science and Technology
Universidade NOVA de Lisboa
Caparica
Portugal

Nuno Preguiça ⓘ
Department of Computer Science,
  Faculty of Science and Technology
Universidade NOVA de Lisboa
Caparica
Portugal

Benjamim Fonseca ⓘ
Universidade de Trás-os-Montes
  e Alto Douro
Vila Real
Portugal

ISSN 0302-9743   ISSN 1611-3349   (electronic)
Lecture Notes in Computer Science
ISBN 978-3-319-99503-8   ISBN 978-3-319-99504-5   (eBook)
https://doi.org/10.1007/978-3-319-99504-5

Library of Congress Control Number: 2018951639

LNCS Sublibrary: SL3 – Information Systems and Applications, incl. Internet/Web, and HCI

This Springer imprint is published by the registered company Springer Nature Switzerland AG
The registered company address is: Gewerbestrasse 11, 6330 Cham, Switzerland

Preface

This volume contains the papers presented at the 24th International Conference on Collaboration Technologies, CRIWG 2018. The conference was held during September 5–7, 2018, in Costa da Caparica, Portugal. The conference is supported and governed by the Collaborative Research International Working Group (CRIWG), an open community of collaboration technology researchers. Since 1995, conferences supported by CRIWG have focused on collaboration technology design, development, and evaluation. The background research is influenced by a number of disciplines, such as computer science, management science, information systems, engineering, psychology, cognitive sciences, and social sciences.

This year, CRIWG received 32 submissions, which were carefully reviewed by Program Committee members. Each submission has received between three and four reviews. In all, these proceedings include 11 submissions that were selected as full papers and six that were selected as work in progress. The selected submissions present relevant and interesting research works in different stages of development. We believe their presentation at the conference led to interesting discussions and they will foster future research works.

The papers published in the proceedings span different areas of collaborative computing research, from collaborative learning to collaboration through social media and virtual communities. The CRIWG 2018 papers were evenly balanced between Europe and America (mainly Latin America): eight papers with authors from Europe and six from America, including collaborations between Brazil and the USA and between Brazil and Portugal. There was also a substantial contribution from Asia, with five papers. More specifically, this year, there was a strong participation from Portugal, Brazil, and Japan (each country with four papers). The remaining papers are individual contributions from Chile, Denmark, France, Germany, Ireland, Mexico, and Thailand.

As editors, we would like to thank the authors of all CRIWG 2018 submissions, and particularly to those whose papers were accepted. Moreover, we thank the Keynotes, Dr. Claudia-Lavinia Ignat and Prof. Volker Wulf, who were kind enough to provide very excellent presentations of their very relevant work. We also want to thank the Steering Committee for the opportunity to organize the conference and all the help provided during this process, and to the members of the Program Committee for carefully reviewing the submissions. Last but not least, we would like to acknowledge the effort of the organizers of the conference. Our thanks also go to Springer, the publisher of the CRIWG proceedings, for their continuous support.

September 2018

Armanda Rodrigues
Benjamim Fonseca
Nuno Preguiça

Organization

Program Committee

Nikolaos Avouris	University of Patras, Greece
Marcos R. S. Borges	Federal University of Rio de Janeiro, Brazil
Ivica Boticki	FER UNIZG, Croatia
Luis Carriço	Universidade de Lisboa, Portugal
Cesar A. Collazos	Universidad del Cauca, Colombia
Raymundo Cornejo	CONACYT-UACH, Mexico
Gj De Vreede	University of South Florida, USA
Yannis Dimitriadis	University of Valladolid, Spain
Orlando Erazo	Universidad Técnica Estatal de Quevedo, Ecuador
Micaela Esteves	IPLeiria, Portugal
Jesus Favela	CICESE, Mexico
Mikhail Fominykh	Independent, Norway
Benjamim Fonseca	UTAD/INESC TEC, Portugal
Kimberly García	Siemens, USA
Marco Gerosa	Northern Arizona University, USA
Ramiro Gonçalves	INESC TEC and Universidade de Trás-os-Montes e Alto Douro, Portugal
Cédric Grueau	Polytechnic Institute of Setúbal, Portugal
Francisco J. Gutierrez	University of Chile, Chile
Joerg Haake	FernUniversität in Hagen, Germany
Valeria Herskovic	Pontificia Universidad Católica de Chile, Chile
Ramon Hervas	Universidad de Castilla La Mancha, Spain
Ulrich Hoppe	University Duisburg-Essen, Germany
Gwo-Jen Hwang	National Taiwan University of Science and Technology, Taiwan
Claudia-Lavinia Ignat	Inria, France
Tomoo Inoue	University of Tsukuba, Japan
Seiji Isotani	University of São Paulo, Brazil
Marc Jansen	University of Applied Sciences Ruhr West, Germany
Ralf Klamma	RWTH Aachen University, Germany
Michael Koch	Bundeswehr University Munich, Germany
Tun Lu	Fudan University, China
Stephan Lukosch	Delft University of Technology, The Netherlands
Wolfram Luther	University of Duisburg-Essen, Germany
José Martins	Universidade de Trás-os-Montes e Alto Douro, Portugal
Alejandra Martínez	Universidad de Valladolid, Spain
Sonia Mendoza	CINVESTAV-IPN, Mexico
Roc Meseguer	Universitat Politècnica de Catalunya, Spain

Contents

Findings When Converting a Summative Evaluation Instrument to a Formative One Through Collaborative Learning Activities

Gustavo Zurita[1], Nelson Baloian[2(⊠)], Oscar Jerez[3], Sergio Peñafiel[2], and José A. Pino[2]

[1] Department of Information Systems and Management Control,
Faculty of Economics and Business, Universidad de Chile,
Diagonal Paraguay 257, Santiago, Chile
gzurita@fen.uchile.cl

[2] Department of Computer Science, Universidad de Chile,
Beaucheff 851, Santiago, Chile
{nbaloian, spenafie, jpino}@dcc.uchile.cl

[3] Teaching and Learning Centre, Economics and Business Faculty,
Universidad de Chile, Diagonal Paraguay 257, Santiago, Chile
ojerez@fen.uchile.cl

Abstract. Although illiteracy has been in constant decline over the last decades, there are too many reports about people having problems to identify the main ideas contained in texts they read. Reading comprehension is essential for students, because it is a predictor of their academic or professional success. Researchers have developed computer supported learning activities for supporting students develop their reading comprehension skills with varying degrees of success. One of the various advantages of having students work on electronic documents is that computers can help teachers monitor students' work. One of the problems of these systems is poor usability due to sophisticated human-computer interaction paradigms emulating activities students perform in traditional learning activities for improving reading comprehension with pen and paper. In this paper we report on a research which implements a learning activity based on answers with multiple choice similar to a questionnaire, which is easy to implement in computers and easy to interact with. Although multiple choice questionnaires are associated to summative evaluations, the implemented learning activity uses them within a collaborative learning activity in which students have to justify, first individually then collaboratively, their choice with a short text. The developed system was used and evaluated in a real learning situation; one of the most interesting findings is not only that students who have to justify their option with a text perform better than those who have not, but that the pertinence of the text to the question does not play a major role. This suggests that just asking the students to justify their answers requires them to do a thinking process which otherwise they would not do.

Keywords: Reading comprehension · Collaborative learning
Multiple selection

© Springer Nature Switzerland AG 2018
A. Rodrigues et al. (Eds.): CRIWG 2018, LNCS 11001, pp. 1–16, 2018.
https://doi.org/10.1007/978-3-319-99504-5_1

1 Introduction

During last years, statistics show a constant decline in reading and writing illiteracy in the world, and especially in developing countries. For example, the webpage https://ourworldindata.org/literacy/ contains several charts showing how the illiteracy rate has been falling in many countries in all continents. The trend turns dramatically sharp during the second half of the last century.

However, although more people can read a text, the reports are not so encouraging when it comes to reporting results about the understanding that people achieve about the texts they read in their schools [1]. Also, in developed countries we can see same concern about people understanding the content of what they read. As an example, it has been reported that "far too many American students remain poor readers" [2].

In the past, computer-based systems have been developed to support training of reading comprehension with reported good results. In [3] authors identify the advantages of using computer-assisted systems in educational programs for children as motivating factors [4] and tools for obtaining high level of attention [5]. Computer based systems for supporting the improvement of reading skills are mostly aimed at addressing the learning of strategies which experts have identified as conducive to improve reading comprehension [6]. Some of the most used strategies are to have students read a text trying to determine its main message by means of summaries or keywords, have the students construct alternative representations of the text - such as drawings, conceptual maps, mental images - and answer questions about the text [7].

A previous paper presents work based on the strategy of training the reading comprehension by highlighting the words inside a piece of text which represents the key idea contained in it [8]. However, this experience has shown that the approach of using constructed development responses has its disadvantages, especially when applied to massive courses. In this sense, an activity in which the students could respond through the selection of multiple choices would make the whole process easier, since the evaluation of the correctness of the answers becomes simple. Multiple-choice tests have some advantages [9]. However, they also have criticisms [10] related to the fact that a constructed response is supposed to require more complex skills from the student than a multiple-choice answer, thus allowing a student to perform a more demanding and complete learning activity.

On the other hand, authors of [11, 12] show there is equivalence between constructed responses and multiple choices. The justification for this statement is that for these authors, one way for the student to generate a response in a multiple-choice questionnaire is that the student must first build a response, then verify/check against possible alternative responses, thereby doing a significant learning activity.

In various papers, authors describe experiments in which students answering a multiple-choice questionnaire are asked to justify their decision for various reasons, like detecting false positives (choosing the right answer for a wrong reason) [13] or for stressing the student's reasoning process [14].

In this inquiry, we wanted to explore how the need to justify the answer to a multiple-choice questionnaire affects students' performance. Furthermore, we also wanted to study the quality of the comments provided by them. For these purposes, we designed a learning activity in which students had to read texts and answer a multiple-choice questionnaire where they also had to provide a short text justifying their choice for the right answer. This activity was done in 3 phases: first individually; then again individually but after looking at the answers and the justifying texts provided by their groupmates; and finally, discussing the right choice and justifying text with their groupmates having all members of the group to choose a common option. This learning activity was supported by a technological tool named RedCoMulApp which we developed (described in detail in Sect. 3).

The content of this article is organized as follows. Section 2 explains the relevant theories, methods and techniques used as design requirements for the reading comprehension activity converted to a formative activity. Section 3 presents the design of the reading comprehension activity, along with the description of the RedCoMulApp application. Section 4 describes the preliminary experiments and Sect. 5 concludes the paper.

2 From Multiple Choice to Reading Comprehension Learning Activity

In a previous learning activity, students had to read a text in an electronic document displayed on iPads, and mark the words of the text which represent the key idea contained it [8]. However, this experience has shown that the approach of using constructed development responses has its disadvantages, especially when applied to massive courses. Some of these disadvantages are the following:

- It is difficult for students to develop a response built from mobile computer systems.
- It is time-consuming for the teacher to evaluate answers from all the students.
- It is difficult to monitor the degree of progress of the answers given by the students: (a) how many have already responded, and (b) the correctness of the answers.
- It takes much effort and time for the teacher to give appropriate feedback to all students based on their answers.

There were also problems related to Human-Computer Interaction when students had to "mark" with a virtual pen the words of the text displayed by the iPad. In this sense, an activity in which the students can respond through the selection of multiple choices, would make the whole process easier; since the evaluation of the correctness is simple. In fact, according to [10], the advantages of multiple choice tests are:

- They are easy to apply.
- Their results are trustworthy.
- Because they are standardized, they are applied in the same way to all students.
- They are objective.

We can also add that if we are aiming at implementing a computer-based system, multiple-choice tests are easy to build. However, some authors [9, 10] also express some criticisms:

- It is possible to choose the right answer without real knowledge.
- Typically, students do not receive specific feedback, apart from the general results.
- The evaluator could be a non-expert in the subject and decide to take out questions regardless of pedagogic arguments.

The criticisms are related to the fact that a constructed response is supposed to require students' complex skills. Therefore, a student performs a significant learning activity. However, as mentioned above, [11, 12] show there is equivalence between constructed responses to multiple choices. Marsh et al. [13] argue that in a multiple-choice test students not only have to mark the option she/he considers to be the right one but also to justify it.

There is a common test of student selection for almost all universities in Chile, called PSU. An important part of it consists of reading comprehension, measured by multiple-choice questions. This evaluation is summative, that is, it is meant to measure what the students know. Based on [14], it is possible to convert an activity with summative evaluation into a formative one if the evaluation is used as feedback for the student to reflect on and reformulate their original answers. Moreover, this can be done collaboratively to take advantage of the benefits offered by Collaborative Learning (CL) not only in the academic but also in the social and psychological realms [15]:

Social benefits:

- CL helps to develop a social support system for learners;
- CL leads to build diversity understanding among students and staff;
- CL establishes a positive atmosphere for modelling and practicing cooperation; and
- CL develops learning communities.

Psychological benefits:

- Student-centered instruction increases students' self-esteem;
- Cooperation reduces anxiety; and
- CL develops positive attitudes towards teachers.

Academic benefits:

- CL Promotes critical thinking skills;
- CL involves students actively in the learning process;
- Classroom results are improved;
- CL models appropriate student problem solving techniques;
- Large lectures can be personalized; and
- CL is especially helpful in motivating students in specific curricula.

Multiple-choice tests are mainly used for summative evaluations, since often the feedback the student receives is the number of correct answers only and not the explanations. In this inquiry we modified multiple-choice tests to include both aspects mentioned above, namely collaboration and justification of the right option. In particular, we modified the PSU summative evaluation in order to make it a formative evaluation instrument.

2.1 Reading Comprehension

Students who use reading comprehension strategies (such as prediction, think-aloud, text structure, visual representation of text, key words selection, etc.), improve their understanding of the message, identify the essential and relevant parts of it, and/or are able to express opinions or comments [16]. Accordingly, the design of the Red-CoMulApp application has the following features:

(1) Use the advantages of **short messages** (microblogging).
(2) Implement **real-time monitoring** to manage the follow-up of the elementary stages.
(3) Implement **collaborative learning** with groups of 2 to 5 students who will work together to answer the multiple choices questionnaire.

In an educational context, **short messages** (microblogging, or tweets) can be used to express ideas, paraphrase or criticize a concept [17]. Short messages provide support for students' collaborative work, since they allow posing questions, share ideas and state answers.

One of the main contributions of software applications as a scaffolding for learning activities is the **real-time monitoring** that the teacher can have on the level of progress and achievement of her students, allowing her to act as a catalyst to produce changes in the educational activity or in pedagogy [18].

Nowadays, university leaders are recognizing the need for **collaborative learning** inside the classroom, to increase student success [19]. The goal of collaborative learning techniques is to support learning for a specific educational objective through a coordinated and shared activity, by means of social interactions among the group members [20, 27]. Research has shown that proper design of collaborative learning tasks can improve motivation levels, ease communication and social interaction [21, 28], support coordination and increase the level of students' learning achievement [22, 23], and support face-to-face work using mobile devices [21, 24, 25].

3 Design of the Reading Comprehension Activity: RedCoMulApp

This section describes the design of the RedCoMulApp collaborative application to support reading comprehension, which can be used under two roles: teacher (Sect. 3.1) and student (Sect. 3.2).

3.1   Teacher's Role

The teacher's role allows creating the learning activity, and a real-time monitoring of the task development. This monitoring allows the teacher to review the progress of the learning activity that students are performing during "Individual", "Anonymous" and "Team Work" phases (phases are presented in the second line of the main window in Fig. 1).

For the **creating of the learning activity**, a teacher performs the following actions using the "Editor" option of the RedCoMulApp (see this option at the top of Fig. 1):

- Input the title of the activity and writing a text specifying the general instructions.
- Upload a text used as a context for the multiple-choice questions.
- Introduce the multiple-choice questions with their corresponding right answers.
- Using the "Users" option, a teacher assigns the students to the activity.
- With the "Groups" option, the teacher assigns the task to work teams, each one composed of two or three students.

For the **real-time monitoring of the task development,** the teacher has access to relevant information during the execution of the learning activity in order to review the progress of the students in each phase by using the "Dashboard" option. For instance, the teacher can know in the "Individual" phase, how many students have chosen the right answers (see the bar diagrams of Fig. 2); or in the "Team work" phase how many work teams have already completed all multiple-choice questions (Fig. 3). The information presented to the teacher will be shown in simple graphic interfaces, such as comparative tables or matrices, bar charts, etc. (Figs. 2 and 3), that are used by the teacher to decide whether to move to the next phase or wait for a significant number of students to complete the current activity stage. In addition, this information allows the teacher to identify the students' level of achievement in each phase, according to answers correctly chosen by the students. For example, if less than 1/3 of the students have successfully completed to answer their questions during the "Individual" phase, then the teacher may proceed to intervene the class, offering feedback to explain the questions, explain the context of the texts, etc. Monitoring and then intervening a face-to-face class can be very effective [29].

Using the "Configuration", "Individual", "Anonymous" and "Team Work" options, the teacher manages the development of the application. In the initial phase of "Configuration", the teacher can create the learning activity.

Then, when the teacher selects the "Go to Next" option (Fig. 1), the phase changes to "Individual", which is when the students receive the text to be read and the questions to answer on an individual basis. Once all the students have finished responding, with the "Go to Next" option the teacher changes the task from "Individual" to "Anonymous"; where the students answer the same questions again but having anonymous access to the answers from two of their classmates (Fig. 4), according to the groups defined with the "Groups" option. Then, the teacher changes phase to "Team Work"

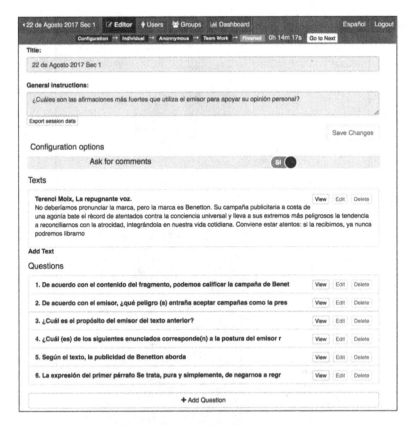

Fig. 1. View of the interface for the teacher's role, showing title of the activity, instructions, the text and the multiple-choice questions with their answers. The task is assigned to the students with the "Users" option. The "Groups" option is used to configure the groups. The teacher monitors the activity using the "Dashboard" option (Fig. 2). The second line shows the phases of the activity. The current one is highlighted in yellow: "Finished". The "Go to Next" option advances from one phase to the following one. (Color figure online)

with the "Go to Next" option. At this stage students meet face-to-face and they answer together the same multiple-choice questions, having access to the answers previously given during the "Individual" and "Anonymous" phases. The students exchange opinions in order to agree on a single answer.

In each of the "Individual", "Anonymous" and "Team Work" phases, the teacher can monitor and manage the activity and performance of students in real time through the "Dashboard" option (Figs. 2 and 3).

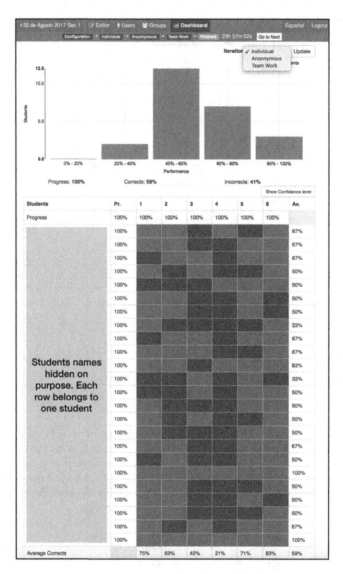

Fig. 2. A view of the monitoring tool showing the performance of the students with the correct answers (green) and the wrong answers (red). This is from an activity performed by 22 students, Sect. 1. The results are of the "Individual" phase, where students got an achievement of 40%–60%. Although this view shows that the RedCoMulApp has finished (status "Finished" in the label), it is possible for the teacher to access the students' performance, since the view is with "Dashboard" option activated, and has chosen the "Individual" phase. (Color figure online)

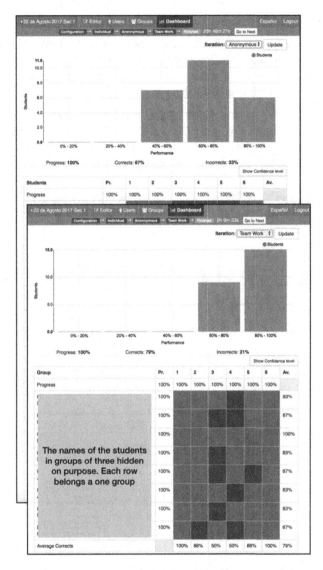

Fig. 3. Two views of the monitoring tool showing the performance of the students with the correct answers (green) and the wrong answers (red) for "Anonymous" (top view partially covered) and "Team Work" (superimposed bottom view) phases. This capture is from an activity performed by 42 students. The views show the activity has finished. The upper view are the results corresponding to the "Anonymous" stage and the third one to the "Team Work" phase. There is an increase in the students' performance from phase to phase, reaching from 40%–60% and 60%–80% in the "Individual" phase (Fig. 2), 60%–80% in the "Anonymous" phase to 60%–80% and 80%–100% of correct answers in the "Team Work" phase. (Color figure online)

3.2   Stages in the Learning Activity – Student's Role

This section describes the "Individual", "Anonymous" and "Team Work" phases which students should go through with RedCoMulApp in order to accomplish the reading comprehension learning activity in that order. As mentioned above, the teacher decides the moment when to move from one phase to the next one.

"Individual" Phase. At this stage, each student individually reads the text provided by the teacher (left hand side view of Fig. 4). As each student answers the questions, the teacher can see the answers (in green if correct, and in red if it is incorrect) in real time in RedCoMulApp using the "Dashboard", as seen in the left hand side view of Fig. 2.

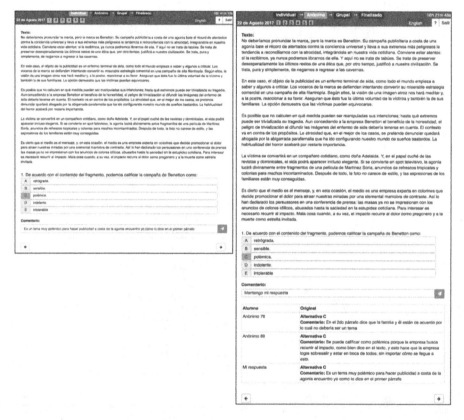

Fig. 4. Two views of the of RedCoMulApp interface in the student's role from a session called "August 22, 2017". At the left, the status in "Individual" phase is highlighted. In the following line labels with numbers 1 to 6 correspond to the six multiple-choice questions of this session. They change color as they are answered. The text to be read is shown in the middle, followed by the first of the 6 questions, along with 5 response options labeled with letters A, B, C, D and E. In this case, the student has selected option C, and in the line below has written a brief justification for his answer. The view on the right corresponds to the "Anonymous" phase, which contains the response of the same student from the view on the left, together with the answers and justifications of his colleagues from whom he receives this information anonymously. (Color figure online)

"Anonymous" Phase. At this stage, students do the same as in the previous stage (reading the text and answering the multiple-choice questions) with the difference that they can see the answers of the other two students of their groups without knowing who they are (see the view on Fig. 4 at the right). Students have then to confirm their previous answer or change them based on what their groupmates have answered.

"Team Work" Phase. At this stage, students see the names of their groupmates and they meet face-to-face to choose a single option together. They can talk to each other, exchange opinions and discuss their disagreements. All students of the group have to select the same option as answer; otherwise, they receive a message from the system to do so.

4   Evaluation of the Reading Comprehension Learning Activity

Subjects and Settings: The evaluation took place at the Faculty of Economics and Business of the University of Chile, with 12th grade students from nine Santiago mid-income high schools, from July to October, 2017 (6 sessions in total, 90 min each). There were 46 students in total, divided in two sections, 22 in the control section and 24 in the experimental section. At the end we used the information associated with 42 students (20 in the control section, 22 in the experimental section) since some of them did not participate in all sessions. Students' age ranged between 15 and 16 years old.

Procedure: In each session, the students worked in a regular classroom during the language class time. During the first session, the teacher gave 5-min basic instructions about the collaborative activity to both control and experimental sections. Students performed a first test activity for 15 min in order to learn how to use the application. This activity consisted in reading a simple short text and answering three questions. After this preparation, students performed the proper activity (intervention), which was recorded by the teacher and three teaching assistants. Each section had six sessions in total.

Activity Description: The activity was designed according to the goals in reading comprehension for students of 12th grade defined by the language area of the Chilean Ministry of Education. Before starting the activity, the teacher explained the methods and techniques of text reading comprehension. Later, during the experimental sessions, students received a 800–900 words text that they had to read and then answer a multiple-choice questionnaire in order to evaluate their level of comprehension of the text they read. In each of the next five sessions, they received a new text to read. The six chosen texts were extracted from the curricular content of the Chilean Ministry of Education along with the corresponding multiple-choice questions. Text and questionnaire were the same for both sections in each session.

In each session, the activity started providing the students with iPads having network access to the RedCoMulApp application, on which they had to log in with their personal account and password. Then, the teacher started the activity on an iPad, activating the "Individual" phase for approximately 20 min, where students individually accessed and read the text. After that, they answered 12–14 associated multiple-choice questions. Once all the students finished this phase, they continued to the "Anonymous" phase for nearly 30 min, where again each student accessed individually the text to answer the same multiple-choice questions as before but having access to the answers of their two groupmates. At this stage, students could confirm their previously selected options or change their answers. Finally, in the "Team Work" phase, which lasted approximately 30 min, the students received from RedCoMulApp the names of their colleagues who in the previous phase saw their answers, and with whom they now meet face to face to answer as a group the same multiple-choice questions. In this phase, students are expected to talk to each other, exchange opinions, and discuss and sort out their disagreements in order to have a group answer.

Both sections (control and experimental) had to perform exactly the same activity except for the experimental section, whose students had to input a short text with an argument justifying the chosen option; the control section did not have to enter any justification.

Results. Comparing the performance in terms of correct answers given by the students who had to justify their answers with a short text (experimental section) with those of the control section, we can see that the difference is statistically significant at 0.000 as shown in Table 1 in favor of the experimental section. This means that students who justified the selection of the option obtained better results.

Moreover, when comparing the correct answers grouped by phase ("Individual", "Anonymous" and "Team Work") the difference is also statistically significant at 0.000 in all cases as shown in Table 1. This implies that when having to justify the given answer during the "Individual" stage the experimental section student had to think more the comprehension of the text than the typical student of the control section. This further work resulted in better answers.

On the other hand, during the "Anonymous", stage the justification text helped the students understand more accurately the selection of answers from their groupmates, with whom they had not talked yet. Finally, during the "Team Work" stage the collaborative work with their groupmates, from whom they already knew their justifications enriched even more their own decision when selecting the right answer.

We also analyzed the quality of the justification given by the students of the experimental section; that is, the degree to which they related the arguments written in relation to whether it covers all the dimensions required for the selection of their answers, whether correct or incorrect. For this analysis, we rated the quality of the justifications to support the selected answers in all 6 sessions, and in all the stages "Individual", "Anonymous" and "Team Work" of the experimental section.

The justification was rated in one of three categories (see Table 2): (a) **Insufficient:** It fails to cover any of the dimensions or elements of the response or choice made, or simply, there was no evidence of coherence between the central idea and the given answer. (b) **Partially Sufficient:** It covers some elements or dimensions of the response or choice made. It is on the right track, but it does not give an adequate justification involving the given answer. (c) **Sufficient:** The given justification is good enough to justify the selected answers. They are in total coherence and can give relevant arguments for their selection.

Table 1. Description of the results, comparison between answers without and with justifications.

Descriptive statistics			
Justifications	*Answers*	*Frequency*	*Valid percentage*
Without justifications (Control section)	Incorrect	781	45.2
	Correct	946	**54.8**
	Total	1,727	100.0
With justifications (Experimental section)	Incorrect	597	32.7
	Correct	1,226	**67.3**
	Total	1,823	100.0

Comparative statistics	
Contrast statistics	*Value for the correct answers figure*
U of Mann-Whitney	2755577.000
W of Wilcoxon	8722362.000
Z	−8.763
Sig. asintot. (bilateral)	**.000**

Comparison of correct answers between control and experimental grouped by phases		
Phase	*Contrast statistics*	*Correct answers*
"Individual"	U of Mann-Whitney	418677.000
	W of Wilcoxon	1389598.000
	Z	−7.248
	Sig. asymptote (bilateral)	**.000**
"Anonymous"	U of Mann-Whitney	206804.000
	W of Wilcoxon	452154.000
	Z	−5.360
	Sig. asymptote (bilateral)	**.000**
"Team Work"	U of Mann-Whitney	255944.500
	W of Wilcoxon	1182785.500
	Z	−3.541
	Sig. asymptote (bilateral)	**.000**

Table 2. Classification of quality of the justifications written by the students of the experimental section in all stages. It is important to note that the number of comments will not match the total of justified answers, because only non-repeated justifications are taken into account, since several were re-used and others were new in subsequent stages such as the "Anonymous" and "Team Work"

Session	#comments	Insufficient	Partially sufficient	Sufficient
1	592	93%	4%	3%
2	397	89%	6%	5%
3	433	88%	9%	3%
4	405	90%	7%	3%
5	449	83%	13%	4%
6	265	86%	10%	4%

Given the results shown in Table 2, we can conclude that the justifications written by the students do not sustain (or are insufficient) for building an argument justifying the decision made when selecting an option. However, it seems the intent of doing it positively influenced the selection made.

5   Conclusions

The results of the experiment confirmed that the learning activity supported by Red-CoMulApp presented in this paper effectively supports the improvement of the students' reading comprehension. Its design was based on converting a summative evaluation learning activity into a formative one using a mechanism which is easy to implement and use.

We can infer that students' performance is positively influenced by their comments production, regardless of their quality. It seems that the cognitive effort of trying to make a statement makes the students choose better answers than those who do not have to produce comments. Will they spend more time thinking on the answers? Will they use upper level cognitive processes? Nevertheless, we did not observe a correlation between the cognitive process of generating short texts and the quality of these texts. The existing positive correlation is between the cognitive process and the text generation process.

It is interesting to observe answers such as "I believe…", or "I think…", or "In my opinion…". These statements seem to validate the widespread existence of the post truth; i.e., the validity of just saying something or based on "my opinion" as a foundation for decisions. The new pedagogic scenario should take into account this post truth belief in which "my opinion" really matters and creates a reality [26].

Another observation is that the apparent widespread availability of "emojis" is introducing a new way of communication, which is not understandable by the traditional analysis of text production.

Thanks to the new technologies, especially mobile devices, people are writing many more characters today than in the past. We can imagine the number of characters a person daily writes for communicating through Whatsapp, Facebook and other social network applications is large by observing them in everyday life. However, we cannot guarantee that people are writing better than in the past. Results obtained in this work tend to show the contrary. Perhaps, a new communication paradigm is emerging, which is worth to study.

Acknowledgements. This paper was funded by Fondecyt 1161200.

References

1. Mullis, I.V., Martin, M.O., Foy, P., Drucker, K.T.: PIRLS 2011 International Results in Reading. ERIC (2012)
2. Slavin, R.E., Cheung, A., Groff, C., Lake, C.: Effective reading programs for middle and high schools: a best-evidence synthesis. Read. Res. Q. **43**(3), 290–322 (2008)

3. Rosas, R., Escobar, J.P., Ramírez, M.P., Meneses, A., Guajardo, A.: Impact of a computer-based intervention in Chilean children at risk of manifesting reading difficulties/Impacto de una intervención basada en ordenador en niños chilenos con riesgo de manifestar dificultades lectoras. Infancia y Aprendizaje **40**(1), 158–188 (2017)
4. Wild, M.: Using computer-aided instruction to support the systematic practice of phonological skills in beginning readers. J. Res. Read. **32**(4), 413–432 (2009)
5. Karemaker, A.M., Pitchford, N.J., O'Malley, C.: Does whole-word multimedia software support literacy acquisition? Read. Writ. **23**(1), 31–51 (2010)
6. Dole, J.A., Duffy, G.G., Roehler, L.R., Pearson, P.D.: Moving from the old to the new: research on reading comprehension instruction. Rev. Educ. Res. **61**(2), 239–264 (1991)
7. Sung, Y.-T., Chang, K.-E., Huang, J.-S.: Improving children's reading comprehension and use of strategies through computer-based strategy training. Comput. Hum. Behav. **24**(4), 1552–1571 (2008)
8. Zurita, G., Baloian, N., Jerez, O., Peñafiel, S.: Practice of skills for reading comprehension in large classrooms by using a mobile collaborative support and microblogging. In: Gutwin, C., Ochoa, S.F., Vassileva, J., Inoue, T. (eds.) CRIWG 2017. LNCS, vol. 10391, pp. 81–94. Springer, Cham (2017). https://doi.org/10.1007/978-3-319-63874-4_7
9. Gunderman, R.B., Ladowski, J.M.: Inherent limitations of multiple-choice testing. Acad. Radiol. **20**(10), 1319–1321 (2013)
10. Park, J.: Constructive multiple-choice testing system. Br. J. Educ. Technol. **41**(6), 1054–1064 (2010)
11. Rodriguez, M.C.: Construct equivalence of multiple-choice and constructed-response items: a random effects synthesis of correlations. J. Educ. Meas. **40**(2), 163–184 (2003)
12. Bennett, R.E., Rock, D.A., Wang, M.: Equivalence of free-response and multiple-choice items. J. Educ. Meas. **28**(1), 77–92 (1991)
13. Marsh, E.J., Lozito, J.P., Umanath, S., Bjork, E.L., Bjork, R.A.: Using verification feedback to correct errors made on a multiple-choice test. Memory **20**(6), 645–653 (2012)
14. Tamir, P.: Some issues related to the use of justifications to multiple-choice answers. J. Biol. Educ. **23**(4), 285–292 (1989)
15. Laal, M., Ghodsi, S.M.: Benefits of collaborative learning. Procedia-Soc. Behav. Sci. **31**, 486–490 (2012)
16. Duke, N.K., Pearson, P.D.: Effective practices for developing reading comprehension. J. Educ. **189**(1/2), 107–122 (2008)
17. Prestridge, S.: A focus on students' use of Twitter–their interactions with each other, content and interface. Act. Learn. High. Educ. **15**(2), 101–115 (2014)
18. Dufresne, R.J., Gerace, W.J., Leonard, W.J., Mestre, J.P., Wenk, L.: Classtalk: a classroom communication system for active learning. J. Comput. High. Educ. **7**(2), 3–47 (1996)
19. Adams Becker, S., Cummins, M., Davis, A., Freeman, A., Hall Giesinger, C., Ananthanarayanan, V.: NMC Horizon Report: 2017, Higher Education Edition (eds.). The New Media Consortium, Austin (2017)
20. Zurita, G., Nussbaum, M.: Computer supported collaborative learning using wirelessly interconnected handheld computers. Comput. Educ. **42**(3), 289–314 (2004)
21. Baloian, N., Zurita, G.: MC-supporter: flexible mobile computing supporting learning though social interactions. J. UCS **15**(9), 1833–1851 (2009)
22. Blasco-Arcas, L., Buil, I., Hernández-Ortega, B., Sese, F.J.: Using clickers in class. The role of interactivity, active collaborative learning and engagement in learning performance. Comput. Educ. **62**, 102–110 (2013)
23. Carpenter, J.P.: Twitter's capacity to support collaborative learning. Int. J. Soc. Media Interact. Learn. Environ. **2**(2), 103–118 (2014)

24. Zurita, G., Baloian, N., Baytelman, F.: A face-to-face system for supporting mobile collaborative design using sketches and pen-based gestures. In: 10th International Conference on Computer Supported Cooperative Work in Design, CSCWD 2006. IEEE (2006)
25. Zurita, G., Baloian, N.: Handheld-based electronic meeting support. In: Fukś, H., Lukosch, S., Salgado, A.C. (eds.) CRIWG 2005. LNCS, vol. 3706, pp. 341–350. Springer, Heidelberg (2005). https://doi.org/10.1007/11560296_27
26. Aparici, R., Marín, D.G.: Comunicar y educar en el mundo que viene (in Spanish). GEDISA (2017)
27. Collazos, C., Guerrero, L., Pino, J.A., Ochoa, S., Stahl, G.: Designing collaborative learning environments using digital games. J. Univers. Comput. Sci. **13**(7), 1022–1032 (2007)
28. Gallardo, T., Guerrero, L., Collazos, C., Pino, J.A., Ochoa, S.: Supporting JIGSAW-type collaborative learning. In: 36th Hawaii International Conference on System Sciences (HICSS 2003). IEEE Press (2003)
29. Baloian, N., Pino, Jose A., Hardings, J., Hoppe, H.U.: Monitoring student activities with a querying system over electronic worksheets. In: Baloian, N., Burstein, F., Ogata, H., Santoro, F., Zurita, G. (eds.) CRIWG 2014. LNCS, vol. 8658, pp. 38–52. Springer, Cham (2014). https://doi.org/10.1007/978-3-319-10166-8_4

Collaborative Learning Environment in Higher Education: A Case Study

Micaela Esteves[1(✉)], Rosa Matias[1], and Angela Pereira[2]

[1] CIIC - Computer Science and Communication Research - ESTG,
Polytechnic Institute of Leiria, Leiria, Portugal
{micaela.dinis,rosa.matias}@ipleiria.pt
[2] CiTUR - Tourism Applied Research Centre - ESTM,
Polytechnic Institute of Leiria, Leiria, Portugal
angela.pereira@ipleiria.pt

Abstract. This article seeks to present a case study regarding collaborative learning (CL) in a higher education environment. CL is an approach of teaching and learning where students at a various performance levels work together in small groups with the aim to solve a problem. With CL students developing not only higher-level thinking skills, but also enhancing the soft skills, such as oral communication, social interaction, among others. Currently, the labour market demands professionals with transversal abilities. In this context, the Polytechnic Institute of Leiria changed the curriculum of Web and Multimedia Development (DWM) technological course to create a collaborative learning environment. The process stated on the 2017/2018 scholar year. The results show that students working in a collaborative environment are more motivated and committed. Furthermore, the importance of real projects and the contact with clients were highlighted during the study.

Keywords: Collaborative learning environment · Higher education
Problem-solving · Transversal skills

1 Introduction

Nowadays, the labour market demands professionals with solid knowledge, generally called technical skills, but also with transversal abilities namely soft skills. Examples of soft skills are thinking and working together on critical issues, to communicate and express technical topics in an understandable way [10]. Higher Education System must help students to accomplish those kinds of skills and to prepare them to active citizenship and for lifelong learning, so they can be successful in their future careers. Furthermore, since the Bologna process the students' rates in the higher education increased, and inevitably the students' population became more diversified. This diversity brought great challenges to teachers, who had to adapt teaching methods to students with different characteristics and backgrounds.

Collaborative Learning (CL) is an educational approach that has many benefits like developing higher level thinking skills, developing oral communication, social interaction and enhancing self-management skills, as well as developing mutual responsibility

A. Rodrigues et al. (Eds.): CRIWG 2018, LNCS 11001, pp. 17–24, 2018.
https://doi.org/10.1007/978-3-319-99504-5_2

[8]. In CL, students work in small groups with the aim to solve a problem. Collaborating in problem-solving provides, through an appropriate activity, reflection, a mechanism that enhances the learning process. Students that work in groups need to communicate, argue and give opinions which leads to a more reflective behaviour and an easier learning [1].

In this context, the Polytechnic Institute of Leiria changed the curriculum of Web and Multimedia Development (DWM) technological course to create a collaborative learning environment. DWM is a course which targets the development of static and dynamic web applications as well as multimedia contents such as images and video. The main curriculum was adjusted with the introduction of a project subject in each semester where students work in groups of five to six elements, collaborating with each other to solve an open-ended problem.

Our goal is to proportionate an environment in which students with different backgrounds can discuss ideas and help each other, so they can deeply understand the theoretical subjects and its practical application. On the other hand, this adjustment pretends to increase the students' motivation, their engagement and consequently reduce the dropout rates and improve the scores.

In this research was used a Case Study methodology which enables the researchers to collect and analyze data within this specific context. The data were obtained by the researchers through written narratives, after the project was concluded. Along the process, interviews were made to students and teachers.

The aim of this paper is to present a case study concerning the use of collaborative learning methodology in context of Portuguese Higher Education. Furthermore, the challenges for teachers and students are argued, also the main results are discussed and is taken into account the considerations of the literature review. The Case Study was implemented in the 2017/2018 school year, in the 1st semester of the course DWM, and adjusted in the 2nd semester. This paper also describes the collaborative learning environment process developed in the 1st semester, identifies the 1st semester problems and the transformations performed in the 2nd semester to overcome them.

In the next section of this paper the motivations for this work are described. Then the related work is outlined, and the project methodology is described. Finally, we present the results of our work and the work plan we will follow aiming to increase the learning effectiveness and students' motivation.

2   Related Work and Motivation

One of the most important skills that today students must have are the transversal ones. Transversal skills are a broad set of knowledge that will prepare individuals to be successful in future career [4]. According to Union European [3], transversal skills also namely soft skills, cover the follow domains: ability to think critically, take initiative, solve problems and work collaboratively.

Current labour market demands that workers develop the skills to connect efficiently with others. High levels of interpersonal skills are necessary since most of enterprises develop work into multiple disciplinary teams, many of them are in different places around the world, in this case they work virtually. All these situations require that individuals understand the rules of interacting with co-workers [2].

To accomplish the employment demands, schools in general and universities, in particular, must promote not only technical skills but also soft skills to prepare all students for life after higher education. Nowadays, the classroom time is mostly spent in a narrow curriculum, where learners are prepared to perform tests, which reduces the time they should spent in learning social skills.

A widespread of students enter in higher education, however about one-third of them will not obtain a degree and most of withdrawals have been found to happen during the first year [4]. The transition into higher education is a hard process for many students. The massification of education since Bologna brings students with different profiles, most of them are uncommitted, are not being driven by curiosity in a particular subject and do not have ambitions to excel in a particular profession, but they want to be qualified for a different job.

CL is a strong educational approach to teaching and learning that involves groups of learners working together to solve a problem, complete a task, or create a product [5, 6, 9]. In a CL setting, learners discuss ideas, exchange opinions and enquire the solutions [7]. It is a student-centred approach which substitutes the traditional teacher-centred approach.

Laal and Ghodsi [5] summarized the benefits of CL into four large areas which are social, psychological, academic and assessment. Social, a community environment is provided to learners where they collaborate with each other by tutors' supervision with the aim to provide a positive atmosphere. Physiological, a cooperation environment benefits students' positive attitudes and self-esteem. Academical, improves students' critical thinking by involving them in the learning process. Finally, introduces new ways of assessment.

In addition, Laal and Ghodsi refers that Collaboration is an interaction philosophy where everyone is responsible for their actions, including learning, respect for each other abilities and contribute for their peers learning [5]. In this context, students are invited to evaluate their contribution to the groups success or failure [8].

These results influenced some of the opinions the research have had when thinking about using a collaborative learning environment for learning.

3 Methodology

In this study it was used a qualitative methodology in which the data collected was obtained by the researchers through direct observation in the field and through written narratives. Also, teachers were interviewed with the aim to know their own opinions, experiences and to identify difficulties. Moreover, students were also interviewed to know their opinions, the perceptions of their engagement in the course and to identify areas for further development.

3.1   1st Semester Design

In the first year, entered in the course DWM forty-seven students which were divided in two practical laboratory classes: practical laboratory 1 (PL1) and practical laboratory 2 (PL2) with, respectively, twenty-six students in the first and twenty-one students in the second. One student with disabilities attended PL2, requiring differentiated treatment and some careful in his integration in class, specially in the group.

The students were assigned to groups in the first class. As students did not know each other, neither teachers, the groups were randomly organized by them. This resulted in nine groups of five to six elements. PL1 had one group with six elements and three groups with five elements and PL2 had one group with six elements and four groups with five elements. Each group had two tutors, a graphical designer and a computer science. The project consist of six hours per week and students were supervised by their tutors. Students in class collaborated with each other, discussing ideas with tutors' guidance.

In the first class of the 1st semester, it was presented to students the project outline, clear enough but without any consideration about the possible solution. Each group should provide its own solution enhancing creativity. The project had three milestones with delivers and public discussions, and a final discussion/presentation at the end of the semester.

In this semester was only done academical projects that consisted in the development of static web sites using technologies such as HTML, JavaScript and CSS.

The assessment resulted in individual performance at the final presentation/discussion. Students peer assessment were done but this was mainly indicative for teachers.

To minimize the students' impact from high to higher education they had once a month a Psychologist support.

1st Semester Results

Although the project development was in a collaborative environment, some faults were observed.

Inside the groups there were a lot of disagreement along the project development and despite the tutors help these problems were not overcome. Consequently, six students drop out and five did not have approved. At the end of the 1st semester it was done an interview to students. Their feedback indicates some disappointment about the project development, namely, the lack of agreement between pairs, the lack of teacher intervention, in this situation. Students also mentioned that they felt demotivated and angry with results. Only one group liked the project and the way they worked together. This group struggled the fact the leader was very important to assign tasks and motivate them to work. All other groups did not have a leader despite the tutors' indications.

In present of these results the researchers decide to change completely the way the project classes work in the 2nd semester. The priorities were groups formation, project context, classroom and project scope.

3.2   2nd Semester Design

The students' distribution by groups were made with a Psychologist help and resulted in eighteen students in PL1, three group with six elements and twenty-two students in PL2, two groups with six elements and two groups with five elements.

In this semester was created an enterprise simulator constituted by a CEO (the teacher responsible for the project subject), a Human Resources department (with the aim to monitor the teams and the way they interact between them), a Design department (responsible for accomplishing the design of all projects) and a Technical department (in charge of the project development with two chiefs, one for each PLs). The students were the employees that worked in groups, with different projects to develop. These groups were distributed by PL1 and PL2 with three groups of six elements in PL1 and two groups of six elements plus two groups of five elements in PL2. All groups had a team leader, and there was a leader in charge of each PL.

Once a month the enterprise direction met to discuss problems inside each group. The enterprise direction is formed by the CEO, the chief of each PL and by two students' leaders from PL1 and PL2.

Four teams were developing projects for local industries. The others were developing academical projects proposed by students but in order to put the project in the market. The project had seven milestones and in each the enterprise direction rewarded the best work.

For teams to work it was prepared a collaborative learning space with an enterprise environment where there was a wall for each team to make the project management (Fig. 1). It was also created a Facebook page where the progress of the company was shown to the community.

Fig. 1. Collaborative learning environment

A student who dropped out in the first semester after speaking with their colleagues decided to return to the course. This was a good signal of the improvement that had been made.

4 Results and Discussion

Our concern throughout the development of this study was to find out what was the best collaborative environment for students learning. The results show that in 2nd semester students were more motivated compared to the 1st semester. From students' interviews, they mention that real problems and regular meetings with the clients were important factors for their learning process. Teachers agreed with students' opinions and considered these important factors for students' motivation and responsibility, leading to their commitment. Consequently, the public recognition of students' work boosted their motivation and proud. These results are in line with the research made by several authors [9, 12, 13], which refer the importance of public recognition to students' motivations.

The problems reported in the 1st semester about the relationships inside groups did not occur in the 2nd semester. Students worked very well as a group team. The reason for this was that elements of groups were more balance. The leadership inside groups contributed to the development of leadership skills, so it was considered important the turnover of leader. This is a transversal skill that every student should put in practice [14]. In this instance, the role of the leader was considered by students very important to assign tasks and verify if everybody perform them.

In the 2nd semester, during the students' presentations, it was observed an improvement of the students' skills such as, a better oral expression and support materials with more quality. Furthermore, students became more active during their colleagues' presentations, making suggestions and detecting small gaps.

The reward in each project milestones had a big impact in students' self-esteem and motivated them to be more productive due to this feeling of pride and achievement. Some of these students had never been acclaimed by anyone along their academic path. Several authors mention the importance of reward for students' motivation and commitment [16, 17].

In the 2nd semester students followed informally an agile software methodology without any kind of theoretical explanation about the method. This was important for project management. The students used post-its in boards with the tasks they were supposed to do and the ones they had done. For these students, it was important to put their hands on and see the results instead of using the software to perform the task itself. Schank, Berman and Macpherson [15] highlighted the importance for students to know how to do things because life requires us to do more than it requires us to know.

The transformation of the classroom to a collaborative learning space was crucial for students to work together, to self-organize their learning and to stimulate brainstorming. By this way, students could generate ideas and come up with creative solutions to solve problems. Harrop and Turpin [11] emphasized the importance of design learning space to promote collaboration and innovation.

The main changes between the 1st and the 2nd semester are summed up in Table 1.

Table 1. Comparing 1st and 2nd semesters

	1st semester	2nd semester
Groups	Without team leader	With team leader
	Groups organized by students	Groups organized with the help of a psychologist
Context	Academic project	Project in real context
	Intermediate presentations	Increase the number of intermediate presentations
	Without rewards	With rewards
	Two tutors by group	Enterprise simulator
Facilities	Classroom	Collaborative learning space
	–	Desk in U shape
	–	Round table
	–	Interactive tables

In teachers' opinions, the students' performance and assessment during the 2nd semester was better. They highlight the students' motivation and the more constructive discussions about their problem solutions. However, besides these positive aspects teachers referred that was important to have more time available to support students work and more teachers in full time work. Since, this type of teaching requires more preparation and more time available.

In general, students' liked learning in a collaborative environment, since they saw a practical application of what they had been learning. Besides, this requires additional efforts that they are not used to. They considered that this methodology will help them in the future career.

5 Conclusions

As teachers we continuous seek for news learning and teaching approaches with the aim to reduce the gap between schools and labour market. Currently, the labour market demands professional with advanced transversal abilities, so educational system must prepare students. With this experience we recommend the use of a collaborative learning environment with enterprises simulators where students work together with the industry and solve real life problems.

In addition, the design of DWM course focused on cross-disciplinary projects development in each semester with the aim to aggregate all the knowledge. Therefore, students benefit from learning by doing in a collaborative environment where they practice their transversal skills.

Our results suggest that students are better prepared for long-life learning and based in our experience in teaching in Higher Education and in the literature review. We believe that the use of this type of methodology can enhance the development of transversal skills that has become a twenty-first-century trend.

References

1. Esteves, M., Morgado, L., Martins, P., Fonseca, B.: The use of Collaborative Virtual Environments to provide student's contextualisation in programming. In: m-ICTE 2006, IV International Conference on Multimedia and Information and Communication Technologies in Education, p. 283 (2006)
2. Riggio, R.E., Tan, S.J. (eds.): Leader Interpersonal and Influence Skills: The Soft Skills of Leadership. Routledge, London (2013)
3. McAleese, M., et al.: Improving the quality of teaching and learning in Europe's higher education institutions. High Level Group on the Modernisation of Higher Education, Report to the European Commission, Luxembourg, pp. 978–992 (2013)
4. OECD: Education at a Glance 2017: OECD Indicators. OECD Publishing, Paris (2017). https://doi.org/10.1787/eag-2017-en
5. Laal, M., Ghodsi, S.: Benefits of collaboration. Soc. Behav. Sci. **31**, 486–490 (2012)
6. Laal, M., Laal, M.: Collaborative learning: what is it? Soc. Behav. Sci. **31**, 491–495 (2012)
7. Srinivas, H.: What is collaborative learning? The Global Development Research Center, Kope, Japan. http://www.gdrc.org/kmgmt/c-learn/index.html. Accessed 21 Apr 2018
8. Laal, M., Naseri, A.S., Laal, M., Khattami-kermanshahi, Z.: What do we achieve from learning in collaboration? Soc. Behav. Sci. **93**, 1427–1432 (2013). (In: 3rd World Conference on Learning, Teaching and Educational Leadership)
9. Esteves, M., Fonseca, B., Morgado, L., Martins, P.: Improving teaching and learning of computer programming through the use of the Second Life virtual world. Br. J. Edu. Technol. **42**(4), 624–637 (2011)
10. Alves, A.C., et al.: Teacher's experiences in PBL: implications for practice. Eur. J. Eng. Educ. **41**(2), 123–141 (2016)
11. Harrop, D., Turpin, B.: A study exploring learners' informal learning space behaviors, attitudes, and preferences. New Rev. Acad. Librariansh. **19**(1), 58–77 (2013)
12. Ames, C.: Classrooms: goals, structures, and student motivation. J. Educ. Psychol. **84**(3), 261 (1992)
13. Linnenbrink, E.A., Pintrich, P.R.: Motivation as an enabler for academic success. Sch. Psychol. Rev. **31**(3), 313 (2002)
14. Brunello, G., Schlotter, M.: Non-cognitive skills and personality traits: labour market relevance and their development in education & training systems (2011)
15. Schank, R.C., Berman, T.R., Macpherson, K.A.: Learning by doing. In: Instructional-Design Theories and Models: A New Paradigm of Instructional Theory, vol. 2, pp. 161–181 (1999)
16. Lopes, D., Esteves, M., Mesquita, C.: Video game interaction and reward mechanisms applied to business applications: a comparative review. In: 2012 7th Iberian Conference on Information Systems and Technologies (CISTI), pp. 1–6. IEEE (2012)
17. Esteves, M., Pereira, A., Veiga, N., Vasco, R., Veiga, A.: The use of new learning technologies in higher education classroom: a case study. In: Auer, M.E., Guralnick, D., Simonics, I. (eds.) ICL 2017. AISC, vol. 715, pp. 499–506. Springer, Cham (2018). https://doi.org/10.1007/978-3-319-73210-7_59

Towards an AUX Evaluation Framework for User Tools in Virtual Communities

Luis Martín Sánchez-Adame[1](✉), Sonia Mendoza[1],
Beatriz A. González-Beltrán[2], Amilcar Meneses Viveros[1], and José Rodríguez[1]

[1] Department of Computer Science, CINVESTAV-IPN,
Av. IPN 2508, Col. San Pedro Zacatenco, Del. Gustavo A. Madero,
07360 Mexico City, Mexico
luismartin.sanchez@cinvestav.mx,
{smendoza,ameneses,rodriguez}@cs.cinvestav.mx
[2] Department of Systems, UAM-Azcapotzalco, Av. San Pablo 180, Col. Reynosa
Tamaulipas, Del. Azcapotzalco, 02200 Mexico City, Mexico
bgonzalez@azc.uam.mx

Abstract. A virtual community is a social group of any size that shares common interests and communicates through the Internet. A user joins a virtual community not only because of its popularity or the quality of its contents, but also owing to the user experience that the platform offers. Anticipated User eXperience (AUX) allows knowing the idealisations, hopes, and desires of the users in a very early stage of any development. Participation is a crucial component in the growth and survival of any virtual community. An essential element for people to participate in a virtual community is that the platform should provide suitable user tools, which are widgets that allow users to interact with their peers. We propose an AUX evaluation framework for user tools, whose intention is to improve their design, and through it, the participation of users.

Keywords: User experience · Anticipated user experience
Virtual communities · Participation · User tools

1 Introduction

Shneiderman et al. [30] present a series of challenges that Human-Computer Interaction researchers must face in the years to come. Those problems are the product of human population growth and all its consequences. One problem states that it is necessary to shift from user experience to community experience. Many research fields (e.g., Sociology, Psychology, and Economics) are advocated the resolution of said problems within communities. However, as this is a broad subject, a multidisciplinary approach seems to be a natural way.

In Computer Sciences, virtual communities, also called online communities or e-communities, are an area of interest. In the scientific literature, we can encounter many definitions of the term "virtual community" [4,8,28,34]. Nevertheless, we chose the one proposed by Lee et al. [19], as we think this expresses

© Springer Nature Switzerland AG 2018
A. Rodrigues et al. (Eds.): CRIWG 2018, LNCS 11001, pp. 25–33, 2018.
https://doi.org/10.1007/978-3-319-99504-5_3

the complexity of virtual communities: "cyberspace(s) supported by computer-based information technology, centred on communication and interaction of participants to generate content, resulting in a relationship being built".

In the design of a prosperous virtual community, usability and sociability are influential factors. Sociability concerns the relationship established among members. Usability refers to how users interact with technology [5,26].

A logical consequence of sociability is participation, an inherent issue of virtual communities. Therefore, there are many studies to comprehend why people participate in a virtual community [13,23,32,37]. Participation is crucial, as the success of a virtual community strongly depends on interaction and cooperation among its users to generate content and contribute to the community [17].

By participating in a virtual community, users interact with businesses, organisations, peers, relatives, and friends to co-create their consumption experience and satisfy their needs [9,20,21].

Dealing with those interactions is a design task, so User eXperience (UX) offers a holistic view to address this endeavour. UX is characterised by two types of factors: hedonic and pragmatic. Hedonic factors include all users' perceptions and responses resulting from the actual and anticipated use of a product, system or service, such as: emotions, beliefs, preferences, behaviours, and accomplishments. Pragmatic factors are a consequence of the characteristics of the system subject to evaluation: usability, functionality, performance, interactive behaviour, and assistive capabilities [1].

AUX deals with experiences and feelings of what the user expects to occur when imagining using an interactive product or system [36]. The purpose of AUX evaluation is to identify whether a given concept can provide the kind of UX anticipated by developers for its future users [31]. The study of AUX has been proven valuable, although few jobs have explored it [3,14,29,33].

The main contribution of this article is a novel AUX evaluation framework through which developers can obtain a knowledge base to create their designs. Such knowledge would have as a source opinions, desires, experience, and idealisations of users. As a consequence, user tools can have a positive impact on the participation of users in virtual communities. By using our framework, developers have the opportunity to focus on the nuances they want of the interaction and communication tools of virtual communities, which would not happen if they decided to use a general-purpose UX framework.

This paper is organised as follows. After analysing related work, in Sect. 3 we present the research methodology used to develop our proposal. Then, in Sect. 4, we describe the preliminary version of our framework for virtual communities. Finally, in Sect. 5, we conclude this work and describe the next steps needed to complete our framework.

2   Related Work

Hassenzahl et al. [10] demonstrated the importance of hedonic and pragmatic factors for software's appeal. They were also pioneers in the evaluation of AUX.

Nevertheless, as an early work, they could not succeed in determining which specific design factors can stimulate the perception of the hedonic quality.

Davis [6] proposed the Technology Acceptance Model (TAM) as a framework for recollecting from possible users the perceived usefulness and ease of use of new technology. Nonetheless, this framework just gets very generic information.

Kukka et al. [16] gathered information and requirements for the integration of social media content into 3D environments. From their AUX evaluation, they identified issues and guidelines that designers of 3D systems should consider. This is a preliminary study that only analyses information about social networks.

Eilu and Baguma [7] extended the framework proposed by Yogasara et al. [36] (base for our proposal described in Sect. 4) to improve the acceptance of mobile phones for voting. Despite the lack of validation, they presented an explanation of how AUX occur, from the perspective of cognitive psychology.

Wurhofer et al. [35] investigated the relationship between predicted and actual driving experiences. They found that many factors influence users' predictions, such as mood and the time of day. This is a study on UX over time, but without any GUI involved.

These works show the value of AUX and how it can be useful to predict design problems. They try in some way to increase the acceptance of a new characteristic or functionality, excepting Wurhofer et al. [35], who like us seek to improve UX. However, they do not offer a systemic way of evaluating and comparing results on the GUI domain. Unlike TAM [6], we do not aim to predict acceptance or the possible added value of a particular technology, but to gather the previous experiences of the users to understand their needs.

3   Research Methodology

The research methodology for the development of our framework is based on the Design Science Research Methodology (DSRM) process model (see Fig. 1) proposed by Peffers et al. [25]. We chose this methodology because its popularity in state of the art and has proved useful in similar problems [17,18,24].

An *Objective-Centred Initiation* has been chosen as a research entry point because our goal is to improve participation in a virtual community. As for *Identification & Motivation*, we have already described the importance of participation for virtual communities and the role of UX in that matter. The *Objective of a Solution*, the second step of the process, is to develop an evaluation framework that helps developers create user tools to improve user interaction, thus encouraging participation. The third step *Design & Development* is the description of our framework (see Sect. 4).

4   Framework

According to Koh et al. [15], communities face challenges from the social perspective (communication, motivation, and leadership) and the practical perspective

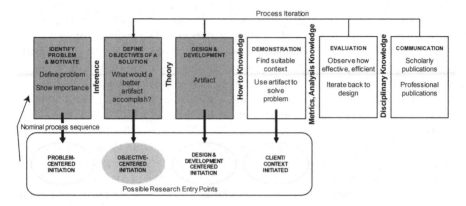

Fig. 1. DSRM process model [25]. In this work we describe the results of the first three stages (coloured in blue) from an *Objective-Centred Initiation*. (Color figure online)

(computer technology). We consider user tools as the intersection of both perspectives (see Fig. 2). User tools are widgets of a virtual community platform that allow users to exchange information and interact with each other, e.g., chats, commenting systems, avatars, recommender systems, and "like" buttons. User tools are part of the platform, a computational support that is crucial to the success of a virtual community [2,11,12,27].

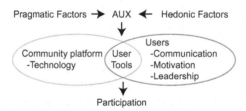

Fig. 2. We aim for improving user tools through AUX, thus increasing participation.

We want to evaluate the impact that these user tools have in users' activities within virtual communities, i.e., to what degree the UX provided by the widgets of a virtual community affects participation. For achieving this goal, we propose a framework organised in six steps (see Fig. 3).

Fig. 3. AUX framework for virtual communities.

Next, we will explain each step of the framework, which is illustrated by developing the example "one user wants to communicate with another user":

- **Set Goals:** It refers to the objectives that developers want to reach. For example, that users achieve a remote conversation as effective as if they were face to face.
- **Identify Tasks:** This step involves defining the stages that the user needs to do in order to achieve the previously defined goals. For example, the user can identify the recipient of the message, open the window or option of direct messages, write the message, and send it.
- **Identify User Tools:** This point concerns establishing which user tools are involved in the tasks already identified. For example, avatars, user profiles, commands, and chat systems.
- **Evaluate AUX:** It consists in conducting an AUX evaluation. We use the criteria described by Yogasara et al. [36]:
  - *Intended Use:* This criterion refers to the usage purpose of each user tool. For example, the way the user believes that a chat works.
  - *Positive Anticipated Emotion:* It concerns pleasant emotions that a user anticipates experiencing as a consequence of interacting with a user tool.
  - *Desired Product Characteristics:* We adapt to our context the principles proposed by Morville [22], which state that a user tool has to be valuable, usable, useful, desirable, accessible, credible, and findable.
  - *User Characteristics:* It has to do with the physical and mental characteristics of the users. For example, designing for a child is not the same as for an older adult.
  - *Experiential Knowledge:* This criterion requires knowing the experience that a user has. This experience is important since users need their prior knowledge to obtain information, and from that, make comparisons. For example, a user may ask whether a new system is better than another already known.
  - *Favourable Existing Characteristics:* It is related to the characteristics that users have already identified as positive in similar tools. For example, a user can say that they like to use the chat from another platform, as it is fast, reliable, and easy to use.
- **Evaluate UX:** This step consists in conducting a UX evaluation. It can be as complicated as necessary, depending on the criteria and tools that will be used. In some cases, the AUX evaluation can be done at a very early stage of development, without having any part of the system or even prototypes. However, once at this stage, it is essential to evaluate all the aspects considered in the AUX evaluation.
- **Compare Results:** Once both evaluations of UX were carried out (anticipated and current), the results obtained must be compared. This contrast will allow developers to make decisions about the design of user tools. For example, juxtaposing the idealised by the users with reality, checking whether their suggestions came to be implemented or not.

5   Conclusion and Future Work

The significant contribution of this study is a work in progress version of a new conceptual AUX framework for user tools provided by virtual communities platforms. Gathering the expectations, hopes, and idealisations of the participants will allow the developers to know the underlying needs, the possible contexts of use, and what participants consider essential to obtain a pleasant experience (AUX). Then, when measuring the current UX of user tools, the results can be juxtaposed and the contrasts observed, e.g., if all the participants agreed that adding a specific characteristic would be good, after implementing it and measuring it, was it indeed positive? The intention of our framework is to help answering that kind of questions. As such, the aim of this study is to propose a way to improve the design of user tools, and in that way, enhance participation.

As future work, we will develop an experimental design to evaluate AUX in several virtual communities. The experiment will consist of three phases. In the initial phase, the participants have to answer an initial survey concerned with their personal data, what virtual communities they know (e.g., Facebook, Reddit, Twitter, a forum, or a video game), and how much time they use them. The second phase will consist of a creativity session in which participants will have to perform a specific task (e.g., send a message to another user) using paper user tools. In other words, several papers cutouts with shapes of standard widgets (e.g., buttons, and text boxes) will be available to the participants, so they will choose the ones they think are necessary, and they will have to explain how their prototype carries out the task. Additionally, every participant has to complete a satisfaction questionnaire, in which we will ask the participants their opinion of the prototype they built. The third and final phase will be a test with real virtual communities, where the participants will have to do the same tasks of the second phase, but this time with actual communities. They also need to fill a final questionnaire about the satisfaction of the task, and how it compares to the prototype they built. It should be noted that we will design the satisfaction questionnaires for the last two phases, allowing us to compare the AUX of tasks from the second phase and the actual UX of tasks from the third phase.

Acknowledgement. We thank CONACyT (Consejo Nacional de Ciencia y Tecnología) for funding Luis Martín Sánchez Adame's doctoral fellowship. Scholarship number: 294598.

References

1. Ergonomics of human-system interaction - part 210: Human-centred design for interactive systems. Standard [9241-210:2010(2.15)], International Organization for Standardization, Geneva, March 2010
2. Apostolou, B., Bélanger, F., Schaupp, L.C.: Online communities: satisfaction and continued use intention. Inf. Res. **22**(4), 1–27 (2017)
3. Bargas-Avila, J.A., Hornbæk, K.: Old wine in new bottles or novel challenges: a critical analysis of empirical studies of user experience. In: Proceedings of the

SIGCHI Conference on Human Factors in Computing Systems, CHI 2011, pp. 2689–2698. ACM, Vancouver (2011)

4. Chen, L.S., Chang, P.C.: Identifying crucial website quality factors of virtual communities. In: Proceedings of the International MultiConference of Engineers and Computer Scientists, vol. 1, pp. 17–19 (2010)

5. Chen, V.H.H., Duh, H.B.L.: Investigating user experience of online communities: the influence of community type. In: 2009 International Conference on Computational Science and Engineering, vol. 4, pp. 509–514, August 2009

6. Davis, F.D.: A technology acceptance model for empirically testing new end-user information systems: theory and results. Ph.D. thesis, Massachusetts Institute of Technology (1985)

7. Eilu, E., Baguma, R.: Anticipated user experience (AUX) framework for improving acceptance of using mobile phones for voting. In: Proceedings of the 10th International Conference on Theory and Practice of Electronic Governance, ICEGOV 2017, pp. 87–96. ACM, New Delhi (2017)

8. El Morr, C., Eftychiou, L.: Evaluation frameworks for health virtual communities. In: Menvielle, L., Audrain-Pontevia, A.F., Menvielle, W. (eds.) The Digitization of Healthcare, pp. 99–118. Palgrave Macmillan, London (2017). https://doi.org/10.1057/978-1-349-95173-4_6

9. Fragidis, G., Ignatiadis, I., Wills, C.: Value co-creation and customer-driven innovation in social networking systems. In: Morin, J.H., Ralyté, J., Snene, M. (eds.) IESS 2010. LNBIP, vol. 53, pp. 254–258. Springer, Heidelberg (2010). https://doi.org/10.1007/978-3-642-14319-9_20

10. Hassenzahl, M., Platz, A., Burmester, M., Lehner, K.: Hedonic and ergonomic quality aspects determine a software's appeal. In: Proceedings of the SIGCHI Conference on Human Factors in Computing Systems, CHI 2000, pp. 201–208. ACM, The Hague (2000)

11. Hummel, J., Lechner, U.: Social profiles of virtual communities. In: Proceedings of the 35th Annual Hawaii International Conference on System Sciences, pp. 2245–2254, January 2002

12. Iriberri, A., Leroy, G.: A life-cycle perspective on online community success. ACM Comput. Surv. 41(2), 11:1–11:29 (2009)

13. Jacobsen, L.F., Tudoran, A.A., Lähteenmäki, L.: Consumers' motivation to interact in virtual food communities - the importance of self-presentation and learning. Food Qual. Prefer. 62, 8–16 (2017)

14. Karapanos, E., Zimmerman, J., Forlizzi, J., Martens, J.B.: User experience over time: an initial framework. In: Proceedings of the SIGCHI Conference on Human Factors in Computing Systems, CHI 2009, pp. 729–738. ACM, Boston (2009)

15. Koh, J., Kim, Y.G., Butler, B., Bock, G.W.: Encouraging participation in virtual communities. Commun. ACM 50(2), 68–73 (2007)

16. Kukka, H., Pakanen, M., Badri, M., Ojala, T.: Immersive street-level social media in the 3D virtual city: anticipated user experience and conceptual development. In: Proceedings of the 2017 ACM Conference on Computer Supported Cooperative Work and Social Computing, CSCW 2017, pp. 2422–2435. ACM, Portland (2017)

17. Lamprecht, J., Siemon, D., Robra-Bissantz, S.: Cooperation isn't just about doing the same thing – using personality for a cooperation-recommender-system in online social networks. In: Yuizono, T., Ogata, H., Hoppe, U., Vassileva, J. (eds.) CRIWG 2016. LNCS, vol. 9848, pp. 131–138. Springer, Cham (2016). https://doi.org/10.1007/978-3-319-44799-5_10

18. Laubis, K., Konstantinov, M., Simko, V., Gröschel, A., Weinhardt, C.: Enabling crowdsensing-based road condition monitoring service by intermediary. Electron. Mark. 1–16, March 2018. https://doi.org/10.1007/s12525-018-0292-7

19. Lee, F.S., Vogel, D., Limayem, M.: Virtual community informatics: a review and research agenda. JITTA: J. Inf. Technol. Theory Appl. **5**(1), 47 (2003)

20. Mai, H.T.X., Olsen, S.O.: Consumer participation in virtual communities: the role of personal values and personality. J. Mark. Commun. **21**(2), 144–164 (2015)

21. McCormick, T.J.: A success-oriented framework to enable co-created e-services. The George Washington University (2010)

22. Morville, P.: Experience design unplugged. In: ACM SIGGRAPH 2005 Web Program, SIGGRAPH 2005. ACM, New York (2005)

23. Nov, O., Ye, C.: Why do people tag?: motivations for photo tagging. Commun. ACM **53**(7), 128–131 (2010)

24. Patrício, L., de Pinho, N.F., Teixeira, J.G., Fisk, R.P.: Service design for value networks: enabling value cocreation interactions in healthcare. Serv. Sci. **10**(1), 76–97 (2018)

25. Peffers, K., Tuunanen, T., Rothenberger, M., Chatterjee, S.: A design science research methodology for information systems research. J. Manag. Inf. Syst. **24**(3), 45–77 (2007)

26. Preece, J.: Online Communities: Designing Usability and Supporting Sociability. Wiley, Hoboken (2000)

27. Preece, J.: Sociability and usability in online communities: determining and measuring success. Behav. Inf. Technol. **20**(5), 347–356 (2001)

28. Preece, J., Abras, C., Maloney-Krichmar, D.: Designing and evaluating online communities: research speaks to emerging practice. Int. J. Web Based Communities **1**(1), 2–18 (2004)

29. Roto, V., Law, E., Vermeeren, A., Hoonhout, J.: User experience white paper. Bringing clarity to the concept of user experience. In: Proceedings of Dagstuhl Seminar on Demarcating User Experience, vol. 22, pp. 6–15, September 2011

30. Shneiderman, B., Plaisant, C., Cohen, M., Jacobs, S., Elmqvist, N., Diakopoulos, N.: Grand challenges for HCI researchers. Interactions **23**(5), 24–25 (2016)

31. Stone, D., Jarrett, C., Woodroffe, M., Minocha, S.: User Interface Design and Evaluation. Morgan Kaufmann Series in Interactive Technologies. Morgan Kaufmann, Burlington (2005)

32. Tella, A., Babatunde, B.J.: Determinants of continuance intention of Facebook usage among library and information science female undergraduates in selected Nigerian universities. Int. J. E-Adopt. (IJEA) **9**(2), 59–76 (2017)

33. Vermeeren, A.P.O.S., Law, E.L.C., Roto, V., Obrist, M., Hoonhout, J., Väänänen-Vainio-Mattila, K.: User experience evaluation methods: current state and development needs. In: Proceedings of the 6th Nordic Conference on Human-Computer Interaction: Extending Boundaries, NordiCHI 2010, pp. 521–530. ACM, Reykjavik (2010)

34. Wang, Y., Li, Y.: Proactive engagement of opinion leaders and organization advocates on social networking sites. Int. J. Strateg. Commun. **10**(2), 115–132 (2016)

35. Wurhofer, D., Krischkowsky, A., Obrist, M., Karapanos, E., Niforatos, E., Tscheligi, M.: Everyday commuting: prediction, actual experience and recall of anger and frustration in the car. In: Proceedings of the 7th International Conference on Automotive User Interfaces and Interactive Vehicular Applications, AutomotiveUI 2015, pp. 233–240. ACM, Nottingham (2015)

36. Yogasara, T., Popovic, V., Kraal, B.J., Chamorro-Koc, M.: General characteristics of anticipated user experience (AUX) with interactive products. In: Proceedings of IASDR2011: The 4th World Conference on Design Research: Diversity and Unity, pp. 1–11 (2011)
37. Zhou, T.: Understanding online community user participation: a social influence perspective. Internet Res. **21**(1), 67–81 (2011)

SciCrowd: Towards a Hybrid, Crowd-Computing System for Supporting Research Groups in Academic Settings

António Correia[1,2(✉)], Daniel Schneider[3], Hugo Paredes[1,2], and Benjamim Fonseca[1,2]

[1] University of Trás-os-Montes e Alto Douro, UTAD, Vila Real, Portugal
ajcorreia1987@gmail.com, {hparedes,benjaf}@utad.pt
[2] INESC TEC, Porto, Portugal
[3] Tércio Pacitti Institute of Computer Applications and Research (NCE), Federal University of Rio de Janeiro, Rio de Janeiro, Brazil
schneider@cos.ufrj.br

Abstract. The increasing amount of scholarly literature and the diversity of dissemination channels are challenging several fields and research communities. A continuous interplay between researchers and citizen scientists creates a vast set of possibilities to integrate hybrid, crowd-machine interaction features into crowd science projects for improving knowledge acquisition from large volumes of scientific data. This paper presents SciCrowd, an experimental crowd-powered system under development "from the ground up" to support data-driven research. The system combines automatic data indexing and crowd-based processing of data for detecting topic evolution by fostering a knowledge base of concepts, methods, and results categorized according to the particular needs of each field. We describe the prototype and discuss its main implications as a mixed-initiative approach for leveraging the analysis of academic literature.

Keywords: AI · Crowd-computing hybrids · Human computation
Hybrid machine-crowd interaction · Knowledge discovery
Mixed-initiative systems · Crowdsourcing

1 Introduction

A major research path in today's computing landscape has been focused on analyzing datasets whose volume, velocity, and variety are so extreme that the current automatic tools are inadequate for their accurate collection, management, and analysis in a reasonable amount of time [17]. As the literature increases at an exponential rate, scholars need to adapt their institutions and practices by improving searching, analytical, and filtering mechanisms to select the most relevant data sources. Nonetheless, manual labor applied on examining variances, correlating evidence, and compiling descriptive statistics is an exhaustive and subjective process [13]. At the forefront are the rapidly advancing techniques of AI such as machine learning running on large collections of data [1]. However, computer algorithms involve expensive training being prone to errors. Dunne and colleagues [14] go even further by arguing that the "current theories

© Springer Nature Switzerland AG 2018
A. Rodrigues et al. (Eds.): CRIWG 2018, LNCS 11001, pp. 34–41, 2018.
https://doi.org/10.1007/978-3-319-99504-5_4

and tools are directed at finding a paper or website, not gaining an understanding of the key papers, authors, controversies, and hypotheses." In this sense, research scholars interested in answering a particular question need intelligent systems robust enough to assist them in exploring always-evolving knowledge representations as a "science of science measurement" [19].

In this work, SciCrowd is introduced as a crowd-powered system prototype under development "from the ground up" towards an open participation model in which a large amount of researchers and crowd workers/volunteers can contribute for improving the way as research data are processed. We assume that crowd-computing hybrids constitute a valuable instrument to address some of the limitations of current applications by enabling us to identify new relations between research topics, authors, and groups [10]. Meaningful categories, filters, and summaries can be generated through mixed-initiative approaches combining human and machine intelligence [13]. Such synergies between mechanical and cognitive operators (the "crowd") can contribute to create open knowledge bases supported by collaborative participation.

The paper is organized as follows. Section 2 provides an overview of key issues in the form of theoretical bridge between crowd and machine intelligence for enhancing research pursuits. Section 3 presents a brief conceptualization of the requirements for SciCrowd as an experimental human-centered hybrid system for scientific discovery. The implementation details are also discussed with emphasis on the SciCrowd's prototype and architecture. This section also provides some exploratory remarks on the results achieved from a survey with crowdsourcing researchers. The paper finishes discussing limitations and future directions that need consideration in the deployment of a crowd-powered, self-organizing system for scientific discovery.

2 Related Work

Scientific knowledge production is being increasingly dependent on collaborative efforts and new forms of collaboration and data analysis are dawning as result of social-technical advances achieved in e-Science through CSCW research [2]. Various approaches have been proposed to leverage crowd work for improving the quality of data. Human crowds can combine Human Intelligence Tasks (HITs) and large-scale database systems such as MTurk[1] to cope with the ambiguity, vagueness, heterogeneity, scale, timeliness, and complexity of scientific data [10]. Empirical studies have emphasized crowdsourcing efforts in domains such as taxonomy development [22], machine learning experiments using MTurk [20], and scientific discovery games (e.g., Foldit[2]) [6]. In addition, several crowd-powered systems have been presented in the literature. For instance, GATE Crowdsourcing Plugin [12] offers infrastructural support for supporting a massive pool of users on mapping corpora to microtasks while automatically generating crowdsourcing interfaces for classification and annotation. CrowdScape [21] measures crowd behavior and outputs though interactive

---

[1] https://www.mturk.com/.

[2] https://fold.it/portal/.

visualization and mixed-initiative machine learning. Moreover, Apolo [8] allows interactive large graph sensemaking by combining machine learning and visualization. On the other hand, PANDA [9] is a hybrid algorithmic-crowdsourcing platform for academic knowledge discovery.

Mixed-initiative systems have been introduced as interactive, intelligent approaches that combine the strengths of human interaction with the algorithmic power of AI to solve problems that could not be solved by either computers or humans alone [11]. In this kind of systems, human work is both used directly to complete HITs and as feedback for machine learning classifiers training to complete that work in the future. Such hybrid approach can be particularly fruitful in crowd science projects to refine machine-extracted metadata while providing evidence on demand by using automatic classification techniques enabled by human crowd workers who can process, filter, classify, and verify the information [10].

3   On the Deployment of SciCrowd: Targeting Crowd-Enabled Scientific Discovery

A paradigmatic shift in information systems design that can be taken into account in the design and development of a crowd-computing system for scientific discovery involves the consideration of IT artifacts and social practices as central units of research [15]. Theoretically grounded from a design science perspective, such approach includes goal-directed collective activities, routines, and resources to create explicit knowledge by means of reflection and concept formation (e.g., linguistic signs, organizational schemes, technical artifacts) as socially situated practices.

Research tasks such as performing a systematic literature review involve a set of laborious, time-consuming, and sometimes wasteful efforts. This includes the identification of relevant sources, data extraction, and quality assessment [5]. In this scenario, relevant sources and data dimensions can be ignored during the process. Thus, suitable crowd-powered systems are required to produce, share, filter, and combine scientific discoveries. In the literature, crowdsourcing has been closely related to processes, task characteristics, and participants [10]. Tinati and colleagues [7] identified numerous factors when designing citizen science platforms, including task specificity, community development, task design, and engagement. The authors pointed out to the likelihood of using periodic feedback, roles and privileges, and task context as motivational factors. In addition, the environment must be easy to use, fast, intuitive, and reliable. Crowd aspects (including size, type, social structure, behavior), quality control, and temporal issues (e.g., daily devoted time) assume particular importance on the design of crowd-powered systems [10]. Hybrid classifiers must be trained according to the crowd behavior and the system must enable the crowd to selectively supplement weak regions of the classifier [16].

3.1   Baseline System Design and Prototyping

SciCrowd is a system prototype based on a crowd-enabled model [4] that supports the entire process of research data analysis. In this approach, crowd members are exposed to situations involving human factors like expertise and motivation. HITs are created by users and associated to collaboration features (e.g., annotation). Our ultimate goal is to build a mixed-initiative interface for (and by) researchers and citizen scientists. Figure 1 presents the system prototype towards the design of a web-based interface for extracting facts from publication records through human-machine interaction. In this scenario, a contributor can be aware of new papers in the system or insert a new entry, see who is online in the system, edit publication metadata, set conceptual units and descriptions, and getting access to data categorized by machine.

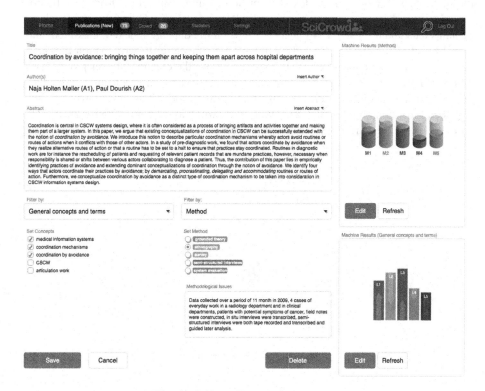

Fig. 1. SciCrowd's system prototype.

Currently, the prototype comprises a limited set of features that range from edit a publication record automatically extracted from DBLP[3] or added manually by users to the settings panel (e.g., group roles) and main page. Publication details can be visualized pressing the "show" button, which opens an internal page that allows to insert data about a paper. For instance, consider the following scenario. A paper on "medical informatics" could be classified by subarea (e.g., cognitive aging), method, setting, key concepts, findings, and social-technical aspects concerning a certain technology (e.g., a Wiki intended to support knowledge exchange in public health). All these data could be filtered considering specific research purposes. For example, a user could be interested

---

[3] http://dblp.uni-trier.de/.

on understanding relations among concepts and related areas in machine learning for medical purposes and/or identifying features in health care systems implemented by Portuguese researchers in a certain period.

Our approach to extract information from public data sources is based on a previous proposal for a hybrid human-computer scientific information extraction pipeline [23]. As initially addressed by Correia and colleagues [18] and followed in further proposals [9], the preprocessing stage includes the automatic extraction of metadata from each paper using DBLP. To test the effectiveness of our information extraction algorithm, metadata from papers were indexed using a structure that comes from two bibliographic reference management systems (EndNote, BibTeX). Currently, the database contains data about 28,991,154 papers. How scientific data are indexed, classified, and visualized differs from field to field through an architecture of participation that gain value as more users cooperate [2]. The system allows the creation of user groups with predefined permissions (e.g., edit) by using an authentication mechanism. An innovative feature is being planned for extracting altmetrics [3], including download data and social mentions by country, discipline, and professional status. Figure 2 provides an overview of the current system architecture.

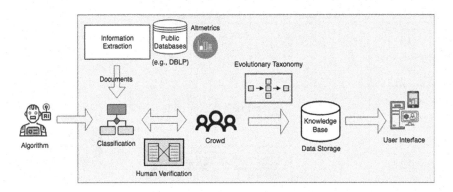

Fig. 2. System architecture.

3.2 Preliminary Evaluation

The initial results of a survey (N = 90 researchers) corroborate the need for developing a crowd-computing system for research data analysis. The sample consisted mostly of researchers from USA (33.3%) with more than 8 years of experience (60%) and a research focus on crowdsourcing (58.9%). All participants (75.5% male, 24.5% female) were asked to participate via e-mail in a total of 3625 e-mail addresses. Google Forms[4] was chosen for collecting responses between September 20, 2017 and April 3, 2018. Researchers pointed out resources (63.3%) and access to information (30%) as the main problems when working on their research tasks. There was some disagreement with regard to the use of crowdsourcing in research activities. Nonetheless, the participants

---

[4] https://docs.google.com/forms/.

identified classification and categorization (45.6%), verification and validation (44.4%), surveys (40%), content creation (36.7%), and information finding (32.2%) as their main types of tasks assigned to crowd workers. When asked about the incentives for participation in crowd-driven research, researchers pointed out the interest in the topic (31.1%), money and extrinsic rewards (16.7%), social incentives (16.7%), and altruism and meaningful contribution (15.6%). Regarding the best practices and the main drawbacks of using crowdsourcing for scientific purposes, participants identified approaches like gamification, need for supervision, real-time collaboration, proper diffusion, and data collection. Participants also indicated legal and ethical limitations that will make it difficult for people to help collect or analyze research data. Examples include privacy (57.8%), accuracy of information (53.3%), protection of intellectual property (40%), and abuse of personal information (37.8%).

The implementation of SciCrowd as a hybrid approach for integrating human inputs into AI systems was also addressed. Almost all respondents stated that it is "very promising" in the scientific context. A participant called our attention to value human input, while other responses emphasized the importance of interdisciplinary identity, transparency, and provenance "to keep track of all versions of the information and knowledge capture, so that the state of knowledge can be rewound and replayed from any point in time to any other point in time". Another participant explicitly demonstrated the potential of crowd-computing hybrids by assuming that "machine learning algorithms could learn from user/volunteer responses in applications where the computer classification skill is below a desirable threshold." A few of the researchers mentioned the risk of enabling machine imposing (wrong) interpretations.

An important implication for design relies on considering diversity (in terms of education and income levels, race, gender) when designing crowd-based human computation systems. Some participants mentioned some problems associated to error tolerance, ethical dilemmas of introducing AI, and crowd bias. An additional set of questionnaire responses showed us some features that can be implemented in Sci-Crowd. Examples include user-friendly AI algorithms, learn from examples, statistical analysis, a semantic search engine exploring scientific literature by specific questions (instead of keywords), visualization of work progress, a graph of papers based on their impact, and ability to identify the "right crowd" (general crowd might not be suitable for specialized tasks like scientific analysis). In addition, participants also indicated a need for more connections (links) between the data, the published papers, the search (query) terms that led a user to the data, and how the data were used and/or analyzed.

3.3   Limitations and Future Work

Some limitations remain unfilled concerning the lack of case studies to validate the system (scarcity of tests and experimental research) by analyzing interaction logs and questionnaires. An approach for the lightweight development of this system relies on involving the crowd in the underlying engineering and design processes. Design and evaluation principles will be further explored, while usability tests are also required to gain insight on work practices that can better inform the development of a robust, hybrid machine-crowd intelligent system. Based on the requirements identified previously, future deployments include hybrid classifiers and learners trained according to the crowd behavior, a public dashboard, a fine-grained classification mechanism that would store and retrieve metadata that could be extracted in the form of graphics and statistics, and a context-aware reputation system. One important problem in this study was that the survey was conducted with researchers who had not used the system, so results are very limited. A new survey and a controlled experiment engaging users on the evaluation of publication records using a crowdsourcing platform such as MTurk constitute important lines of further research.

4　Concluding Remarks

This paper emphasizes the implications for design concerning a crowd-enabled, self-organizing system under development towards achieving a higher level of engagement by researchers and citizen scientists. SciCrowd system's prototype aims to improve the way as publication records are evaluated while harnessing the wisdom of a crowd. The main target relies on improving the effective use of data to solve complex problems at large-scale, and the possibility to adapt this tool to multivariate scientific fields. The crowd can be particularly helpful in this process by indexing metadata and fixing errors while providing new interpretations on the published data through highly detailed and filtered data granules. The outputs can be established on understanding how research communities form and evolve over time. Further steps will be focused on providing features for supporting hybrid reasoning using AI inferring on contributions from crowd members performing HITs such as systematic literature reviews and sciento-metric studies. Despite the prospects for research in crowd science, we must be able to consider incentives, ethical constraints, and social-technical aspects for "closing the loop" in developing crowd-powered scientific computing systems.

Acknowledgements. This work is financed by the ERDF – European Regional Development Fund through the Operational Programme for Competitiveness and Internationalisation - COMPETE 2020 Programme within project «POCI-01-0145-FEDER-006961», and by National Funds through the Portuguese funding agency, FCT - Fundação para a Ciência e a Tecnologia as part of project «UID/EEA/50014/2013».

References

1. Gil, Y., Greaves, M., Hendler, J., Hirsh, H.: Amplify scientific discovery with artificial intelligence. Science **346**(6206), 171–172 (2014)
2. Farooq, U., Ganoe, C.H., Carroll, J.M., Giles, C.L.: Designing for e-science: requirements gathering for collaboration in CiteSeer. Int. J. Hum. Comput. Stud. **67**, 297–312 (2009)
3. Thelwall, M.: Using altmetrics to support research evaluation. In: Proceedings of the International Workshop on Altmetrics for Research Outputs Measurements and Scholarly Information Management, pp. 11–28 (2018)
4. Correia, A., Fonseca, B., Paredes, H.: Exploiting classical bibliometrics of CSCW: classification, evaluation, limitations, and the odds of semantic analytics. In: Proceedings of the International Conference on Human Factors in Computing and Informatics, pp. 137–156 (2013)

5. Kitchenham, B., Brereton, O.P., Budgen, D., Turner, M., Bailey, J., Linkman, S.: Systematic literature reviews in software engineering – a systematic literature review. Inf. Softw. Technol. **51**(1), 7–15 (2009)
6. Cooper, S., et al.: The challenge of designing scientific discovery games. In: Proceedings of the ACM International Conference on the Foundations of Digital Games, pp. 40–47 (2010)
7. Tinati, R., Van Kleek, M., Simperl, E., Luczak-Rösch, M., Simpson, R., Shadbolt, N.: Designing for citizen data analysis: a cross-sectional case study of a multi-domain citizen science platform. In: Proceedings of the ACM CHI Conference on Human Factors in Computing Systems, pp. 4069–4078 (2015)
8. Chau, D.H., Kittur, A., Hong, J.I., Faloutsos, C.: Apolo: making sense of large network data by combining rich user interaction and machine learning. In: Proceedings of the ACM CHI Conference on Human Factors in Computing Systems, pp. 167–176 (2011)
9. Dong, Z., Lu, J., Ling, T.W., Fan, J., Chen, Y.: Using hybrid algorithmic-crowdsourcing methods for academic knowledge acquisition. Clust. Comput. **20**(4), 3629–3641 (2017)
10. Correia, A., Schneider, D., Fonseca, B., Paredes, H.: Crowdsourcing and massively collaborative science: a systematic literature review and mapping study. In: Rodrigues, A., et al. (eds.) CRIWG 2018. LNCS, vol. 11001, pp. 133–154 (2018)
11. Horvitz, E.: Principles of mixed-initiative user interfaces. In: Proceedings of the ACM CHI Conference on Human Factors in Computing Systems, pp. 159–166 (1999)
12. Bontcheva, K., Roberts, I., Derczynski, L., Rout, D.: The GATE crowdsourcing plugin: crowdsourcing annotated corpora made easy. In: Proceedings of the 14th Conference of the European Chapter of the Association for Computational Linguistics, pp. 97–100 (2014)
13. Borne, K.: Collaborative annotation for scientific data discovery and reuse. Bull. Am. Soc. Inf. Sci. Technol. **39**(4), 44–45 (2013)
14. Dunne, C., Shneiderman, B., Gove, R., Klavans, J., Dorr, B.: Rapid understanding of scientific paper collections: integrating statistics, text analytics, and visualization. J. Assoc. Inf. Sci. Technol. **63**(12), 2351–2369 (2012)
15. Rohde, M., Stevens, G., Brödner, P., Wulf, V.: Towards a paradigmatic shift in IS: designing for social practice. In: Proceedings of the DESRIST (2009)
16. Cheng, J., Bernstein, M.S.: Flock: hybrid crowd-machine learning classifiers. In: Proceedings of the ACM CSCW, pp. 600–611 (2015)
17. Zhao, Y., Zhu, Q.: Evaluation on crowdsourcing research: current status and future direction. Inf. Syst. Front. **16**, 1–18 (2012)
18. Correia, A., Santos, J., Azevedo, D., Paredes, H., Fonseca, B.: Putting "human crowds" in the loop of bibliography evaluation: a collaborative working environment for CSCW publications. Procedia Technol. **9**, 573–583 (2013)
19. Börner, K., Scharnhorst, A.: Visual conceptualizations and models of science. J. Informetr. **3**(3), 161–172 (2009)
20. Burrows, S., Potthast, M., Stein, B.: Paraphrase acquisition via crowdsourcing and machine learning. ACM Trans. Intell. Syst. Technol. **4**(3), 43 (2013)
21. Rzeszotarski, J., Kittur, A.: CrowdScape: interactively visualizing user behavior and output. In: Proceedings of the Annual ACM Symposium on UIST, pp. 55–62 (2012)
22. Chilton, L.B., Little, G., Edge, D., Weld, D.S., Landay, J.A.: Cascade: crowdsourcing taxonomy creation. In: Proceedings of the ACM CHI Conference on Human Factors in Computing Systems, pp. 1999–2008 (2013)
23. Tchoua, R.B., et al.: Towards a hybrid human-computer scientific information extraction pipeline. In: Proceedings of the IEEE 13th International Conference on e-Science, pp. 109–118 (2017)

Reframing Taxonomy Development in Collaborative Computing Research: A Review and Synthesis of CSCW Literature 2003–2010

António Correia[1,2](✉), Hugo Paredes[1,2], and Benjamim Fonseca[1,2]

[1] University of Trás-os-Montes e Alto Douro, UTAD, Vila Real, Portugal
ajcorreia1987@gmail.com, {hparedes,benjaf}@utad.pt
[2] INESC TEC, Porto, Portugal

Abstract. Technological evolution impacts the research and development of new solutions, as well as consumers' expectations and behaviors. With the advent of the new millennium, collaboration systems and technologies were introduced to support ordinary cooperative work and inter-dependent, socially and culturally mediated practices as integral units of everyday life settings. Nevertheless, existing classification systems are limited in scope to analyze technological developments and capture the intellectual structure of a field, understood as an abstraction of the collective knowledge of its researchers and their socially mediated activities. Ten years after the introduction of Mittleman et al.'s taxonomy, we build upon earlier work and adopt this classification scheme to provide a descriptive, taxonomy-based analysis of four distinct venues focused on collaborative computing research: ACM CSCW, ACM GROUP, ECSCW, and CRIWG. The proposal consists of achieving evidence on technical attributes and impacts towards characterizing the evolution of socio-technical systems via (and for) taxonomic modeling. This study can also constitute an important step towards the emergence of new, potentially more valid and robust evaluation studies combining Grounded Theory with alternative methods and techniques.

Keywords: Classification · Collaborative computing · CSCW
Grounded Theory · Groupware · Review · Social-technical systems
Taxonomy

1 Introduction

CSCW has been defined by interdisciplinarity from its very beginnings and its focus has changed dramatically (more in the US than in Europe), from traditional studies of work practices to more eclectic approaches such as social networks, disaster management, domestic life, and crowdsourcing [1]. With technologies pervading ordinary settings and increasingly aiding cooperative work arrangements, CSCW has a recurrent commitment on presenting different ways of thinking about technology development, evaluation, and impact on the societal framework. The importance of in-depth studies

© Springer Nature Switzerland AG 2018
A. Rodrigues et al. (Eds.): CRIWG 2018, LNCS 11001, pp. 42–59, 2018.
https://doi.org/10.1007/978-3-319-99504-5_5

examining collaborative settings has been stressed when designing technical artifacts [2]. However, little is known about their successful contributions for technology-driven paradigmatic shifts largely geared by software and hardware industries and research fields [3]. Experimental prototypes have been developed as artifacts by developers working in the field of CSCW and pre-packaged by major vendors for widely available platforms [4]. Nevertheless, the uncertainty motivated by the pace of technology development affects the way as research communities evolve and several gaps remain unfilled concerning the examination of their complex settings.

Evaluating social and collaborative technologies becomes a critical factor to detect changes while anticipating directions as new tools are introduced and deployed [5]. Novel evaluation approaches are needed to uncover not only central aspects related with groupware attributes, success, and failure [6] but also new classes of technologies and functional attributes. Advances in CSCW have spread across journals, conference proceedings, posters, tutorials, book series, technical reports, and social networking services created for scientists. As we enter an age of increasingly larger and noisier data, the challenge here relies on the "tedious and lengthy task" of finding, analyzing and systematizing all relevant issues [9]. Hence, a research effort in the interdisciplinary field of CSCW is thus justified regarding its commitment with the development of innovative technologies by means of ethnographic studies, conceptual work, experiments, and evaluation studies.

Understanding the nature and evolution of collaboration as a social phenomenon is a difficult goal to achieve reading literature only. Nonetheless, systems developed to support or enhance collaboration activities are concrete and can be further examined. Although it seems as an extremely complex process to present an analysis comprehensive enough, a study using Mittleman et al.'s [10] taxonomy is elaborated in the form of hypothesis about the characteristics of collaborative computing in terms of application-level domains and functional attributes. The study also explores concomitant changes resulting from technical deployments to support or enhance collaborative practices. In addition, Grounded Theory [13] is also addressed as a research approach intended to extract new categories for taxonomy development.

In the remainder of this paper we first present a discussion on seminal publications, exploring a taxonomic rationale of collaborative systems. In Sect. 3, we present the methodology used to classify the functional attributes of collaborative systems from literature. Section 4 shows the main results of our study. This section also provides some exploratory remarks on the use of Grounded Theory for taxonomy development, summarizing some of the lessons learned and future directions. Section 5 summarizes and concludes this piece by providing some actionable recommendations.

2 Revisiting Key Contributions on the Nature and Technical Evolution of Collaborative Systems

Tracing the origins of CSCW, Greenberg [14] provided an annotated bibliography comprising general sources, groupware systems, and concepts. The earliest mention is to the Bush's [15] vision of Memex as "a way of structuring and leaving trails through a large, shared information store." Meanwhile, Augment/NLS [16] was envisioned as a research center for augmenting human capabilities through the use of artifacts, language, and training. In the literature, there are a surprising number of examples of groupware systems (e.g., Coordinator [17]). CSCW research during the 90s was focused on creating solutions flexible enough to cope with the "high flexibility, contextualization and variability of human activity" [19]. Over time, it has evolved in response to the social and technological advances, comprising foundations, approaches and languages for a better collaboration experience into multi-user environments and interfaces. As argued by Law and colleagues [20], social software tools and packages produced nowadays are similar to groupware appeared in 90s but more versatile, lightweight, wide-ranging, and dynamic. Although little is known on the adoption and real impact of collaborative systems, it is possible to assume that they had more success outside the workplace [21]. The implementation of such tools involves a "structured, continuous and flexible adaptation" affected by the tendency of users to shape the system to their specific needs [22].

Theoretical frameworks can help us characterize the field of CSCW [8, 23]. Thus, understanding major technology shifts becomes a critical endeavor in a highly volatile community predominantly established on time frames of evolutionary stasis disrupted by short periods of sudden technological waves [3]. Only a small number of studies have already examined impacts on work practices when a collaborative system is introduced. As outlined by Pinelle and Gutwin [4], "a better understanding of how groupware systems have been evaluated in the past can help to frame the discussion of what methods and techniques should be considered for future evaluations". The authors preceded the advent of the 21st century with a review of papers that introduced or evaluated a groupware system from ACM CSCW conference proceedings. Findings included a predominance of synchronous applications and a small number of deployments in real world settings when comparing with academic or research implementations. Furthermore, an emphasis on ongoing evaluations of prototypes comparing to evaluations of completed software packages was also denoted.

A vast set of classification frameworks were proposed in order to organize contributions, "but none of them are comprehensive enough since they focus either on a particular aspect of collaboration or on the specific mechanism that the tools follow" [24]. Such frameworks have several elements in common, including group and individual characteristics, task properties, situation factors, and group processes and outcomes [6]. In the light of this work, Bafoutsou and Mentzas [25] emphasized a number of areas of further consideration that arise when studying collaborative applications, including classification dimensions such as scalability and usability. Evolutionary approaches based on requirements engineering were also proposed for scaffolding groupware implementation [26]. Sarma and colleagues [24] adapted Maslow's hierarchy of needs pyramid to create a classification framework for characterizing collaboration needs. A multifaceted evaluation framework covering relationships underlying communication, collaboration, coordination, work coupling, and joint awareness was also provided [6]. A somewhat similar body of work has sought to propose typologies of collaborative tool capabilities [28], while Antunes et al. [8] proposed a framework for collaborative systems evaluation covering all stages of system development. Further research was reviewed by Grudin and Poltrock [29] regarding the development of taxonomic schemes comprising technology features and collaborative behavior.

3   Method

As we enter an age of increasingly larger and noisier data, too many relevant results and work are hidden in the large volumes of literature annually published. Data serve as evidence to support scientific inquiry and researchers guide their pursuits around data as a foundation for scientific collaboration [30]. CSCW applications are difficult to evaluate [6] since most of the taxonomies existing at the time are inadequate to classify more complex systems that include a large variety of features. As collaborative systems and technologies evolve and become more complex, it is much harder to evaluate them appropriately with a clear perception of their practical implications.

This work relies on the premise that despite technologies may change frequently, classes of systems may endure for much longer [31]. It is also assumed that previous results and implications for designing a system can also be useful on the design of another type of system. Classify papers according to a taxonomy is one of the stages of the formal process outlined by Kitchenham [32] for conducting a Systematic Literature Review (SLR). We followed evidence-based research methods for conducting a feature analysis and collaborative systems evaluation [5, 34]. Thus, the strengths and weaknesses of collaborative computing technology, in terms of how well they provided each of the functional attributes, are discussed. For the purpose of this study, we also discuss the use of Grounded Theory [13] as a "railroad" for CSCW research [35].

3.1   Sample

We reviewed a total of 541 publications from ACM CSCW, ACM GROUP, ECSCW, and CRIWG proceedings. These venues are acknowledged as devoted conferences in the field of CSCW [30] as well as reference venues for regular publication by CSCW authors from both North American and European research communities [3]. The scientific committees and editorial boards of these conferences include some of the most cited authors in the field of CSCW, which makes this set of publication venues an effective sample to evaluate technological variants. The period of analysis was limited to the publication years between 2003 and 2010 and this review only included papers that introduced and/or evaluated a collaborative system [4]. Excluded papers include posters, tutorials, doctoral consortium abstracts, prefaces, special issue introductions, book reviews, and panels. Studies with a strong sociological focus (e.g., [1]) were not included at this stage due to the emphasis on technical aspects. Table 1 presents the overview of the papers we have considered for analysis.

Thematically, the reviewed papers cover a diverse range of studies. However, we acknowledge several limitations of this study, including the 8-year timeframe and the relatively small sample size. Thus, this review can only cover a small portion of all related literature and we cannot entirely exclude sampling bias as a result. Nonetheless, we believe that we have obtained a representative sample and the rationale for choosing this period is based on several factors. First, our main goal is developing a historical

Table 1. Retrieved papers and publication years.

Conference	Range (conference editions)	Records
CRIWG	2006–2008	72
ECSCW	2005–2007	37
ACM CSCW	2004–2008	215
ACM GROUP	2003–2010	217

perspective in the research by looking back at the changes that have occurred in the field of CSCW. A further reason relies on the fact that the first known bibliometric study devoted to collaborative computing research in this century was published by Holsapple and Luo in 2003 [7], as recently mentioned by Correia and colleagues [11]. In addition, some of the most widely used social networking services were launched in this period. It is also worth noting that the lack of access to the content of more recent papers brings difficulty to the process since we need to read the full text of each paper to extract functional attributes.

3.2 Classification Process

The taxonomy used for analysis was adopted from Mittleman and colleagues [10] to shortly compare collaborative systems and research prototypes together with the functionalities implemented within each system. The selection of this taxonomy was based on a systematic review of evaluation frameworks [36]. The classification scheme for collaborative technologies [10] divides a set of application-level domains into *jointy authored pages*, *streaming tools*, *information access tools*, and *aggregated systems*. The last category consists of a combination of the first three types of technologies in order to optimize them while supporting cooperative work practices in settings for which is necessary more than a single technology. On the other hand, the comparison scheme relies on nine core capabilities for collaboration affordances. First, the *core functionality* provided by a tool can range from creating and/or sharing a single text page to video/audio stream. *Content* describes the type of contributions or data structures. Examples include text messages, URL, pictures, data stream, and hypermedia. *Relationships* among contributions can range from collection to list, tree, and graph. Moreover, *supported actions* represent the things that users can do on content and relations (e.g., modify content, remove data, receive contributions). *Synchronicity* can be explained by when participants are working at the same time (synchronous) or different time (asynchronous). *Identifiability* is another action parameter characterized by the degree to which contributors can determine who executed an action (e.g., full anonymity). *Access control* deals with the configuration of user's privileges to execute actions, while *session persistence* is the degree to which contributions persist or disappear in the system. *Alert mechanisms* deal with the interruptions (notifications) suffered by the user when a new contribution is made into the system. Finally, *awareness* is the perception of users about what each member develops and the contextual knowledge that they have about what is happening within the system [10].

Feature analysis is a recognized evaluation method in software engineering and can be understood as "a qualitative form of evaluation involving the subjective assessment of the relative importance of different features plus an assessment of how well each of the features is implemented by the candidate tools" [34]. The classification process consisted on gathering descriptive metadata related to a publication and adding contextual knowledge to each record. As can be seen in Fig. 1, a total of 1480 papers published in CSCW devoted venues between 2003 and 2010 were indexed by year, ID, name of the author(s), title of the paper, and conference categorization using DBLP and ACM Digital Library information sources. The classification and comparison schemes for collaborative systems [10] were thus applied on 541 papers speculating on the social and organizational impact of collaboration technologies. Such primary studies include the design, deployment, and evaluation of new (or already introduced) systems, tools, and architectures. Once data were categorized and organized, each paper was screened and evaluated taking into account the classes and functional attributes that were either present or absent [34]. The sample was then revisited using Grounded Theory [13] as an experimental approach for extracting new categories.

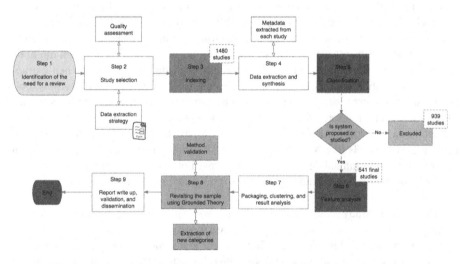

Fig. 1. Stages of the classification process (adapted from Kitchenham [32]).

4   Findings

As a research community mainly constituted by behavioral scientists and system developers, CSCW has a long tradition in conceptualizing collaboration dynamics and proposing technology-based tools. The development of communication networks led to the emergence of social interaction support systems in a broad-spectrum of application domains ranging from healthcare and emergency response to ludic scenarios [21]. The analysis of the functional attributes by conference (Fig. 2) demonstrates an interest of ECSCW by awareness, notification mechanisms, and access controls. Our results go beyond previous reports, showing that the ACM CSCW conference discarded awareness in some systems but makes use of alert mechanisms and permanent contributions. A similar pattern of results was obtained in CRIWG proceedings from 2006–2008. In turn, ACM GROUP shows greater emphasis on text sharing with hyperlinks and asynchronous tools, representing a major outlet to study awareness. Nevertheless, CSCW is a very dynamic field and the research focus continually changes over time. As the analyzed periods are different for each conference, some differences can be due to the time periods rather than to conceptual focuses.

Work processes in cooperative ensembles require a coordination of resources with high levels of interdependency between tasks [40]. As a socially oriented process, cooperative work is ordinarily enabled by a shared database, requiring an active construction process by participants into a mutual information working space to reach a common ground [41]. Text sharing was the most pronounced feature in our sample. For instance, electronic patient record systems, three-dimensional digital media design environments, and activity-tracking tools promote social interaction and engagement through text sharing. In addition, collaborative applications with both text sharing and conferencing features demonstrated growing indicators at the end of the previous decade. Examples include avatar-based meeting support tools and robots with computer vision such as Lunar rover robot [39]. The results found clear support for hypermedia as the most adopted type of data structure that may be used to a particular collaboration. On the other hand, we speculate that the decrease of data stream might be due to the expansion of this type of functionality provided by WWW. When extrapolating to the different associations that users can establish among contributions, collection was the most visible implementation by programmers of collaborative systems. This indicator can reinforce the notion of a lack of structure in certain components of collaboration technology. Adding content (e.g., a new blog entry) is noticeably high, being present in tools like ActivitySpotter [42]. Results also showed a high expression in the ability to comment in groupware systems. For instance, a group of users can produce annotations in mutual digital documents and support decision-making while reducing the cost of reading a document [27].

The present study confirmed the Pinelle and Gutwin's [4] findings about the prevalence of synchronous systems in the collaborative work sphere. Such kind of systems were followed by tools with both synchronous and asynchronous features. In addition, asynchronous applications were then slightly introduced, demonstrating a growth and optimistic perspectives reflected in platforms such as Amazon Mechanical Turk[1]. This finding is in line with the fact that the conception of collaboration has changed during the last decade, being more multi-tasking, asynchronous and flexible given the opportunities that recent technology offers to the users [23]. Although collaborative systems have a strong focus on identifying users who perform shared actions, tools where the user acts anonymously or can choose to be anonymous or identified have shown indicators of remarkable growth. Access controls denoted preeminence signs on the inclusion of authentication mechanisms. With this feature, security and privacy issues can be enhanced by preventing unauthorized or malicious

---

[1] https://www.mturk.com.

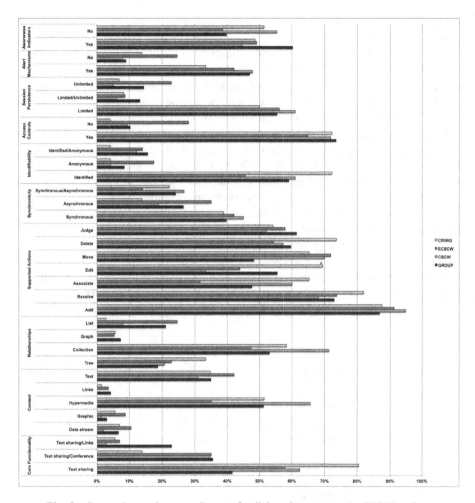

Fig. 2. Comparison scheme attributes of collaborative systems in CSCW outlets.

access to resources and users may increase their trust using collaboration technology. From the data in Fig. 2, it is apparent that there was little difference between tools providing awareness compared to those that did not make use of this feature. However, awareness has been a critical topic in CSCW research and developers should be mainly focused on the implementation of this feature appropriately. From this data, we can also see high values for notification/alert mechanisms and permanent sessions.

Collaborative computing research has been expanded from studying group work in organizations or workplaces to the home, including the effects of life disruptions on home technology routines [37]. Social networking has been also a topic of intensive interest at work [38]. Technologies where users can edit text collaboratively and use hyperlinks have been growing in the literature. Some examples are online social tagging, gift exchange and mind mapping/brainstorming systems (e.g., GroupMind [18]). A preference by group dynamics and a steady increase of social tagging, video conferencing, and search engines were noted. Moreover, audio conferencing and desktop/application sharing tools clearly express a decrease. Aggregated systems showed a peak in 2005 before decreasing in the last years, while shared file repositories grown up in 2009. Syndication tools followed the same path, and conversation systems were more addressed between 2003 and 2004. Nevertheless, polling tools had more influence in 2007, while shared editors remained stable all years. Figure 3 details the results of our analysis on the classes of collaborative systems and technologies by venue.

Concerning the scope of ECSCW, this venue addressed desktop/application sharing, followed by aggregated systems and conversation tools with remarkable indicators on video conferencing. Nevertheless, ACM CSCW put the focus on polling tools, conversation tools, shared editors, desktop/application sharing, and syndication tools. On average, we found many studies spread over conversation systems, social tagging tools, aggregated systems, search engines, and shared editors in ACM GROUP conference proceedings. Interestingly, CRIWG showed a large number of group dynamics tools, aggregated systems, polling tools, and shared editors. Curiously, all research venues published most of their studies on group dynamics. Regarding the categories with the lowest values (e.g., audio conferencing), this may be related with a focus of intensive research on these systems until the beginning of the 21st century, resulting in a consequent slowdown by achieving stabilized solutions. Oppositely, an explosion in

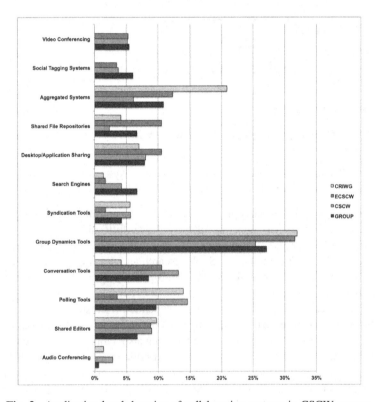

Fig. 3. Application-level domains of collaborative systems in CSCW venues.

the use of social networking sites, question answering systems, social bookmarking, microblogs, wikis, virtual worlds, crowd computing, and Web conferencing tools brought opportunities for studying online behavior. This fact is also consistent with the growth of social tagging systems, search engines, video conferencing, and syndication applications.

4.1 Grounded Theory for Taxonomy Development in CSCW: A 'Sleeping Dragon' Wanting for Awakening

A taxonomic evaluation can characterize the most addressed systems and functional attributes by venue. However, further research is needed updating taxonomic categories in a systematic way considering the changing requirements of collaboration. From a general examination on DBLP, both ACM CSCW and ACM GROUP divide their tracks into particular categories that range from collaborative software development to crowdsourcing and citizen science, healthcare and emergency response, social media, tangible interfaces, home and family technology, Wikipedia studies, MOOCs, games and virtual worlds, policy, cybersecurity, Q&A sites, etc. Conversely, ECSCW publications are mostly based on field-based studies using methods intended to inform the development of technologies from the ground up, presenting fieldwork on multiple scenarios such as heritage and homecare.

Despite their utility, such categories are very generic, being difficult to obtain qualitative data with high level of detail. Measuring scientific production is a hard task that needs a comprehensive, theoretically grounded and practically valuable conceptualization of its structure and evolution [33]. Despite the efforts in the creation of conceptual frameworks, taxonomies, ontologies, and thesauri to represent knowledge about consolidated and emerging topics, existing classification systems fail on capturing the intellectual structure of a scientific field, understood as an abstraction of the collective knowledge of its researchers. The main challenge relies on the following question: How do researchers, venture capital investors, program managers and students keep up with advances in the expanding field of CSCW? This is particularly complex to manage since we are nowadays overwhelmed by findings of thousands of scholars. Long-term classification of massive data collections can be considered as a challenging issue for research communities, institutions and disciplines regarding the inherent difficulty of recognizing gaps, trends, patterns, concepts, "ghost theories", and social-technical aspects.

We assume that Grounded Theory [13], a methodology originated in sociology, can be particularly useful in CSCW (as discussed by Muller and Kogan [35]) to make sense of large volumes of data from scientific publications. In the particular structure of work in which an individual is making sense of literature, both domain and type of data to be extracted are previously known. However, new categories can emerge from distinct ways we analyze our data, as well the strategies we use for finding evidence. Based on the Muller and Kogan's [35] guidelines for working with data in Grounded Theory, we returned to our initial sample and categorized three years of research in collaborative computing through a series of data-driven operations conducted to develop a high-quality description in which open and axial codes were gradually developed and grouped into categories and dimensions of analysis. Table 2 provides an example of the descriptive codes used to perform this exploratory analysis. Each paper was screened and a set of categories was then extracted and organized on the basis of a semantic relationship to the data presented in the collection form.

After performing the extraction of categories from a total of 145 publications from ACM GROUP 2010 (36), ECSCW 2009 (23), and ACM CSCW 2008 (86), we formulate a set of considerations. For taxonomy development, it was possible to obtain new categories that can be added to current classification schemes (e.g., [10]) while contributing to the development of a rigorous and comprehensive evaluation framework for collaborative computing. For instance, *selective undo* in collaborative applications appeared as a new functional attribute. Specialized and modularized division of labor was associated to success factors in online creative collaboration (peer production) in the context of collaborative animated movies and open source software development. Perhaps, concepts like *articulation work* and *coordination by avoidance* can be ignored from new researchers in the field. Thus, we consider the record and contextualization extremely important. We also found possible associations between terms like *genre ecologies* ↔ *community regulation, participatory citizenship* ↔ *timeline collaboration, virtual worlds* ↔ *phatic communication, version control* ↔ *collaborative conflict resolution, boundary negotiating artifacts* ↔ *cyberinfrastructure*, and *workspace awareness* ↔ *real-time collaborative 3D design*. Table 3 summarizes the main categories extracted from literature in this preliminary approach to the use of Grounded Theory [13] for CSCW research evaluation.

New types of systems emerged from applying Grounded Theory [13]. Some examples are games, home technology, or tabletop displays. Describe a system is also relevant for who are interested on experimenting a certain tool for particular purposes considering its main features described with high detail. From *scheduling patients* in a medical information system to *collaborative filtering*, several features have already appeared. In general, Grounded Theory [13] can be particularly useful as a method for unveiling new kinds of taxonomic units from publication records with higher levels of granularity. However, researchers in HCI and CSCW will need to inform their choices and problems to be solved with a strong knowledge of the research literature [35].

4.2   Lessons Learned and Future Directions

Any evaluation process suffers from errors due to perception abilities to process data, depending on the homogeneity and standardization of a field of study. A clear limitation of a taxonomy-based study is the lack of socio-technical dimensions that can be extracted using open codes. The granularity of the taxonomy restricted the focus to functional attributes instead of social requirements that represent a central focus of CSCW research. Nonetheless, the lack of categories at the application-level led to the necessity of making some adaptations and classification choices to evaluate a system, since the Mittleman et al.'s [10] taxonomy does not directly cover several collaborative systems. In addition, this taxonomy does not consider the work context representation and management that today is almost mandatory. The lack of categories to classify certain systems resulted in a hard process of decision-making about what categories are best suited for a particular evaluation scenario. For example, Dogear Game [12], a social bookmarking tool, is classified as a social tagging system because its functional

Table 2. Data collection form (adapted from Muller and Kogan [35]).

Paper ID	P1
Source	ACM GROUP
Year	2010
General concepts and terms	Specialized division of labor Modularized division of labor Essential complexity Online creative collaboration Peer production Online communities
Contributions	Systematic research agenda Success factors in open-source software projects
Results, insights, and implications for design	Large software projects require many skill sets and, therefore, many people Success factors in open-source software projects include planning and structure, reputation and experience, communication and dedication Success rates were low for both open source software projects and collabs (less than 20%)
Method	Qualitative (semi-structured interviews and participant observation)
Sample	N = 17 animators (amateurs, students, and professionals), age (16 to 29), genre (male) N = 892 collab threads
Variables	Ratings and popularity of completed collabs Themes as content guidelines for the project (e.g., music video, single narrative, comedy sketches) Specs as technical specifications for the project (e.g., dimensions, frame rate, audio streaming) Authorship criteria determining which artists get "co-author" credit (e.g., best submissions, most helpful, voting) Restrictions identifying prohibited content types for the project (e.g., violence, nudity, profanity) Gatekeeping rules govern who can join the project (e.g., leader's pick, experience baselines, tryouts) Communication preferences providing instructions for contacting the leader (e.g., email, IM, phone/voice)
Research agenda	What are the underlying principles allowing online creative collaboration to succeed, and how well do they transfer from one domain to another? Although the applicability of identified principles to open-source software and collabs is promising, more work is needed to test them in still other domain
System(s) proposed or evaluated	Newgrounds
Application-level domain	Multi-author system for animated movies and games
Features and functional attributes	Post a collab thread describing the project and inviting community members to join Submit completed animations for judgment by other members
Other tools mentioned	Wikipedia SourceForge Slashdot
Notes	Roles (leader, artist, co-author) Interview quote#1 ("A collaboration can't succeed without [communication]")

basis consists in the ability to create tagged resources and additional metadata about enterprise data despite its game-based incentives and mechanisms.

The sample chosen may need broadening to more years and sources where CSCW research is already published in order to increase construct validity on the use and development of Grounded Theory [13] in taxonomy creation and research evaluation. In the future, we aim to collect a larger, yet filtered, sample while identifying new ways to interpret prior research since there is also a large body of studies involving collaborative computing research published in journals such as the CSCW journal and other conferences (e.g., CHI).

Making sense of the social-technical dimensions of collaboration by exploiting the evolution of concepts can help newcomers (and experts) in the field of CSCW since the diversity of concepts is a known problem in the field [1]. Despite the effort to achieve a comprehensive analysis of CSCW technologies based on a scientific valid taxonomic model that may help researchers, developers and general public in understanding groupware features, manual classification is tremendously difficult due to the high human effort spent in the classification tasks, causing judgment deviations. Inconclusive results and time-consuming processes are complex issues for this kind of studies. Mittleman et al.'s [10] classification schemes require further research making additions and revisions while bringing them to a state where their taxonomic units can account for more collaborative tools while enabling better informed design.

5   Concluding Remarks

Understanding CSCW as a socio-technical design space is a big challenge. While making sense of technology can be a relatively easy task, collaboration represents a phenomenon that requires intensive analysis of concepts and contexts. This study explored collaborative systems evaluation techniques by analyzing a wide variety of publications from ACM CSCW, ACM GROUP, ECSCW, and CRIWG. However, this paper does not represent an attempt to summarize the state-of-the-art in collaborative computing research. On the other hand, it provides an initial springboard for the analysis of large volumes of scientific data published every year through a dynamic interplay between a set of strategies and methods. In the future, we aim to evaluate collaborative systems and cooperative work conceptualizations from multivariate views. In this context, analytical techniques and methods must be reinvented systematically and recursively to cope with the advancements in CSCW due to its interdisciplinary nature. Therefore, it is critical to understand how data itself is subjectively situated and used in other disciplines [30]. This breadth raises a number of questions, including the challenge of understanding the structure and evolution of science by reviewing the past while developing current conceptualizations and models of scholarly activity [33]. Finally, we can also assume that distilling such data using Grounded Theory [13] while adopting a mixed-initiative approach based on machine learning and crowdsourcing can constitute an effective approach to cope with the different social-technical dimensions in the field of CSCW while helping researchers and the general public to be aware of its evolution.

Table 3. General concepts, methods, and system attributes identified from CSCW literature.

General concepts and terms

crowdsourcing, wisdom of crowds, collective intelligence, CMC, collaboration, coordination (e.g., coordination by avoidance), CSCL, boundary objects/negotiating artifacts, situated practice, privacy, disruption, awareness (e.g., workspace, situational), user-centered design, articulation work, usability, social presence, communities of practice, interruptions, practice turn, division of labor (e.g., specialized, modularized), mutuality, common ground, conflict, consensus-building, regulation (e.g., social, community), social translucence, distributed cognition, legitimate peripheral participation, peer production, spatial flexibility, sustaining ubiquity, implications for design, active negotiation of shared understanding, online identity, mediating artifacts, shift roles, policy (e.g., healthcare policy), identity, persuasion, implicit interaction, enjoyment, social engagement, social influence, resilience, routines, sustainability, behavioral change, social dilemma, community responsiveness, telepresence, social interaction, reciprocity, appropriation, online ties, people-centeredness, self-presentation, ecologies, distance, distributed and interdisciplinary research (e.g., medical teams), cohesion, information seeking, shared representations of information, degree centrality, context, stigmergy, peripheral augmentation, managing anthropological strangeness, online creative collaboration, collaborative reflection, partially distributed teams (e.g., asymmetric), social relationship interactions, group recommendation, multitasking, cross-institutional and -cultural collaboration, essential complexity, social exchange, social clues, relaxed-space-time, social proxies, phatic communication, ontology, group composition factors, workarounds, in-group membership, HCI4D, lurker, defamiliarization, operational transformation, group formation, worker's standardized operation, grammar of action, consistency maintenance, center/periphery principle, interaction trajectories, collaboration and technology readiness, collaboration engineering, workflow and interaction patterns, timeline collaboration, boundaries, trans-disciplinary and trans-cultural interactions, ideas as design artefacts, information flow, networked communities, work organization, activity mapping, resource sharing, supporting thick practices, externalization, use of physical space, use of bodies, collaborative conflict resolution, geographically distributed software development, model versioning, refactorings, conceptual foundations on CSCW program, remote presence, object-focused collaboration, character sharing, conceptions of sharing, model-based adaptive product and process engineering, socio-technical and collaborative design, organization of scientific work, business multimodal communication, distributed knowledge-intensive work and representation, promotion, organizational behavior, trustworthiness, temporal and spatial organization, attention, mobile conversation, voice memories, community empowerment, underserved communities, physical spaces, requirements engineering, widescale interaction, commiseration, geographical communities, collective behavior, social creativity, socio-temporal stages, content and input redirection, sense of unity, metaphorical relationships between online and offline interactions, shared virtual workspace, shift change, information sharing, transactive memory, human categorization, mental categories, socially constructed information, user-contributed metadata, focused physical interaction, representation of reality, core mechanic, micro goals, marginal challenge, social play, group navigation, accountability, lexical mimicry, trust linguistic politeness, communication (e.g., interpersonal, ad hoc), responsiveness, availability, emotion and affect, social telepresence, deictic cues, body motion, asymmetry, media space, information processing, information overload, community interactions, shared public discourse, close online-offline integration, leadership, collabs, online team-building, jumpstarting relationships, small groups, instances, grouping patterns, context-linked, group decision-making, time-critical science tasks, hybrid ecology, trustmixed reality, socio-political hybridity, intellectual teamwork, distributed work, spam, interpersonal attraction, deception, high-interdependency tasks, design implications, human mediation, virtual organization, interdependencies, team climate, collaborative tie strength, local lag, tightly-coupled interaction, expert collaboration, visual feedback, temporal constraints, dominance, interpersonal critical feedback, feedback-seeking behavior, stability, social visualization, trust, accuracy, motives, expertise, coverage, sources, personalization, group search, groupization, group hit-highlighting, sensemaking, constructs of technology, activity context, organizational context, system and workplace design context, synchronous communication, communication overload, transaction costs, help-seeking, structure, position, functional tie-diversity, predictive power of time, patterns of conversational interactions, text similarity, structure and models of discourse, material artifacts, representational artifacts, redundancy, communication networks, modularity, non-profit social services, organizational structure, event handling, personal assistance, routine work, intimacy, connectedness, degree of ownership, familiar expectations, visibility, accountability, socially responsible behaviour, ambiguity, multi-synchronous interaction, concurrent changes, user account models, personalization, context-sensitive information needs, communal knowledge, technology-assisted fundraising, contextualized discussions, self description and expression, impression formation, reuse, user motivation, open sharing, audience, user profiles, attitudes, disrupted environments, knowledge management

Methods and theories

qualitative, quantitative (e.g., quantitative analysis of user behavior), mixed-method, semi-structured interviews, participant observation, case study, survey, interaction logs (e.g., logs of systems usage), progressive scenarios, laboratory experiments, questionnaires, grounded theory, content analysis, simulation experiments, ethnomethodology (e.g., in-depth field observation, ethnographic data analysis), action research, psychological and ergonomic studies, quasi-experiment, system evaluation, latent semantic analysis, social network analysis, attribution theory, the locales framework, exploratory study (e.g., deployment), field trial, design methods (e.g., participatory design, scenario-based design), conversation/discourse analysis, theoretical model, data collection, longitudinal field tests, discursive method work, agile methods, empirical studies, socio-technical walkthrough, progressive scenarios, gesture analysis, cognitive work analysis

Application-level domains

email, crisis informatics and emergency response, socially-organized social networking sites, multi-author systems (e.g., animated movies), healthcare technology (e.g., electronic health/patient records), collaborative design and 3D digital media design tools, meeting support tools (e.g., avatar-based, integrated), mobile technology (e.g., mobile services for hospital staff), collaboratively edited online encyclopedias (e.g., wikis), online communities (e.g., open source software), surface computing (e.g., shared tabletop displays, tangible interfaces), supply chain management systems, virtual worlds and immersive collaborative virtual environments, assistive technology, multimodal interfaces, multi-display environments, human-robot interaction (e.g., museum guide), recommender systems, question answering, e-science and cyberinfrastructure (e.g., research technology prototypes, collaboratories, laboratories, laboratory notebooks), instant messaging, video conferencing, context-aware computing, ubiquitous and pervasive computing, wearable computing, whiteboards (e.g., augmented), photoware, enterprise social software (e.g., enterprise resource planning), file-sharing services, knowledge repositories and databases (e.g., code repositories, sequence databases, host of animations), collaborative tagging systems, home and family technology (e.g., shared family calendars), urban computing, persuasive technology, information systems (e.g., geographic, medical), GPS and location-based systems, blogging and microblogging, electronic document systems, courseware, version control systems, discussion forums, awareness displays and widgets, collaborative games (e.g., massively multiplayer online games, fitness video games), virtual assistants, notification systems, machine learning, data mining, evolutionary algorithms, text-chat environments, place-based systems for group meetings, interpersonal exchange systems (e.g., online gift exchange), ambient personal information and communication systems, reputation code search applications, task management systems, proactive displays, large displays, flashlight displays, timeline-planning tools, model versioning systems for collaborative conflict resolution, group memory-aid for software developers, information visualization kiosks, public displays, proactive display applications, digital graffiti systems, VNC telescope, persuasive real-time portable systems, multi-synchronous applications, charitable technologies, connections management systems, user-generated content sites, teleconferencing, synchronous social interaction environments, conscription devices, living arts displays

Features and functional attributes

collaborative filtering, selective undo, upload a file, add a file to a collection, file sharing, download a file, view metadata about a file, recommend a file to another user, read, dynamic update, transmission of text messages (e.g., SMS), record audio and video (e.g., consultations), photo capture and sharing (e.g., mobile-collocated), calendar information sharing, rating, speech recognition and synthesis, reminders, classification and categorization (e.g., topics, activities, code recorded sessions), intelligent assistance, digital media creation and submission (e.g., 3D animations), express preferences, event notification (e.g., context linked), chat (e.g., asynchronous chat), awareness indicators, comment, access control, ask questions, group consensus function (e.g., automatic), telepointing, televiewing, blog posts, subjective observations provided by users, embedded charting, scheduling and planning, timeline (e.g., events, tasks), comment, collaborative play, group video communication, smart splitting, information extraction, text analysis, barnstars, FAQ, social feedback community visualization, task availability, status manager (predict the status of a user), visibility of people's communicative state, list sharing, sharing memories, event aggregator, Thinklets, take notes (e.g., paper-based artifacts for mobile information access), RFID (e.g., sketches, tag models), sociometric sensors and badges, reputation and popularity, security system, automatically display gestures, content and spatial mapping, create individual and collaborative templates, collab threads, context tree, automatically extracted emotional information, space logging, automatic route-finding enhanced by user input, configurable sharing suggestions, meeting support (e.g., lightweight group meetings), real-time text display, WYSIWYG editing (e.g., geographic content), edit history, social summaries of complex multimedia materials, social search and navigation (e.g., crawler search for files through or by clicking a tag), social tagging and bookmarking (e.g., tag geographic objects in an interactive map, tag cloud, suggesting tags that have been applied to a type of object), data curation, annotation, support electronic health records (e.g., charts), personal health record allowing patients to register healthcare-related values (e.g., glucose), registering and coordinating patients, communication, social networking, profile offerings, screen saver, camera, microphone, contact info, auto-complete dialog based on entered text, view finder, ability to browse thumbnails and view photos in full size, multi-tiered policy environment, navigate documental artifacts according to predefined process maps, neighborhood, user reflection, override, interface combining text instructions with map segments on individual pages, text and other information on top of a map, live discussions, archiving materials, mobile maps, route planning and presentation, activity streams, printing, edit profile, expert identification

Acknowledgements. This work is financed by the ERDF – European Regional Development Fund through the Operational Programme for Competitiveness and Internationalisation - COMPETE 2020 Programme within project «POCI-01-0145-FEDER-006961», and by National Funds through the Portuguese funding agency, FCT - Fundação para a Ciência e a Tecnologia as part of project «UID/EEA/50014/2013».

References

1. Schmidt, K.: Divided by a common acronym: on the fragmentation of CSCW. In: Wagner, I., Tellioğlu, H., Balka, E., Simone, C., Ciolfi, L. (eds.) ECSCW 2009. Springer, London (2009). https://doi.org/10.1007/978-1-84882-854-4_14
2. Wulf, V., Rohde, M., Pipek, V., Stevens, G.: Engaging with practices: design case studies as a research framework in CSCW. In: Proceedings of the ACM Conference on Computer Supported Cooperative Work, pp. 505–512 (2011)
3. Grudin, J.: Punctuated equilibrium and technology change. Interactions **19**(5), 62–66 (2012)
4. Pinelle, D., Gutwin, C.: A review of groupware evaluations. In: Proceedings of the IEEE International Workshops on Enabling Technologies: Infrastructure for Collaborative Enterprises, pp. 86–91 (2000)
5. Hamadache, K., Lancieri, L.: Strategies and taxonomy, tailoring your CSCW evaluation. In: Carriço, L., Baloian, N., Fonseca, B. (eds.) CRIWG 2009. LNCS, vol. 5784, pp. 206–221. Springer, Heidelberg (2009). https://doi.org/10.1007/978-3-642-04216-4_17
6. Neale, D.C., Carroll, J.M., Rosson, M.B.: Evaluating computer-supported cooperative work: models and frameworks. In: Proceedings of the ACM Conference on Computer Supported Cooperative Work, pp. 112–121 (2004)
7. Holsapple, C.W., Luo, W.: A citation analysis of influences on collaborative computing research. Comput. Support. Coop. Work **12**(3), 351–366 (2003)
8. Antunes, P., Herskovic, V., Ochoa, S.F., Pino, J.A.: Structuring dimensions for collaborative systems evaluation. ACM Comput. Surv. **44**(2), 8 (2012)
9. Jacovi, M., Soroka, V., Gilboa-Freedman, G., Ur, S., Shahar, E., Marmasse, N.: The chasms of CSCW: a citation graph analysis of the CSCW conference. In: Proceedings of the ACM Conference on Computer Supported Cooperative Work, pp. 289–298 (2006)
10. Mittleman, D.D., Briggs, R.O., Murphy, J., Davis, A.: Toward a taxonomy of groupware technologies. In: Briggs, R.O., Antunes, P., de Vreede, G.J., Read, A.S. (eds.) CRIWG 2008. LNCS, vol. 5411, pp. 305–317. Springer, Heidelberg (2008). https://doi.org/10.1007/978-3-540-92831-7_25
11. Correia, A., Paredes, H., Fonseca, B.: Scientometric analysis of scientific publications in CSCW. Scientometrics **114**(1), 31–89 (2018)
12. Dugan, C., Muller, M., Millen, D.R., Geyer, W., Brownholtz, B., Moore, M.: The Dogear Game: a social bookmark recommender system. In: Proceedings of the ACM International Conference on Supporting Group Work, pp. 387–390 (2007)
13. Glaser, B., Strauss, A.: The Discovery of Grounded Theory. Adeline, Chicago (1967)
14. Greenberg, S.: An annotated bibliography of computer supported cooperative work. ACM SIGCHI Bull. **23**(3), 29–62 (1991)
15. Bush, V.: As we may think. Atl. Mon. **176**(1), 101–108 (1945)
16. Engelbart, D.: A conceptual framework for the augmentation of man's intellect. In: Howerton, P. (ed.) Vistas in Information Handling, vol. 1, pp. 1–29. Spartan Books, Washington, DC (1963)
17. Winograd, T., Flores, F.: Understanding Computers and Cognition: A New Foundation for Design. Ablex, Norwood (1986)

18. Shih, P.C., Nguyen, D.H., Hirano, S.H., Redmiles, D.F., Hayes, G.R.: GroupMind: supporting idea generation through a collaborative mind-mapping tool. In: Proceedings of the ACM Conference on Supporting Group Work, pp. 139–148 (2009)

19. Ackerman, M.S.: The intellectual challenge of CSCW: the gap between social requirements and technical feasibility. Hum.-Comput. Interact. **15**(2), 179–203 (2000)

20. Law, E.L.C., Nguyen-Ngoc, A.V., Kuru, S.: Mixed-method validation of pedagogical concepts for an intercultural online learning environment: a case study. In: Proceedings of the ACM Conference on Supporting Group Work, pp. 321–330 (2007)

21. Schmidt, K.: The concept of 'work' in CSCW. Comput. Support. Coop. Work **20**(4–5), 341–401 (2011)

22. Orlikowski, W.J.: Learning from notes: organizational issues in groupware implementation. In: Readings in Human-Computer Interaction, pp. 197–204 (1995)

23. Lee, C. P., Paine, D.: From the matrix to a model of coordinated action (MoCA): a conceptual framework of and for CSCW. In: Proceedings of the ACM Conference on Computer Supported Cooperative Work & Social Computing, pp. 179–194 (2015)

24. Sarma, A., Van Der Hoek, A., Cheng, L.T.: A need-based collaboration classification framework. In: Proceedings of the ACM Conference on Computer Supported Cooperative Work (2004)

25. Bafoutsou, G., Mentzas, G.: Review and functional classification of collaborative systems. Int. J. Inf. Manag. **22**, 281–305 (2002)

26. Pumareja, D.T., Sikkel, K.: An evolutionary approach to groupware implementation: the context of requirements engineering in the socio-technical frame. Technical report TR-CTIT-02-30, Centre for Telematics and Informational Technology, University of Twente, Enschede (2002)

27. Guibert, S., Darses, F., Boujut, J.F.: Using annotations in a collective and face-to-face design situation. In: Wagner, I., Tellioğlu, H., Balka, E., Simone, C., Ciolfi, L. (eds.) ECSCW 2009, pp. 191–206. Springer, London (2009). https://doi.org/10.1007/978-1-84882-854-4_11

28. Weiseth, P.E., Munkvold, B.E., Tvedte, B., Larsen, S.: The wheel of collaboration tools: a typology for analysis within a holistic framework. In: Proceedings of the ACM Conference on Computer-Supported Cooperative Work, pp. 239–248 (2006)

29. Grudin, J., Poltrock, S.: Taxonomy and theory in Computer Supported Cooperative Work. In: The Oxford Handbook of Organizational Psychology, vol. 2, pp. 1323–1348 (2012)

30. Pace, T., Bardzell, S., Fox, G.: Practice-centered e-science: a practice turn perspective on cyberinfrastructure design. In: Proceedings of the 16th ACM Conference on Supporting Group Work, pp. 293–302 (2010)

31. Jirotka, M., Lee, C.P., Olson, G.M.: Supporting scientific collaboration: methods, tools and concepts. Comput. Support. Coop. Work **22**(4–6), 667–715 (2013)

32. Kitchenham, B.: Procedures for performing systematic reviews, vol. 33, pp. 1–26. Keele University, Keele, UK (2004)

33. Börner, K., Scharnhorst, A.: Visual conceptualizations and models of science. J. Informetr. **3**(3), 161–172 (2009)

34. Marshall, C., Brereton, P., Kitchenham, B.: Tools to support systematic reviews in software engineering: a feature analysis. In: Proceedings of the 18th ACM International Conference on Evaluation and Assessment in Software Engineering, p. 13 (2014)

35. Muller, M.J., Kogan, S.: Grounded Theory Method in HCI and CSCW, pp. 1–46. IBM Center for Social Software, Cambridge (2010)

36. Cruz, A., Correia, A., Paredes, H., Fonseca, B., Morgado, L., Martins, P.: Towards an overarching classification model of CSCW and groupware: a socio-technical perspective. In: Herskovic, V., Hoppe, H.U., Jansen, M., Ziegler, J. (eds.) CRIWG 2012. LNCS, vol. 7493, pp. 41–56. Springer, Heidelberg (2012). https://doi.org/10.1007/978-3-642-33284-5_4

37. Dimond, J.P., Poole, E.S., Yardi, S.: The effects of life disruptions on home technology routines. In: Proceedings of the 16th ACM International Conference on Supporting Group Work, pp. 85–88 (2010)
38. Lampe, C., Ellison, N.B., Steinfield, C.: Changes in use and perception of Facebook. In: Proceedings of ACM CSCW, pp. 721–730 (2008)
39. Dabbish, L.A., Wagstrom, P., Sarma, A., Herbsleb, J.D.: Coordination in innovative design and engineering: observations from a lunar robotics project. In: Proceedings of the 16th ACM International Conference on Supporting Group Work, pp. 225–234 (2010)
40. Bayerl, P.S., Lauche, K.: Technology effects in distributed team coordination – high-interdependency tasks in offshore oil production. Comput. Support. Coop. Work 19(2), 139–173 (2010)
41. Schmidt, K., Bannon, L.: Taking CSCW seriously. Comput. Support. Coop. Work 1(1–2), 7–40 (1992)
42. Lim, B.Y., Brdiczka, O., Bellotti, V.: Show me a good time: using content to provide activity awareness to collaborators with ActivitySpotter. In: Proceedings of the ACM International Conference on Supporting Group Work, pp. 263–272 (2010)

Bundles: A Framework to Optimise Topic Analysis in Real-Time Chat Discourse

Jonathan Dunne[1]($\boxtimes$)(iD), David Malone[1], and Andrew Penrose[2]

[1] Hamilton Institute, Maynooth University, Maynooth, Ireland
jonathan.dunne.2015@mumail.ie, david.malone@mu.ie
[2] IBM Technology Campus, Dublin, Ireland
apenrose@ie.ibm.com

Abstract. Collaborative chat tools and large text corpora are ubiquitous in today's world of real-time communication. As micro teams and start-ups adopt such tools, there is a need to understand the meaning (even at a high level) of chat conversations within collaborative teams. In this study, we propose a technique to segment chat conversations to increase the number of words available (19% on average) for text mining purposes. Using an open source dataset, we answer the question of whether having more words available for text mining can produce more useful information to the end user. Our technique can help micro-teams and start-ups with limited resources to efficiently model their conversations to afford a higher degree of readability and comprehension.

Keywords: Chat segmentation · Topic modelling · Regression

1 Introduction

We live in an information age, and consumer-based services and applications generate more text-based data. As we embrace both collaborative and social communication, we converse more often via text-based communication [2,4]. For both business and recreational purposes real-time chat discourse appears to be part and parcel of our lives.

However, for businesses irrespective of size, using such collaborative and social means of communication, can be an overwhelming experience [6]. This is due in part to the large volumes of text-based data that are generated by such applications and services. Recent studies have shown that almost 350,000 tweets are created every minute of every day. Globally 2.5 quintillion bytes of data are produced [5]. The growth in social media messaging is not confined to tweet messages. A recent study [9] by the Harvard business school has shown that over 2.5 billion users communicate with at least one messaging app (e.g. WhatsApp, Facebook). This figure will rise to 3.6 billion users in the next few years. Therefore, for this study, we consider techniques that may help teams make sense of their message based data.

A. Rodrigues et al. (Eds.): CRIWG 2018, LNCS 11001, pp. 60–75, 2018.
https://doi.org/10.1007/978-3-319-99504-5_6

Topic modelling is a frequently used process to discover semantic structure within a text corpus. Topic modelling is used across multiple disciplines [12] as a vehicle to grow business insights [7]. For example, if a business can mine customer feedback on a particular product or service this information may prove valuable [3]. One of the recommendations when employing topic modelling techniques is that the more data available for analysis, the better the overall results. However, even in the age of big data, practitioners may have a requirement to text mine a single conversation or small text corpus to infer meaning.

In this paper, we propose a framework that both micro teams and SMEs can use to deliver a significant level of topic modelling terms, from real-time chat discourse data, while utilising their limited resource cohort. The core idea of this framework is for topic mining practitioners to partition their conversations using a novel technique. Such a method can provide a higher number of words (19% on average) for topic summarisation tooling. For small teams with a limited pool of test resources, leveraging such segmentation techniques can provide not only more words for text mining but an improved level of readability than using an entire message corpus alone.

This paper contains research conducted on an open-source real-time chat corpus. Through the study of this dataset we investigate (a) If by partitioning messages based on their inter-arrival time, can a more significant number of distinct words be returned for use by topic modelling software? (b) Does a higher number of words provide a level of readability that is easier for humans to comprehend? (c) Can we use the results of this work to predict an optimal topic cluster size? Using the results of this study for our framework, a topic mining solution can be developed to provide an enhanced level of understanding for small message corpora.

The rest of the paper is structured in five sections: Sect. 2 gives some description of study background and related works. Section 3 describes the enterprise dataset. Section 4 provides analysis and methodology. It is followed by Sect. 5 that explains the result. Finally, the conclusion and future work are described in Sect. 6.

2 Background and Related Research

2.1 Natural Language Processing

Tokenisation is a process of converting a sequence of characters (e.g. message discourse) into a series of tokens (strings with an assigned meaning) [21]. Therefore, before any analysis is conducted on a text corpus, the text is divided into linguistic elements such as words, punctuation, numbers and alpha-numerics [32].

Stop words are words which are filtered out before or after processing of text discourse [25]. Stop words typically refer to the most common words in a language; there is no consensus or master list of agreed stop words. The website "ranks.nl" provides lists of stop words in forty languages [10]. Luhn, one of the pioneers in the field of information retrieval, is credited with creating the concept of stop words [27].

Stemming is a method of collapsing inflected words to their base or root form [26]. For example, the words: fishing, fished and fisher, could be reduced to their root fish. The benefit of stemming can be seen as follows: If one is interested in term frequency, it may be easiest to merely count the occurrences of the word fish rather than its non-stemmed counterparts.

Lemmatisation is the process of grouping together the inflected words, for analysis as a single entity [28]. On the surface this process may look like the opposite of stemming; however, the main difference is that stemming is unaware of the context of the words and thus, cannot differentiate between words that have other meanings depending on context. For example, the word "worse" has "bad" as its lemma. This link is missed by stemming as a dictionary lookup is needed. Whereas, the word "talk" is the root of "talking". This reference is matched in both stemming and lemmatisation.

2.2   Corpus Linguistics

Corpus linguistics is the study of language as expressed in corpora (i.e. collections) of "actual use" text. The core idea is that analysis of expression is best conducted within its natural usage. By collecting samples of writing, researchers can understand how individuals converse with each other. One of the most influential studies in this field was conducted by Kučera and Francis [23]. The authors analysed an American English Corpus, that involved analysis techniques from linguistics, psychology and statistics.

2.3   Topic Modelling Tools

Latent Semantic Analysis (LSA) is a method that allows for a low-dimension representation of documents and words. By constructing a document-term matrix, and using matrix algebra, one can infer document similarity (product of row vectors) and word similarity (product of column vectors). The idea was first proposed by Landauer et al. in 1998 [24].

In 1999 Hofmann proposed a statistical technique of two-mode and co-occurrence data [19]. In essence, his Probabilistic Latent Semantic Analysis model (PLSA), allowed a higher degree of precision for information retrieval than standard LSA models. This is due to the introduction of a novel Tempered Expectation Maximisation technique that used a probabilistic method rather than matrices for fitting. However, one drawback of the PLSA method, is that, as the number of words and documents increase, so does the level of overfitting.

Latent Dirichlet allocation (LDA) is a generative statistical model that allows topics within a text corpus to be represented as a collection of terms [13]. At its core, LDA is a three-level hierarchical Bayesian model, in which each item in an array is modelled as a finite mixture over an underlying set of topics. Blei et al. first proposed the idea in 2003.

2.4   Linear Regression

Linear regression is a statistical technique to model the relationship between two or more variables. Typically, one or more explanatory (or independent) variables expressed as X, are used to predict the a response (or dependent) variable expressed as y. Where one independent variable is used, the process is known as simple linear regression. Where more than one independent variable is used the process is known as multiple linear regression.

At a high level, both sets of variables are plotted in the form of a scatter plot, and a least squares line is fitted between the points on the graph. This approach attempts to fit a straight line between the points plotted. If the two sets of variables have a linear relationship, a suitable linear functional can be obtained in the following form:

$$\hat{Y}_i = \hat{\beta}_0 + \hat{\beta}_1 X_i + \hat{\epsilon}_i \tag{1}$$

Linear regression was first proposed by Galton in 1886 [17].

2.5   Studies Related to Topic Modelling of Small Text Corpora

Jivani conducts a comparative study of eleven stemmers, to compare their advantages and limitations [20]. The study found that there is a lot of similarity regarding performance between the various stemming algorithms. Additionally, a rule-based approach may provide the correct output for all cases, as the stems generated may not always be accurate words. For linguistic stemmers their output is highly dependent on the lexicon used, and words outside of the lexicon are not stemmed correctly.

Naveed et al. [29] investigates the problem of document sparsity in topic mining in the realm of micro-blogs. Their study found that ignoring length normalisation improves retrieval results. By introducing an "interestingness" (level of re-tweets) quality measurement also improves retrieval performance.

The Biterm topic model is explicitly designed for small text corpora such as instant messages and tweet discourse [33]. Conventional topic models such as LDA implicitly capture the document-level word co-occurrence patterns to reveal topics, and thus suffer from the severe data sparsity in short documents. With these problems identified, Yan et al., proposed a topic model that (a) explicitly models word co-occurrence patterns and (b) uses the aggregated patterns in the whole corpus for learning topics to solve the problem of sparse word co-occurrence patterns at document-level.

Yin et al. [35] discuss the problem of topic modelling short text corpora such as tweets and social media messages. The core challenges are due to sparse, high-dimensional and large volume characteristics. The authors proposed a Gibbs Sampling algorithm for the Dirichlet model (GSDMM). The authors demonstrated that a sparsity model could achieve better performance than either K-means clustering or a Dirichlet Process Mixture Model for Document Clustering with Feature Partition.

Sridhar [31] presents an unsupervised topic model for short texts using a Gaussian mixture model. His model uses a vector space model that overcomes the issue of word sparsity. The author demonstrates the efficacy of this model compared to LDA using tweet message data.

Topic Modelling of Short Texts: A Pseudo-Document View by Zuo et al. [36] propose a probabilistic model called Pseudo-document-based topic model (PTM) for short text topic modelling. PTM introduces the idea of a pseudo-document to implicitly aggregate short texts against data sparsity. By modelling these pseudo-documents rather than short texts, a higher degree of performance is achieved. An additional sparsity enhancement is proposed that removes undesirable correlations between pseudo-documents and latent topics.

The idea of 'Bursty' topics (i.e. posts published in a short time window follow a similar topic distribution) within microblogs (Twitter) has been considered by both Diao et al. [16] and Yan et al. [34].

Schofield and Mimmo [30] investigate the effects of stemmers on topic models. Their research concluded that stemming does not help in controlling the size of vocabulary for topic modelling algorithms like LDA, and may reduce the predictive likelihood. The authors suggest that post-stemming may exploit nuances specific to corpora and computationally more efficient due to the smaller list of words for input.

3   Data Set

Topic modelling and text mining of social media/collaboration messaging have been shown to provide insight into the subjects people discuss as part of their online communication. By segmenting instant message text in a novel way, before topic modelling, we demonstrate how a higher degree of understanding can be achieved by the results of topic model outputs.

For this study, we topic modelled three complete chat conservations from an open source Ubuntu developer IRC channel [11]. For each conversation, IRC messages were read, we noted an initial salutation, a valediction and a grouped topic discussed in-between the greeting and farewell messages. For this study, only conversations with related topic content were considered. We note that chat conversations with mixed chat messages (i.e. 'entangled chat conversations') are beyond the scope of this study and will not be considered here.

Table 1 provides a summary of the number of total words, the non-stopped words, the distinct non-stopped words and the percentage of words available for analysis.

This study aims to answer the following questions. First, can we segment a chat conversation in such a way as to provide a greater number of distinct words for topic modelling algorithms? Second, if a reasonable segmentation method can be found, is the output from a topic model easier to infer meaning, then modelling the entire conversation alone? Third, is there a relationship between the topic modelling cluster size and the number of words Input/Output from topic modelling?

Table 1. Summary of dataset conversation metrics

Metric	Chat 1	Chat 2	Chat 3
Total messages	46	70	59
Total words	292	436	484
Non-stopped words	158	239	262
Distinct non-stopped words	111	168	186
% Words for analysis	38	39	38

3.1   Conversation Segmentation

A question for practitioners of topic modelling is, *how can we maximise the number of words for analysis?* We know from prior research that text mining algorithms may require some form of text pre-processing prior to topic modelling. Pre-processing may include at least one of the following: Tokenisation, stop words removal, stemming and lemmatisation. The removal of words as part of this pre-processing step usually is not an issue for a large text corpus, due to the number of words available. In the case of small text corpora, the problem may be more acute. For our study, stemming and lemmatisation was not conducted.

We recorded the inter-arrival time of instant message posts within the Ubuntu IRC channel, and grouped messages by short and long inter-arrival times. For successive messages with a zero minute inter-arrival time, we define this collection of messages as a burst. For messages with a one minute or greater inter-arrival time, we define this group of messages as a reflection. We then perform text mining on each burst and reflection period and then aggregate the output terms. For topic text mining, we used the tool biterm, which is suited to modelling small text corpora.

3.2   Topic Modelling Comprehension

After a conversation has been (a) segmented into burst and reflection periods, (b) these periods topic modelled and (c) the results aggregated, we consider the efficacy of the output.

We accept that the terms output from a topic model algorithm is not explicitly designed for a readable summary. Instead, they are designed to give a user an indication of the terms used in a text corpus. Nevertheless of interest is how

Table 2. Summary of differences between questionnaire samples

Sample 1	Entire chat - topic modelled
Sample 2	Burst & reflections - topic modelled
Sample 3	Entire chat - stop words removed
Sample 4	Entire chat - no text pre-processing

a user can understand the output of text mining. Our approach is to prepare four sets of text as follows; (1) each conversation is modelled with biterm (as a whole) and the mined terms output into a single collection, (2) the bursts and reflections from each conversation are modelled individually, the terms are then aggregated into a single collection, (3) each conversation with the stop words removed and (4) the raw conversation (i.e. without any pre-processing). Table 2 summarises the level of pre-processing conducted for each sample.

We then asked twenty four test subjects to summarise each of the four text sets belonging to a single conversation. Additionally, we asked each participant to comment on which of the four text sets was easiest to summarise. Next, we asked each subject, whether they felt set one (all terms topic modelled) or set two (bursts and reflections topic modelled) was most natural to summarise. Finally, we asked each subject to describe why they felt the text set chosen in the second question was easiest to summarise. Results of a meta-study on sample sizes for qualitative studies [8] show there is variability in sample size depending on the subject domain. For our questionnaire, twenty-four individuals were selected, and each conversation was randomly distributed among the users.

Finally we compared the readability of every text set for each conversation using a number of known readability tests such as; Dale-Chall [15], Coleman-Liau [14], Flesch-Kincaid [22] and Gunning Fog [18].

3.3   Term Cluster Size Prediction

Topic modelling algorithms use a unique set of words from a corpus for analysis. Also, we know that the process of text mining may be, in part non-deterministic. In other words, random sampling is often used to generate a term list. One of the goals of text mining is to ensure that a sufficient number of words are output in each topic cluster. The intuition is that the more unique words that are provided, perhaps the easier the output will be to understand.

Biterm, outputs topic mined terms as 'topic clusters'. Each cluster has a maximum size of ten terms. If one hundred words are input for analysis, the intuition is that ten clusters will be output with a ten distinct words. However, due to the underlying random nature of the sampling algorithm used, this is not always the case. Therefore, it is necessary to use a range of cluster sizes to obtain the optimal number of terms. We define 'optimal output words' as the number of words that is closely equivalent to the number of words used for biterm analysis. We define the 'optimal # clusters', as the smallest number of clusters that contains the optimal output words.

Linear regression is a method to determine the relationship between two or more variables where one variable is dependent, and the additional variables are independent. A hypothesis test (are two or variables correlated) is conducted, and a p-value is computed. Depending on the size of the p-value, the hypothesis of a relationship/no relationship can be accepted or rejected. We used the lm function found in the base R package [1] and performed a linear regression test.

We will use linear regression to explore the relationship between the number of unique words input, the biterm cluster size and the unique terms output. For example, if we model the unique words input to biterm, the cluster size that provides the unique optimal set of terms and the count of these text mined terms, a linear model could be used to predict optimal term cluster size.

3.4 Limitations of Dataset

The dataset has some practical limitations, which are now discussed. The process of aggregating chat messages into a cohesive conversation is a subjective one. Every effort was made to assign messages to their most appropriate thread. We recognise that the process is subjective. Additionally, the post times for the Ubuntu chat were measured in hours and minutes only. As a result, we defined our burst and reflection periods as timed in zero and one minute or greater duration respectively.

The chat conversations that form part of this case study are from an Ubuntu IRC developer channel. While we hope these examples will be representative of technical discussion channels, it seems unlikely they will be typical of all types of channels.

4   Results

4.1 Conversation Segmentation

Table 3 shows a summary of the topic modelling work conducted on each of the three conversations. In the first experiment, the entire discussion was mined. In the second experiment, the burst and reflections were modelled separately.

For conversation one, a total of 96 terms were output by biterm when modelling the entire text, whereas 87 and 60 terms respectively were output from the burst and reflection analysis. A total of 51 (17%) more terms were output from the combined burst and reflection analysis than modelling the entire conversation.

For conversation two, a total of 129 terms were output by biterm, whereas 118 and 93 terms respectively were output from the burst and reflection analysis. A total of 82 (19%) more terms were output from the combined burst and reflection analysis than modelling the entire conversation.

For conversation three, a total of 143 terms were output by biterm, whereas 145 and 94 terms respectively were output from the burst and reflection topic mining. A total of 96 (20%) more terms were output from the combined burst and reflection analysis than modelling the entire conversation.

In the third experiment, the stop words were removed from each of the three chat conversations, no segmentation was conducted.

4.2 Topic Modelling Comprehension

Recalling the survey questions asked in Sect. 3 part B: Of the four text samples, which sample did you find easier to summarise? And of samples 1 and 2, which

Table 3. Summary of text mining analysis: entire conversations vs burst and reflections

Metric	Chat 1	Chat 2	Chat 3
Total words	292	436	484
Non-stopped words	158	239	262
Distinct non-stopped words	111	168	186
Distinct non-stopped terms output	96	129	143
# Words not analysed	196	307	341
% Words for analysis	38	39	38
% Actual terms output	33	30	30
Total burst words	185	226	287
Non-stopped burst words	98	143	163
Distinct non-stopped burst words	91	118	154
Distinct non-stopped terms output	87	118	145
# Burst words not analysed	94	108	142
# Bursts	7	11	8
% Words for analysis	49	52	54
% Actual terms output	47	52	51
Total reflection words	107	210	197
Non-stopped reflection words	61	99	99
Distinct non-stopped reflection words	60	95	94
Distinct non-stopped terms output	60	93	94
# Reflection words not analysed	47	115	103
# Reflections	7	12	9
% Words for analysis	56	45	48
% Actual terms output	56	44	48

Table 4. Summary of text sample questionnaire answers (Q1 & Q2)

Question	Sample 1 - biterm (all text)	Sample 2 - biterm (burst & reflections)	Sample 3 - (stop words removed)	Sample 4 - (full text)
One: of the 4 text samples, which sample did you find easier to summarise? (1/2/3 or 4)	0	0	2	22
Two: of samples 1 and 2, which sample did you find easier to summarise? (1 or 2)	0	24	NA	NA

sample did you find easier to summarise? Table 4 shows a summary of the answers to the questions asked of the test subjects. Before the questionnaire, the subjects were asked to summarise the four samples. The questions were asked directly after the summarisation task. As we can see for question one, the majority of users found sample 4 easiest to summarise. For question two, the respondents answered unanimously in favour of sample 2.

Fig. 1. Word cloud of answers from question 3

Question three asked: For the sample, you chose in question two, why did you find that text sample easier to summarise? Fig. 1 shows a word cloud generated from the answers respondents provided. When stop words were removed, the following terms appeared most frequently: easier (8 times), text (6), words (5) and flow/natural/understand/words (all 5).

To further understand the readability of text output from our topic mining experiments, we conducted some readability tests (Dale-Chall, Coleman-Liau, Flesch-Kincaid and Gunning Fog) against each of the four text samples for all three conversations. Figure 2 shows a bar chart of mean readability index scores. In all cases, a lower score indicates a more readable text sample. Intuitively we can see that text sample 1 had the highest score across all indices, and text sample 4 had a lowest. Text sample 2 had a lower index score than sample 1 in all readability tests.

4.3   Term Cluster Size Prediction

Our third research question asked, "Can we use the results of our topic modelling to predict an optimal topic bundle size?" We mentioned previously that obtaining an optimal number of terms (i.e. an output number of distinct words that matches an input number of distinct words) from biterm is an iterative process.

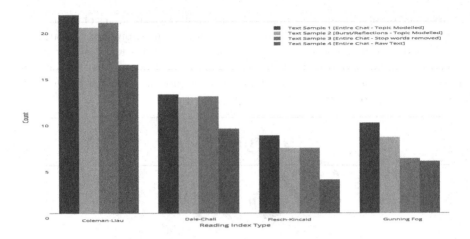

Fig. 2. Mean readability index score of each text sample

For each burst, reflection and complete segment we topic modelled multiple cluster numbers to obtain the optimal number of distinct words. Once an optimal cluster size was found, the number of clusters was noted. We then used Linear regression to determine if there is a strong relationship between the number of distinct words output and the cluster size. In order words can we create a linear function to predict the number of topic clusters, if the optimal number of terms are known?

Table 5. Linear regression coefficient table

Coefficients	Estimate	Std. error	t value	Pr(>t)
(Intercept)	0.934	0.122	7.606	3.45e−10
Optimal.Terms	0.058	0.003	18.201	<2e−16

Table 5 shows the output of the Linear regression analysis. We also note the following additional outputs; Residual standard error: 0.818, Multiple R-squared: 0.855, Adjusted R-squared: 0.853 and p-value: <2.2e−16. From the output we can see that the equation to fit our linear model is as follows:

$$Number\ of\ Clusters = 0.934 + 0.058(Optimal.Terms) \qquad (2)$$

Figure 3 shows the four goodness-of-fit plots generated from our linear regression model. These plots are used in conjunction with the results of the Linear coefficients table to determine the suitability of the model. We shall discuss these results of the model in more detail in the next section.

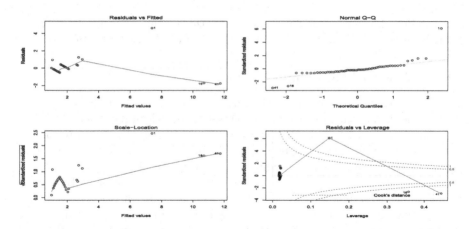

Fig. 3. Residuals vs fitted, Q-Q plot, scale-location & residuals vs leverage

5 Discussion

5.1 Conversation Segmentation

Our first research question asked, can we segment a chat conversation in such a way as to provide a higher number of unique words for topic modelling algorithms? Table 3 shows that the mean proportion of words available for analysis for topic modelling of an entire conversation is 38%, this is due to the considerable number of stop words that are removed as part of pre-processing. Likewise, the mean number of terms output from biterm is 31% a reduction of 7%.

Conversely, when both burst and reflections are aggregated, the mean proportion of terms available for analysis is 51%. Furthermore, the mean proportion of terms output from biterm is on average, 50% a reduction of only 1%.

There is evidence to suggest that segmenting conversations into shorter segments provides a greater number of words for topic analysis due to the lack of duplicate words found in each smaller segment. We note that stop words are removed irrespective of the segment size.

Some interesting points are raised by our analysis. When stop words are removed, duplicate occurrences of the same word are also discarded. However, in the case of a more substantial text corpus, some duplicate non-stop words remain, these words are ignored by text mining tools. We see this is not the case with burst and reflection text segments. In fact, for conversation 2, 143 non-stopped words were retained. A further 25 non-stop duplicate words were ignored. In all other cases, the number of duplicate words ignored by biterm after stop words were removed was less than 10.

Furthermore, we observed that the number of burst and reflections created might have little significance on the number of terms output. Conversations 1 & 3 had a similar number of segments (i.e. between 7 and 9), while conversation 2 had 11 burst and 12 reflections respectively. While no formal correlation tests were conducted, when we look at the segment size and the % terms output, there seems little positive or negative relationship between the two variables.

5.2   Topic Modelling Comprehension

Our second research question asked: If a reasonable segmentation method can be found, is the output from a topic model easier to understand, than modelling the entire conversation alone? In other words, even if more words can be output as part of our improved segmentation technique, how does this translate into comprehension by both a human and for general readability.

Table 4 summarises the answers to the first two survey questions asked by the 24 individuals who took part in our topic modelling comprehension experiment. Unsurprisingly we can see that the majority of respondents picked sample 4, as the easiest to summarise. The consensus was that with all words available and with grammar respected (to a degree) sample 4 was easiest to summarise for the majority. However, we note that two respondents picked sample 3 (stop words removed). The feedback from these two participants was that the samples with fewer words were easier to understand, this may be because these two individuals were not Ubuntu experts.

For survey question 2 the unanimous feedback from all users was that sample 2 was much easier to read than sample 1. A word cloud produced from the short answers provided, clearly indicate that a combination of our segmentation technique and biterm preserved the natural flow of the conversation to the degree that it was easier to summarise the text sample than sample 1.

Turning to the readability tests conducted, we can see that sample 4 produced the lowest mean index score indicating that the unprocessed chat was the most readable based on the four tests conducted. Except for the Gunning Fog index, sample 2 had equal or lower readability scores than sample 3.

It would be over-simplistic to state that when more words are available, it is easier for a human to understand a text segment based on a list of topic terms. However, it seems reasonable to assert that when more words are available and when words are placed in a similar order as to how they were typed, it is easier for humans to comprehend. What was interesting to note for short burst and reflection segments, (i.e. ten words or less) the input order of words was the same as the output terms produced by biterm. That is to say the word at the start of the sentence had the highest log-likelihood value, while the word at the end of the sentence had the lowest log-likelihood value.

We note that the goal of this research question was not to provide a readable summary based on text mined terms. Instead, the goal was to assess the understanding of text samples to humans when varying degrees of topic mining is conducted.

5.3   Term Cluster Size Prediction

Our third research question asked: Can we use the results of our topic modelling experiments to predict the optimal cluster size? Previously, we discussed the problem of determining the number of clusters that will return the highest number of distinct words from the biterm analysis. We also mentioned that the optimal cluster number could be obtained only by iteratively trying a range of sizes.

Table 5 provides the output of a linear regression experiment whereby we used the optimal terms to predict cluster size. The first point to note is that the p-value for optimal.terms was $<2e-16$, this figure indicts a strong regression effect. Additionally, we note that the multiple R-squared and adjusted R-squared values were 0.855 and 0.853. These values indicate the model is an excellent fit for our data.

Figure 3 depicts four goodness-of-fit plots to assess the goodness of fit of our model graphically. The residuals Vs fitted plot shows our model passes through the majority of fitted values quite well. It appears that a small number of points are outside the fitted line. The normal Q-Q plot shows the standardised residuals fitted against a normal distribution line. For the most part, almost all values fit the line. There are a number of exceptions, such as a few small and large residuals. This plot indicates the model would almost all values however there would be some uncertainty of fitted very small and very large values. Finally, three observations had leverage greater than 0.1.

We mentioned previously that biterm topic clusters contain ten terms, and that due to random variation of the tooling, it is not always possible to obtain the same level of distinct output terms as were input. For example, dividing the number of distinct words for analysis by ten and using this result as the optimal # of clusters, does not provide the same amount of output words. However, we did not know to what degree of fit a linear model would provide. In our case, a good fit was obtained.

The main benefit of such a linear model is as follows: Determining the optimal cluster size can be a time-consuming task, especially for large datasets. Even using a rule of thumb such as a 'divide input distinct words by ten' as a starting point, multiple iterations of biterm may be required. By using a linear model, the task of determining the optimal term cluster size may be expedited. In the case where the optimal cluster size needs to be computed at scale, a linear model may be more effective than iteratively computing the size using specialised hardware.

6   Conclusion

The purpose of this study was to examine topic modelling for small text corpora (i.e. Instant message conversations). We found that by segmenting messages into periods of intense (bursts) and non-intense (reflections) communication that these segments, when used in conjunction with a text mining tool can be used to provide a higher number of output terms than modelling the entire corpus of messages at once. Furthermore, we found that message inter-arrival time can be used to determine both burst and reflection periods.

We also found that terms output from topic modelling bursts and reflection periods, when aggregated, are easier to understand than topic modelled terms from the entire message corpus. Additionally, we saw that all four readability tests, topic modelled terms output from aggregated burst and reflection analysis have a lower readability index compared to terms mined from the entire corpus.

Finally, the relationship between optimal output words and the optimal # clusters had a strong regression effect. In other words, we can use the optimal terms to predict the required number of topic clusters. This result can have a positive benefit for topic modelling practitioners, as it may reduce the iterative approach needed to find the number of topic clusters that produce the largest distinct number of words.

Both SMEs and micro-teams can use the above result to deliver high-value topic mining outputs from their group chat discourse. Teams can focus initially on a corpus-based approach for a particular channel/space. The advantage of a more extensive corpus approach is that topic modelled outputs can be assessed in context. Where word collocations exist, this knowledge can be directly applied to place a higher value on terms generated from topic mining tools.

In future work, we shall model burst and reflection period's on a corpus basis to infer the optimal duration.

Acknlowdgements. The authors would like to personally thank the 24 individuals who took part in our topic modelling comprehension experiment.

References

1. Fitting Linear Models. http://bit.ly/2dvqYet
2. Texting Statistics (2015). http://bit.ly/2kjHeF8
3. Improving the Consumer E-commerce Experience Through Text Mining (2015). http://bit.ly/2z8eYyv
4. We Just Don't Speak Anymore (2015). http://bit.ly/2yDXzJ6
5. Expect More Chatbots (2016). http://bit.ly/2z771cJ
6. How to Deal with Social Media Overwhelm (2016). http://bit.ly/2yN5e8r
7. Gain Business Insight with Big Data (2017). http://bit.ly/2zPxmcC
8. Qualitative Sample Size (2017). http://bit.ly/2hWeh3R
9. Social Messaging: Catalysing the Next Wave of Digital Revolution in Communication (2017). http://bit.ly/2FekIpz
10. Stopword Lists (2017). http://bit.ly/2jwKvDa
11. Ubuntu IRC Logs (2017). https://irclogs.ubuntu.com/
12. The Value and Benefits of Text Mining (2017). http://bit.ly/2zJcDcl
13. Blei, D.M., Ng, A.Y., Jordan, M.I.: Latent Dirichlet allocation. J. Mach. Learn. Res. **3**(Jan), 993–1022 (2003)
14. Coleman, M., Liau, T.L.: A computer readability formula designed for machine scoring. J. Appl. Psychol. **60**(2), 283 (1975)
15. Dale, E., Chall, J.S.: A formula for predicting readability: instructions. Educ. Res. Bull. **27**, 37–54 (1948)
16. Diao, Q., Jiang, J., Zhu, F., Lim, E.P.: Finding bursty topics from microblogs. In: Proceedings of the 50th Annual Meeting of the Association for Computational Linguistics: Long Papers, vol. 1, pp. 536–544. Association for Computational Linguistics (2012)

17. Galton, F.: Regression towards mediocrity in hereditary stature. J. Anthropol. Inst. Great Br. Irel. **15**, 246–263 (1886)
18. Gunning, R.: The Technique of Clear Writing. McGraw-Hill, New York (1952)
19. Hofmann, T.: Probabilistic latent semantic analysis. In: Proceedings of the Fifteenth Conference on Uncertainty in Artificial Intelligence, pp. 289–296. Morgan Kaufmann Publishers Inc. (1999)
20. Jivani, A.G., et al.: A comparative study of stemming algorithms. Int. J. Comput. Technol. Appl. **2**(6), 1930–1938 (2011)
21. Jurafsky, D., Martin, J.H.: Speech and Language Processing, vol. 3. Pearson, London (2014)
22. Kincaid, J.P., Fishburne Jr., R.P., Rogers, R.L., Chissom, B.S.: Derivation of new readability formulas (automated readability index, fog count and flesch reading ease formula) for navy enlisted personnel. Technical report, Naval Technical Training Command Millington TN Research Branch (1975)
23. Kučera, H., Francis, W.N.: Computational Analysis of Present-Day American English. Dartmouth Publishing Group, London (1967)
24. Landauer, T.K., Foltz, P.W., Laham, D.: An introduction to latent semantic analysis. Discourse Process. **25**(2–3), 259–284 (1998)
25. Leskovec, J., Rajaraman, A., Ullman, J.D.: Mining of Massive Datasets. Cambridge University Press, Cambridge (2014)
26. Lovins, J.B.: Development of a stemming algorithm. Mech. Transl. Comput. Linguist. **11**(1–2), 22–31 (1968)
27. Luhn, H.P.: Key word-in-context index for technical literature (KWIC index). J. Assoc. Inf. Sci. Technol. **11**(4), 288–295 (1960)
28. Manning, D.A.C.: Introduction. In: Manning, D.A.C. (ed.) Introduction to Industrial Minerals, pp. 1–16. Springer, Dordrecht (1995). https://doi.org/10.1007/978-94-011-1242-0_1
29. Naveed, N., Gottron, T., Kunegis, J., Alhadi, A.C.: Searching microblogs: coping with sparsity and document quality. In: Proceedings of the 20th Acm International Conference on Information and Knowledge Management, pp. 183–188. ACM (2011)
30. Schofield, A., Mimno, D.: Comparing apples to apple: the effects of stemmers on topic models. Trans. Assoc. Comput. Linguist. **4**, 287–300 (2016)
31. Sridhar, V.K.R.: Unsupervised topic modeling for short texts using distributed representations of words. In: VS@ HLT-NAACL, pp. 192–200 (2015)
32. Webster, J.J., Kit, C.: Tokenization as the initial phase in NLP. In: Proceedings of the 14th Conference on Computational Linguistics, vol. 4, pp. 1106–1110. Association for Computational Linguistics (1992)
33. Yan, X., Guo, J., Lan, Y., Cheng, X.: A biterm topic model for short texts. In: Proceedings of the 22nd International Conference on World Wide Web, pp. 1445–1456. ACM (2013)
34. Yan, X., Guo, J., Lan, Y., Xu, J., Cheng, X.: A probabilistic model for bursty topic discovery in microblogs. In: AAAI, pp. 353–359 (2015)
35. Yin, J., Wang, J.: A Dirichlet multinomial mixture model-based approach for short text clustering. In: Proceedings of the 20th ACM SIGKDD International Conference on Knowledge Discovery and Data Mining, pp. 233–242. ACM (2014)
36. Zuo, Y., et al.: Topic modeling of short texts: a pseudo-document view. In: Proceedings of the 22nd ACM SIGKDD International Conference on Knowledge Discovery and Data Mining, pp. 2105–2114. ACM (2016)

An Analysis of Sign Language Group Communication and Support of Such Communication by Projecting the Upper Body of the Signer

Pedro Passos Couteiro[1] and Shin Takahashi[2(✉)]

[1] College of International Studies, University of Tsukuba, Tsukuba, Japan
[2] Department of Computer Science, University of Tsukuba, Tsukuba, Japan
shin@cs.tsukuba.ac.jp

Abstract. Effective sign language communication requires not only seeing the signer's hand, but also seeing facial expressions and body position, especially when communicating in groups. Here, we address the needs of those who use sign language in group settings. First, to better understand issues surrounding sign language group communication, we interviewed sign language users and performed in-loco observations of group communication. Then, we devised a support system projecting the signer's upper body onto a screen and compared group communication with and without the support system. The results revealed that participants found it difficult to see signers sitting adjacent to them, to follow quick turns in conversation, and to identify the next signer in time. Although signers preferred not to employ our system as their principal communication tool, they found it useful to identify the current signer.

Keywords: Sign language · Group communication · Turn-taking

1 Introduction

Effective sign language communication requires a clear view of the signer's hands, face, and body orientation [9]. This can be easily achieved in one-to-one settings by having signers stand face-to-face, but it is not as easy in groups. The traditional approach to group sign language communication is that participants should form a circle, affording clear views of everyone. Although this is effective for small groups of four or five people, in larger groups individuals find it increasingly difficult to see each other well and identify the signer-in-turn at a given moment.

Of course, those who use spoken languages face the same problems in larger settings; individuals may find it difficult to speak loudly enough so that everyone in a large audience can hear, so microphones may be used. If there is only one main speaker, one microphone may be adequate, but at large conferences several microphones may be passed around, or microphones may be attached to all seats,

A. Rodrigues et al. (Eds.): CRIWG 2018, LNCS 11001, pp. 76–90, 2018.
https://doi.org/10.1007/978-3-319-99504-5_7

allowing all speakers to project their voices when needed. The same approach could be used when communicating in sign language; all participants could be recorded using individual cameras and the images projected onto a large screen. However, this would be costly and the necessary infrastructure may be lacking.

Given the relatively few studies on sign language group communication [7] and possible video supports, it remains unclear how such approaches might affect communication and what types of problems could arise. For example, a signer who is required to face a device or screen might find the lack of feedback from others problematic. Also, research has revealed [1] that signers tend not to take turns until they establish a mutual gaze; turn-taking would be compromised if all participants are expected to look at a screen instead of at each other. Because both space and viewpoint play important roles in sign languages [3], compressing an essentially tridimensional language onto a bidimensional screen might cause information loss and reduce overall comprehension.

Here, we sought to support in-person sign language group communication. First, to identify problems sign language communicators face in large groups, we conducted interviews and performed observations in-loco. Then, we explored the possible effects of mobile cameras combined with screen projection on communication. Although we worked with only a small group, we tried to reproduce problems encountered by larger groups. Here, we describe how technology can aid sign language group communication.

2   Related Work

Several studies have focused on support technologies enhancing sign language communication.

Yonehara and Nagashima [19] found that fluent signers read non-manual signs such as facial expressions using central vision, and capture manual signs with peripheral vision. However, while native signers may spend 80% to 90% of their time looking at the other signer's face, non-native signers tend to look more at the hands than the face while communicating. The amount of time spent looking at the signer's face tends to increase as sign language fluency improves. This points to the clear need for views of not only the hands of signers, but their full upper bodies, as the face is the most common gaze target when signing, and the gaze per se imparts information relevant to communication.

Of special interest in this context are studies on sign language that used a conversation analysis approach. Coates and Sutton-Spence [4] suggested that instead of the 'one-at-a-time' type of system such as that described by Sacks et al. [15] for those using spoken languages, signed languages might be more permissive of overlaps, and signers might orient to a 'collaborative floor.' In such an environment, any approach seeking to identify and display only one signer at a time might be flawed; several concomitant signers might be more acceptable. However, although several studies [11] have suggested that overlap is acceptable, recent research [2,5,7,12] on sign language turn-taking has revealed one-at-a-time behavior closer to that suggested by Sacks et al. [15], and that signers deploy several strategies to solve overlap problems. If this is indeed the case, projecting only the main speaker might be of value.

The spread of 4G technology and the development of increasingly powerful smartphones render virtually any device capable of real-time video transmission of a quality adequate for sign language communication. Currently, the deaf community [6] uses several video chat applications including Glide [8] and Skype [16] to engage in remote sign language communication. Several studies have explored how the deaf employ mobile technologies; long before real-time video transmission enabled remote sign language communication, the hearing-impaired enthusiastically adopted mobile devices, recognizing the possibilities afforded by visual media, texting, and picture-sending and display [17].

Kikuchi and Bono [10] investigated telecommunication between two mixed groups of signing and non-signing (deaf and hearing) individuals. The groups were remotely located and relied on screens for communication of sign language in groups concomitant with spoken communication; some participants encountered delay issues.

3   Methods

3.1   Interviews and In-Loco Observations

Interviews with two sign language users explored their experiences in group settings, challenges faced, and possible supports they would like when using sign language in groups. Both interview subjects were male college students in their early twenties, one of whom was deaf and the other was hearing.

In-loco observations were conducted by the author at the University of Tsukuba Sign Language Circle. This circle is composed of both hearing and hearing-impaired students, enrolled not only at the University of Tsukuba but also at the Tsukuba University of Technology, which supports hearing- impaired students, and thus has a large number of such students. In terms of sign language skills and background, members of the circle were very diverse, reflecting the entire spectrum from deaf students who used Japanese Sign Language as their first language to hearing students who had just started learning sign language and were still unable to effectively communicate without the support of spoken Japanese. The meetings thus featured a mix of spoken Japanese, Japanese Sign Language (JSL), and Signed Japanese[1]; when members who could not fully express themselves in sign language were communicating, others performed simultaneous translation. Additionally, when profoundly deaf members who did not have fully functional oral abilities were signing, hearing members with good sign language skills spoke aloud any words they thought some members might not understand when following the signs alone. We sought to better understand the dynamics of group communication in an environment where a sign language served as a common language. We observed seating arrangements, gazing, turn-taking, motion, and conversation strategies.

---

[1] Signed Japanese is a manually coded form of Japanese that uses signs of Japanese Sign Language [20].

3.2   Experiment

We performed an experiment to better understand the dynamics of sign language group communication and the possible effects of mobile cameras and screen projection on such communication. A group of sign language speakers discussed certain topics over two 15-min periods, first without any aid and then with the support of mobile devices serving as individual cameras and a screen projecting the speaker-in-turn. The topics were chosen by participants from a list of topics provided at the beginning of the experiment. Participants first discussed the creation of a new holiday in Japan, and then discussed a subject they would remove from the Japanese middle-school curriculum.

Because the number of participants was small (five), they were asked to sit in a row to simulate the seating arrangement of a group with more participants. The room arrangement is shown in Fig. 1.

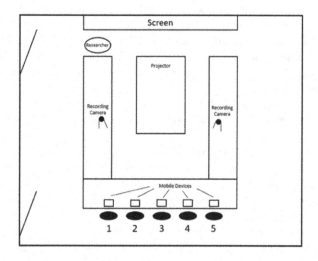

Fig. 1. Experiment arrangement

During the second 15-min session, a smartphone or a tablet was placed in front of each participant, on a stand, to ensure that the upper body was adequately captured by the front camera. Each device was connected via a video-conferencing application to the researcher's computer, which thus displayed all transmitted images. The screen of each mobile device displayed its own front camera image; participants could thus see how they were being captured.

The researcher's computer displayed the image of the signer-in-turn in real time. The mobile device source displayed was manually controlled, thus changing as the conversation proceeded and different participants took their turns signing. The entire conversation was recorded by two cameras placed as shown in Fig. 1.

After both 15-min sessions had concluded, participants were asked to answer a questionnaire (free description) and underwent individual 5-min interviews exploring their views of the experiment and their experience with sign language group communication involving support technologies.

The entire experiment, including questionnaires, explanations, and interviews, was conducted in the Japanese language with Signed Japanese translation as needed. All English text presented here has been translated from the original Japanese.

We explored participant age, sign language background, and hearing condition, and then proceeded as follows:

1. In terms of the first 15-min session (without any form of support):
   - 1.1 Was it easy to talk? (1–7)
   - 1.2 Could you participate adequately? (1–7)
   - 1.3 Could you understand other members' views? (1–7)
   - 1.4 How visible was each person? (1–7 for each seat)
   - 1.5 What was your extent of participation? (1–7)
   - 1.6 If you felt any problem or difficulty during conversation, please describe the issue (free description).
2. In terms of the second 15-min session (with support):
   - 2.1–2.5: The same as questions 1.1 to 1.5
   - 2.6 Was the image quality adequate to allow you to understand the sign language? (1–7)
   - 2.7 Was the support useful? (1–7)
   - 2.8 Please explain why the support was or was not useful (free description).
   - 2.9 If you encountered any problem or difficulty during conversation, please describe that issue (free description).
3. In terms of sign language group communication:
   - 3.1 Do you ever use sign language in groups? In what kinds of situations? (free description).
   - 3.2 Do you encounter any problem or difficulty when using sign language in groups? If yes, please describe the issue (free description).
   - 3.3 If there a support that you would like when using sign language, please describe it. Please do not concern yourself as to whether the support is or is not feasible (free description).

In the visibility questions (1.4 and 2.4), the score 1–7 corresponds to 0% to 100%. In other questions, the score 1–7 corresponds to 'Strongly Disagree' to 'Strongly Agree'.

We recruited five participants, all of whom were undergraduate students and aged 20–26 years (four males and one female). Three were hearing-impaired; all considered themselves to be fluent in sign language and were able to communicate without the aid of spoken Japanese throughout the entire experiment. All provided written informed consent prior to enrolment.

4 Results

4.1 Interviews and In-Loco Observations

In the preparatory interviews, both subjects described difficulties in seeing every-one simultaneously, and noted that this might be why some participants do not receive all information being exchanged. They identified two different sources of such difficulty. The first was simple sight obstruction, and the second was not knowing where to look; one interviewee commented that participants could "lose some of the conversation when the signer changes and I have not yet figured out who is now signing."

When asked about the strategies used to deal with these problems, both subjects stated that their favored approach to sight obstruction was to ensure the group was as circular as possible. Although this sometimes worked, *it may be difficult to achieve, depending on the number of people involved, the size of the room, and the types of tables and chairs available. The choice of long tables for three people, or small individual tables, is relevant when choosing a room for Sign Language Circle activities; individual tables are better. However, when a presentation requires the use of a screen, the need to open one side of the room means that the circle changes to a V- or U-shaped arrangement, forcing participants to sit side-by-side, rendering it more difficult to obtain mutually clear views.*

In terms of the second issue, interviewees noted that when turn changes are extremely hard to follow, they might (in the worst-case scenario) "ask members to raise their hands and wait for other participants to turn toward them before they start to sign." They noted that sometimes, *when participants start signing in what might be considered a natural flow, either two people start signing at the same time without realizing it, or part of the group does not realize that someone has started signing, and thus keeps the conversation going in another direction.*

When specific content is considered important, and the group wants to ensure that everyone is following the topic, the interviewees stated that they usually have the signer in question stand and move to the front of the group, where s/he is visible to everyone and can lead the talk. Although this is effective, both interviewees noted that *it is time-consuming waiting for the person to move, and that while this technique may work for specific relevant announcements, it is impossible to use when the group needs to decide something collectively, such as the date or content of the next meeting.*

In-loco observations revealed that, apart from the problems described above, meetings were characterized by a great deal of moving of tables and chairs around the room, reflecting both dissatisfaction with the view of the signer-in-turn, and also individual clearing of a position when it was that individual's turn to communicate.

In terms of possible support technologies, both interviewees expressed desire for a feature that would render them easily visible to other participants without the need to move around the room; this would both improve overall understand-ing and reduce the time used to wait or to move furniture.

Finally, both interviewees noted that although Sign Language Circle activities usually involve 10–20 people, who can thus sit in a circle, conferences or lectures requiring people to sit in rows would particularly benefit from such support; in such cases, clear views of all speakers are impossible.

4.2 Experiment

Questionnaire Answers. Tables 1 and 2 shows the questionnaire answers after both of the turns[2].

In the first 15-min session, the participant in position 2 found it necessary to constantly change the view-point to the right and left, and thus lost parts of the conversation. Another participant who scored a maximum for all questions found communication easy, because all participants well-understood hearing impairment, but noted that it was rather difficult to see everyone.

In the second 15-min session, the participant in position 2 noted the same problems as in the first session; the constant directional changes caused loss of parts of the conversation. Another participant referred to feeling confused when having to wait for the screen to change before beginning to sign.

In terms of whether the support was useful or not, one participant referred to becoming more aware of his/her own speech, noting that this was good. The same participant noted that when sitting in a line, it is sometimes difficult to know who is signing at a given moment, and found the support useful in this context, in addition to making signing easier to see in general. In terms of negative aspects, two participants stated that the screen change times were too slow; they lost the beginning of the sign and often preferred to look at the signer directly. One participant complained about the delay between a sign and its display on the screen. Another participant referred to wanting to look directly at the person signing, noting that the screen was unsatisfactory. Finally, one participant observed that the screen was not necessary due to the small number of participants, but commented that it would be useful in a larger setting with more than 20 people.

Table 1. Participants' answers regarding group talking without support

	Questions								
	1.1	1.2	1.3	1.4					1.5
				1	2	3	4	5	
p1	6	7	7	-	5	6	5	6	5.5
p2	4	3	5	4	-	5	5	5	2
p3	7	7	7	-	7	-	7	7	7
p4	7	7	7	7	7	7	-	7	5
p5	6	6	7	7	7	7	6	-	5

---

[2] The answers given to the free writing questions are omitted due to space limitation.

Table 2. Participants' answers regarding group talking with support

	Questions										
	2.1	2.2	2.3	2.4					2.5	2.6	2.7
				1	2	3	4	5			
p1	3.5	5	5	-	5	6	5	6	5.5	4.5	1
p2	4	4	5	4	-	5	5	5	3	4	2
p3	7	7	7	7	7	-	7	7	7	5	7
p4	7	7	7	7	7	7	-	7	4	7	5
p5	6	6	7	7	7	7	7	-	6	6	5

Conversation Analysis

First Session—Without Support. During the first 15-min session, it was apparent that signers accustomed to group communication had already developed favored strategies, including actions respectful of other members; there was no need to ask them to do this.

For example, at the exact moment conversation started, all three participants in the middle (positions 2, 3, and 4) pushed themselves backwards even when not requested to. It was not possible to retreat far from the original straight-line arrangement, but even a 30-cm backward push was crucial to afford clear views of participants in positions 1 and 5. These participants also gradually rotated toward the group, until they faced almost completely sideways.

Nonetheless, some participants struggled at several times during conversation, leaning forward to see a member who was more than two positions away. Also, the neutral positions adopted during conversation were usually inadequate to allow conversation with adjacent members. When the signer-in-turn was the person immediately next to them, all participants turned their chairs a few degrees toward him/her, to see the signing better.

Participants at the ends (positions 1 and 5) pushed their chairs forward to see signing from an angle rather than from the side. Signers in the other positions, however, did not exhibit the same behavior, perhaps aware that if they did so they would most likely obstruct the views of the more outside members; they limited themselves to turning in their places without horizontal movement.

A pattern that was observed many times was that when conversation was led principally by the two most distant participants (1 and 5), all other participants alternated their head and eye directions from right to left and vice versa. Participants were accustomed to this style of conversation and quickly adapted, moving their heads to the opposite direction as soon as a sentence concluded, knowing that an answer would most likely be forthcoming from the opposite direction. Although this allowed participants to follow all sentences completely, it meant that when conversation took an unexpected turn, the participants would be facing the wrong way. This is illustrated in Fig. 2; when conversation was led by 1 and 5 for some time (Fig. 2(a) and (b)), 2, 3, and 4 would turn their heads in the

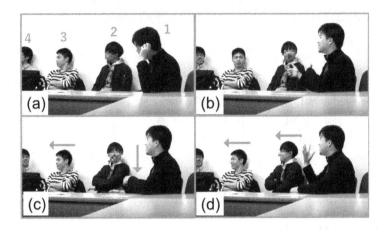

Fig. 2. Unexpected turn-taking causes participants to lose signing signals

opposite direction as soon as any sentence finished, here marked by 1 lowering his/her arms (Fig. 2(c)). However, just after doing so, 1 unexpectedly continued; 2 and 3 were facing the wrong direction for a period and thus lost the beginning of 1's continued signing (Fig. 2(d)).

Appropriately seeing the person right next to oneself was an issue for some participants. On more than one occasion, participants failed to take the turn from participants sitting by their sides. In some cases, participants would tap the shoulders of persons whom they wished to take the turn, as a last resort.

Second Session—with Support. Participants had mixed reactions toward the mobile devices and the main screen. Participants in positions 1 and 5, who previously ended up sideways to better see the group, did not turn in as much as before, probably because they knew that if they did so the cameras would not catch their signing.

Although some participants used the screen to see signing by other participants, they faced each other directly most of the time, ignoring the screen and the devices. However, participants did refer to the screen on several occasions.

When participants failed to correctly predict where the next signing would come from, and ended up facing in a direction from where no-one was signing, they would sometimes use the screen to recognize the signer-in-turn and then face in the correct direction. Also, participants located between two signers who were alternating turns, and who thus needed to constantly turn their heads, decided to look at the screen for as long as that conversation continued.

Usually, participants opted for direct conversation without using the screen; most problems evident in the first session remained evident, including the difficulty of seeing adjacent participants. As shown in Fig. 3, on one occasion, the participant in position 1 was unable to see the signs by the participant in position 2 (Fig. 3(a)), who had turned to better face the rest of the group. Because one comment was funny and made all other participants laugh, the participant

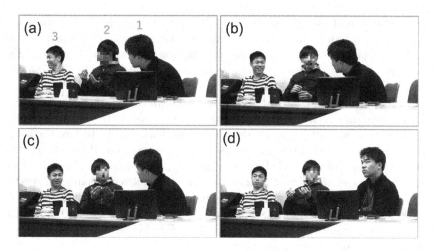

Fig. 3. Repetition of signing, and subsequent use of the screen

in position 1 stopped the conversation and asked the participant in position 2 to repeat it (Fig. 3(b)); participant 2 then turned to a more neutral angle where signing would be visible from position 1 and repeated the comment (Fig. 3(c)). Interestingly, the next time the participant in position 2 became the focus of conversation, participant number 1 opted to use the screen, instead of looking at participant 2 directly (Fig. 3(d)), perhaps as a reaction to the previous failure. Although this allowed participant 1 to correctly understand participant 2, participant 2 turned in the direction of participant number 1 when signing, probably expecting visual feedback, but participant 1 was looking at the screen and thus did not give such feedback, as shown in Fig. 3(d). Participant 2 was somewhat distressed, but due to his desire for anonymity, we cannot show the expression of participant 2.

Interviews After the Experiment. With regard to using sign language in groups, most participants noted that they find it difficult to see signers well when a group contains 10 or more people. One participant noted that "the problem usually involves people sitting close, not those further away." When features of a space force some signers to sit in a straight line, the mutual views of all such signers are obstructed. Another participant mentioned the need to "constantly move the gaze around the group."

With regard to participation in the experiment, participant 5 expressed difficulty seeing what participant 4 was signing, because participant 4 would turn to the left. Participant 2 also referred to having "difficulty managing my gaze, as it was necessary to go back and forth between participant number 1, on the left, and participants 3, 4, and 5, on the right." Although able to follow the conversation most of the time, participant 2 noted that "there were moments when parts of the conversation were lost because of that [head-turning]."

Participants had mixed reactions to the offered support. Two commented that it was useful and would be especially good on occasions where there are more than 20 participants, but others said the system was almost useless. Two participants stated that screen-changing was too slow; they lost the beginnings of signings if they followed conversations on the screen. One participant complained of the time delay between signing beginning and appearing on the screen. Two of the participants referred to preferring direct views, with one commenting "even if a screen was available, in a conversation, I would like to face the signer directly, so I would opt for a direct view over a screen even if the direct view was somewhat obstructed and the screen not." One participant who did not use the screen for most of the time commented that "the screen changes disturbed me, because they intruded into my peripheral vision and distracted me." Two participants referred to wanting to see reactions, with one noting the need to "see other participants' reactions while they talk; this would be impossible if staring at a screen."

On the positive side, almost all participants commented that although they would not use the screen as the principal means of following the conversation, quick glances at the screen were useful to see who was signing at any given moment. Also, two of the participants stated that it was useful for seeing signing when they could not obtain a clear view.

5   Discussion

5.1   Sign Language Group Communication Issues

We observed several patterns of sign language group communication. Signers were very aware of the obstacles they faced and adopted various strategies to benefit both them and other members, such as pushing backwards when sitting in a straight line or avoiding moving forward when they believed this would obstruct the view of others.

Although these strategies were successful to some extent, limitations were apparent. Group communication can be unsatisfactory if a circular arrangement is impossible due to the room size, type of furniture, or number of participants. Also, some strategies cannot be used by all participants. Body rotation was common to improve the views of others, but served to worsen the views of some participants, as the signer tended to turn in the direction in which most participants are located.

A need for rapid head and eye movement was evident, and some signers considered this difficult. The experiment revealed that the usual strategy was to move the gaze as soon as possible in the direction of the next expected signer. Overall, this strategy reduced missed signing, but failed when unexpected turn-taking occurred.

In general, both the questionnaire responses and interviews revealed that signers experienced most difficulties understanding adjacent signers. This may be attributed to two factors. First, sign language is usually viewed from the front; a side view is associated with significant information loss, especially that imparted by facial expressions and other non-manual messages. The other factor, evident in the experiment and expressed by two participants, is that when participants turn their bodies to be better seen by group members, some members actually have a poorer view than before. Rotation of distant participants does not have a strong effect, but even minor rotation of an adjacent participant may render it very difficult to see the hands and face of that person.

Such difficulties not only render signing comprehension difficult, but also compromise turn-taking. The experiment revealed that when participants wanted to take the turn from an adjacent person, they realized that traditional strategies such as a specific gaze or hand movement would not be perceived by the current signer, and were forced to touch the signer.

Although parallel signing was not observed in the experiment, possibly because of the small number of participants, the subjects mentioned that it is sometimes difficult to prevent it; two participants might start signing at the same time while not realizing it. As discussed in Sect. 2, overlap is a recurrent issue [2,4,5,7,11,12] in the sign language literature. Although some recent studies [2,5,7,12] have suggested that a one-at-a-time turn-taking is favored during sign language conversations, all of these studies evaluated groups of fewer than five speakers. In larger settings, overlaps may be more difficult to prevent, even if conscious efforts are made by the participants.

Compared with spoken languages, in which messages are by default broadcast, and two simultaneous utterances invariably disturb each other, simultaneous sign language comments might not necessarily constitute an overlap in the sense that multi-party attention is required to detect the situation; some instances might even be unobserved by the speakers. McIlvenny [13] found that maintaining a shared floor must be continually addressed by employing conscious and explicit efforts, including actions such as tapping and waving.

In large settings, such strategies may be insufficient, which explains participants' comments that when content is considered important to the entire group, the signer moves to a spot where a clear view is possible for all group members. Although this approach is effective, it slows conversation and renders group interaction even more difficult, as all signers are forced to face the same direction rather than each other. Several participants noted that dealing with situations where many signers are present is complex, and some sort of support would be appreciated.

5.2   Signer, Upper Body Screen Projection as a Support

Projecting the signer-in-turn in an effort to facilitate group conversation led to diverse reactions. Although all participants remained in conversation principally by looking directly at the other members of the group, the screen was not useless, as revealed by some answers to the questionnaire.

Even if the screen did not control the conversation, it was useful to identify the signer-in-turn. No participant viewed the screen continuously, but several participants took quick glances to verify who was signing. One participant commented that the screen was useful both to understand signing per se and to identify the signer-in-turn.

All participants commented that they did not use the screen as the principal conversational tool because of the lack of visual feedback from other participants. Looking at the screen prevented participants from seeing the reactions of other signers, and was of particular concern to the signer-in-turn, who would see only him/herself. Simultaneous screening of all participant images was suggested, but attracted mixed reactions. One participant said this would not be helpful, because s/he would try to see everything that was happening at the same time and would become lost. Another stated that even if all participants were on the screen, s/he would still prefer to look directly at the signer. Some participants commented that such an approach was reasonable and that they would like to try it. However, although the approach may work for groups of up to 10 people, such groups might be able to communicate effectively even without support. With larger groups of 20 or more, it is hard to imagine how showing all members at the same time on a screen would be either feasible or desirable.

Although concern with the lack of reactions from others when signing was expected, failure to use the screen had an unexpected effect. During the experiment, participant 1, who had previously failed to see the signing of participant 2, decided to look at the screen to improve understanding of the conversation, but when participant 2 was signing again, s/he turned toward participant 1, who was now looking at the screen instead, creating discomfort for participant 2.

In terms of the technical features of the support, two participants felt that screen changes between signers were too slow. This could possibly be addressed via automatic signer recognition followed by a rapid screen change; however, it is not clear how an automatic recognition algorithm would deal with overlap. Also, sign language users deliver confirmatory and feedback signs in the same manner as spoken language users; avoiding erroneous recognition of such signs may be problematic.

Also, one participant was bothered by the time delay of signing. Previous research [14] has shown that the delay usually tolerated by signers is about 150 ms, considerably more than the 45 ms tolerated by spoken language users. However, the experimental time delay was less than 150 ms, perhaps explaining why only one of the five participants considered it problematic. During the interview, the participant stated that seeing signing on the screen after performing signing or directly seeing signing made him/her uncomfortable. Thus, although the time delay tolerated by sign language users is about 150 ms, this may be reduced when signers are exposed to both original and delayed sources simultaneously, creating discomfort that is absent when the signer has access to only the delayed source.

Overall, signers desired support when communicating in groups. Simple signer upper-body projection onto a screen facilitated signer viewing and recognition, but signers were very concerned about the lack of feedback (the inability to see the reactions of non-signing members). The participants agreed that the screen would be useful in settings with 20 or more people, such as lectures. Also, regardless of whether the screen helped make signing more visible to participants, it was helpful to identify the signer.

6   Conclusion

When in large groups, signers find it difficult to obtain clear views of all participants, and may struggle to correctly recognize who is the principal signer at any moment; fast head and eye movements are used to understand the content being shared in conversation. Also, simultaneous sign language utterances may break the turn-taking mechanism, creating parallel conversations.

Signers find it especially difficult to see adjacent signers because of poor visualization angles, leading to loss of information (such as facial expressions). The views of aligned participants are also obstructed. When participants sit in rows facing the same direction (as during lectures), it is impossible to obtain clear views of some signers.

Projecting the signer's upper body onto the screen facilitated signing visualization, and also indicated who was the speaker-in-turn, allowing participants to face the correct direction rapidly. However, several obstacles in terms of feedback and the reactions of others remain.

The lack of feedback was perceived as negative by all participants. Participants could not see the reactions of others on the screen, and those who were not using the screen experienced negative emotions when they tried to look at another member who was staring at the screen. However, the participants acknowledged that in larger settings, such effects are unavoidable and must be endured to some extent.

To address the remaining issues, it will be necessary to ensure that participants looking at a signer on a screen impart and receive feedback to/from the signer and others. Automatic signer recognition is desirable. Finally, even if the signer-in-turn is not projected, there is a clear need for a form of support allowing participants to correctly recognize the signer-in-turn faster.

References

1. Baker, C.: Regulators and Turn-Taking in American Sign Language Discourse. On the Other Hand, pp. 215–236. Academic Press, New York (1977)
2. Bono, M.: Multimodal analysis for sign language conversation: from two case studies on three party conversations. Jpn. J. Lang. Soc. **13**(2), 20–31 (2011)
3. Bono, M.: Space and viewpoint in Japanese signed discourse: sign language studies meet gesture studies. Jpn. J. Sign Linguist. **17**, 1–10 (2008). in Japanese
4. Coates, J., Sutton-Spence, R.: Turn-taking patterns in deaf conversation. J. Sociolinguist. **5**(4), 507–529 (2001)
5. De Vos, C., Torreira, F., Levinson, S.C.:Turn-timing in signed conversations: coordinating stroke-to-stroke turn boundaries. Front. Psychol. **6**, article no. 268 (2015)
6. Deaf Unity: Top 10 Apps For Deaf People—Free Downloads to Change Your Life (2016). https://deafunity.org/article-interview/top-10-apps-for-deaf-people/

7. Girard-Groeber, S.: The management of turn transition in signed interaction through the lens of overlaps. Front. Psychol. **6** article no. 741 (2015)
8. Glide—Live Video Messaging (2017). http://www.glide.me
9. Herrmann, A., Steinbach, M.: Nonmanuals in Sign Language. John Benjamins Pub Co., Philadelphia (2011)
10. Kikuchi, K., Bono, M.: An analysis of participation framework in multi-party sign language conversation under tele-communication environment. Contact Situations, Participants, and Interactions: Language Management in Contact Situations, vol. 9, pp. 41–50. Chiba University Graduate School of Humanities and Social Sciences Research Project Reports No. 238 (2011, in Japanese)
11. Lackner, A.: Turn-Taking und Dialogstruktur in der Oesterreichischen Gebärdensprache. Eine Gesprächsanalyse der Salzburger Variante. Das Zeichen. vol. 81, pp. 90–104 (2009, in German)
12. McCleary, L., Leite, T.A.: Turn-taking in Brazilian sign language: evidence from overlap. J. Interact. Res. Commun. Disord. **4**(1), 123–154 (2013)
13. McIlvenny, P.: Seeing conversations: analyzing sign language talk. In: Situated Order: Studies in the Social Organization of Talk and Embodied Activities, pp. 129–150. University Press of America, Washington, D.C. (1995)
14. Nagasaki, Y.: Shuwa Kenkyu he no Jouhou Kougaku-teki apuroochi. Language **8**, 60–67 (2009). in Japanese
15. Sacks, H., Schegloff, E.A., Jefferson, G.: A simplest systematics for the organization of turn-taking for conversation. Language **50**, 696–735 (1974)
16. Skype (2017). http://www.skype.com/en/new/
17. Summet, V.H.: Facilitating communication for deaf individuals with mobile technologies. Ph.D. disseration, Georgia Institute of Technology (2010)
18. Sutton, V.: SignWritting for Sign Languages (2017). http://www.signwritting.org
19. Yonehara, A., Nagashima, Y.: Experimental study about variety of gaze point depend on JSL Proficiency. In: Proceedings of the Human Interface Symposium, pp. 233–236 (2002)
20. Signed Japanese. https://en.wikipedia.org/wiki/Signed_Japanese

Remote Video Figure Achieves Smooth Cooperative Movement in a Bidirectional Telepresence Robot Environment

Tomoo Inoue[(✉)] and Zijie Yuan

University of Tsukuba, Tsukuba, Japan
inoue@slis.tsukuba.ac.jp

Abstract. This paper presents a study of telepresence robot environment where each of two remote sites has a telepresence robot from the other. By situating the telepresence robots in the relatively same positions of the remote users in both sites, collaborative physical environment can be realized when the users wear head-mounted displays to see the robots' views. Such an environment has been implemented as a prototype system. Because how to achieve physical cooperative movement between a telepresence robot and a human is an issue to be studied in this environment, an experimentation of passing by each other with the prototype system was then conducted as an example of cooperative movement. It was observed that the movement was smoother when watching the video from the telepresence robot than when watching the other telepresence robot in front of the user. It suggests the usefulness of nonverbal cues through video combined with the recognition of partner's position.

Keywords: Cooperative work · Positional relationship · Nonverbal cue
Telepresence robot

1 Introduction

Spatial collaborative work is a type of collaborative work in which multiple persons interact in physical space. A type of spatial collaborative work is the one that workers actually move in space such as theatrical performance, team sport, team dancing, and so on, unlike the 3D collaborative work that shares 3D workspace but that workers do not move from their fixed positions. In this cooperative work that includes movement in physical space, a worker decides and takes action in response to the partner's position and moving direction. In team dancing, a team should look well-organized and keep a beautiful shape as a group. It needs fine coordination of the workers' positions and movement. In team sport, a player needs to quickly respond to the partner's and the opponent's positions and movement for offence and defense. In remote spatial cooperative work with physical movement, to know the partner's position and moving direction is thought to be also necessary.

Such spatial collaborative work is common and can be seen in daily life, but realizing it remotely is another thing. In this research, we focus on a bi-directional telepresence robot environment to realize abovementioned spatial collaborative work

© Springer Nature Switzerland AG 2018
A. Rodrigues et al. (Eds.): CRIWG 2018, LNCS 11001, pp. 91–104, 2018.
https://doi.org/10.1007/978-3-319-99504-5_8

remotely. Among various setups employing video, virtual reality and/or robot, there is no setup informing the remote partner's position and moving direction for both participants.

First, we have designed and implemented the bi-directional telepresence robot environment. It consists of a pair of telepresence robots situated in each remote site. The position of the robot is synchronized with the remote worker so that the partner's position is visible. Then experimentation of passing by each other with the telepresence robot, which is an example of spatial collaborative work with physical movement, has been conducted to investigate the effect of employing remote video figure.

2   Related Works

People perform various cooperative works in their lives. Cooperative work includes from conversation to collaborative assembly work that requires physically fine coordination. A lot of studies have been conducted for years to support such various cooperative works in remote settings.

2.1   Video-Supported Remote Collaborative Work

One of the merits video is used for remote communication is it conveys rich information including subtle expressions and gestures. Other features of the video have been also explored. Eye contact is often used in communication, thus achieving eye contact in video communication is one of the major topics [1]. Video is easily editable to increase connectedness, for example by applying common background of the screens [2], or applying the local background to the background of a remote participant [3]. Another research direction is to overcome the limitation of a flat screen that it is difficult to depict 3D positions. Arranging large screens circular around users for displaying remote users increased the sense of co-presence [4]. Other type of displays than a flat screen was also proposed, one of which was the image projection to physical objects [5]. In sum, the video is good at conveying nonverbal cues, but not so good at showing spatial positions or dynamic movement in a communication space.

2.2   Virtual Reality-Supported Remote Collaborative Work

Virtual reality (VR) has also been used to support remote collaborative work [6–8]. One was a telepresence system displaying 2 remote groups of participants into a single virtual space on a large screen. Each group of participants was captured and shown stereoscopically through 3D glasses [9]. By placing 3D avatars of remote users around the local user, all users could immerse themselves and share the same virtual work space [10]. It was also possible to show the other parties as if they were working in the same space by showing their figures taken by multiple cameras through an HMD [11]. Application of virtual reality achieved spatial cooperative work in shared virtual space, but as it was limited within a virtual space, actual interaction in the physical space cannot be performed.

2.3 Robot-Supported Remote Collaborative Work

A robot has also been used to support remote collaborative work, typically as a physical surrogate of the remote participant. MeBot [12] and iRIS [13] had the movable display which moved according to the movement of the remote operator's head, which could tell where she was looking at. It has become possible for the remote user to have a feeling that she is in the place of the robot, by attaching a camera and a microphone to the robot and presenting the first person's visual and auditory sensation [14, 15]. Remote collaborative work by a surrogate robot includes a study of shaking hands with a remote person through the robot hand [16], and a study of physical cooperative task between a user and a surrogate robot hand of the remote user in both 2 sites [17]. Physical cooperative work is possible with such robots. Because a robot is a physical entity that can move, spatial collaboration including movement can also be possible. However, nonverbal cues can be conveyed within the limitation of the robot mechanism, and to achieve rich nonverbal cues are similar to human is not very easy.

3 Proposal

We propose an environment where a worker in each of the two remote sites immerses to the other site by using a telepresence robot situated there. The two sites are prepared to be the same size and shape. The robot is situated in the same position of a room with the user in another room, and is designed to move exactly the same direction and distance with the user. The environment includes a pair of this linkage between a telepresence robot and a user. In this way, the same positional relationship between the telepresence robot and the local partner is maintained in both rooms.

The video from a camera on the telepresence robot is presented to the user, thereby allowing the user to recognize her positional relationship with the partner from the first-person view. It enables the user to see the remote user's nonverbal cues. This proposed environment achieves spatial physical collaborative work including the position movement, while keep presenting nonverbal cues at the same time.

4 Implemented System

In this paper, we design a robot to move according to the position of the worker at the remote place which means we synchronize the position of the robot with the worker's. By doing this bi-directionally, the worker's positional relationship is synchronized in the two workspaces. We create an environment that allows both workers to recognize the other person's figure from the first-person view by a 360-degree camera installed on the robot. The images taken with that camera to the workers at remote locations are presented through HMD. In this environment, the worker cannot see the robot in the same work space but can see each other's figure by the image sent from the robot. This makes it an environment where physical actions performed by the robot are felt like actions taken by remote parties on the video.

4.1   System Configuration

The configuration of the implemented system is shown in Fig. 1. We prepare two workspaces whose sizes and shapes are the same at two distant remote sites, and place workers wearing HMDs as shown in the figure. At each space, two tracking cameras are set on the diagonal line of the workspaces. The tracking camera acquires the position and orientation of the HMD and the controllers in real time. Information on each position and orientation acquired by this camera is processed by a PC and then send to a remote PC. The PC moves the robot and match the position and orientation of the robot according to the position and the orientation of the user's head at the remote place. In addition, a 360° camera is attached to the robot, and images taken with this camera are transmitted to a remote PC and to be seen by the operator's HMD.

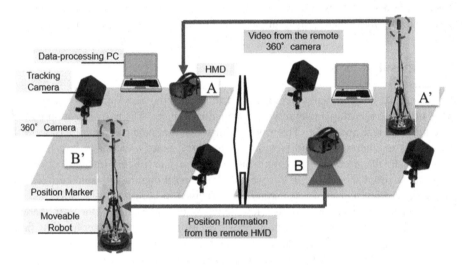

Fig. 1. System configuration

We used HTV's VIVE in this implementation. VIVE can acquire position and orientation information of the HMD and the two controllers by two tracking cameras. VIVE's tracking camera works fine if the distance between the two cameras is less than 5 m. For telepresence robot, we used iRobot Create 2 from iRobot. iRobot Create 2 is a robot capable of rotation in any direction, forward and backward movement. A tripod for the camera whose height can be adjusted is set on the robot, and at the tip of the tripod, a 360° camera called Theta V of RICHO was attached for photographing the first-person video image. Figure 2 shows the created telepresence robot.

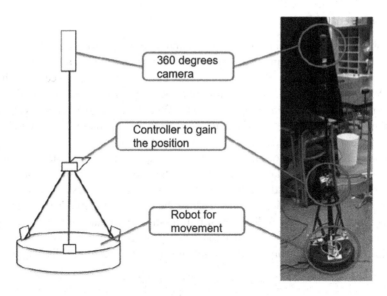

Fig. 2. Telepresence robot

4.2   Synchronizing Robot

In this system, the same coordinate systems are prepared for the worker and the robot in the two workspaces. Each position is represented on Unity [18] by the x coordinate and z coordinate, and the direction is by the angle to the y axis. We call the workplaces Spot A and B. We place one robot and a worker in each spot. Through this system, the coordinate and rotation of worker A will be sent to robot B also the same information of worker B will be sent to robot A. After data processing by the PC, the robots can synchronize both the position and direction with the remote worker in Fig. 3.

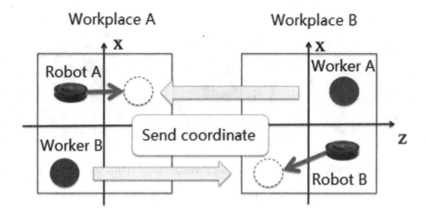

Fig. 3. Position synchronization of robots

4.3   Movement of Robot

The iRobot Create 2 Robot can rotate around and move forward and backward. Specifically, by programming with Python, it is possible to set arbitrary rotational speeds from −500 mm/sec to 500 mm/sec for each of the right wheel and the left wheel. When both wheels are given forward speed, the robot advances and retreats when both wheels are given backward speed. When rotating the robot, by applying opposite speeds to the left and right wheels respectively, the robot does not move and rotates on the spot (see Fig. 4).

In our system, we control the robot by switching the state where static is added to forward, backward, and rotation depending on the situation. For the robot can only move forward and backward, we have to calculate the coordinates between the robot and its goal to get the direction and the distance the robot should move to. And then the robot will rotate as the data. When the current robot's coordinates are are (z, x), the goal's coordinates are $(z2, x2)$, and the direction is the positive direction of the x-axis is $0°$, the following equation using atan 2 (arctangent 2) to determine the angle of the direction of travel.

$$Direction = atan2(x2 - x, z2 - z) \tag{1}$$

When the traveling direction obtained by this formula deviates by more than $5°$ from the direction of the robot, we make the robot rotate to the traveling direction within an error of $5°$.

After that, we calculate the distance between the two coordinates and move the robot forward or backward until the distance is less than 10 cm. Coordinates are calculated every 0.1 s and then the signal for movement will be printed. The speed of the robot is designed according to the distance between the robot and its operator in the same coordinate system as follow. (The speed of the iRobot Create 2 Robot ranges from 100 mm/sec to 300 mm/sec.)

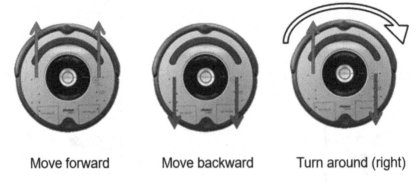

Move forward   Move backward   Turn around (right)

Fig. 4. Movement of robot

If the distance between two coordinates is less than 10 cm, the robot will not move. If the distance between two coordinates is 10 cm to 30 cm, advance or retreat at 100 mm/s.
If the distance between two coordinates is 30 cm to 50 cm, advance or retreat at 200 mm/s.
If the distance between two coordinates is 50 cm to 100 cm, advance or retreat at 250 mm/s.
If the distance between two coordinates is 100 cm or more, advance or retreat at 300 mm/s.

By doing this, we synchronize the position of the robot with the worker within 10 cm of error. As described above, since the robot rotates in the traveling direction and moves forward and backward to adjust the position, when the robot moves laterally with the worker facing forward, the robot moves in the traveling direction and a delay occurs due to the rotation. Since the robot rotation speed is set at 200 mm/s, the robot diameter is about 35 cm, and the maximum rotation angle of the robot at the time of positioning is 90°, it occurs delay about 1.5 s.

4.4   Communication Method

In our system, we set one PC as server, another one as client and the coordinates will be sent once per 0.1 s according to Socket communication method. We use 3D vector coordinates to build up our development environment. The x-axis and the z-axis are the plane, the y-axis is the height in the direction perpendicular to the plane. It means that when aligning the position of the HMD which is worn by the operator, the robot at the remote place can move to the same position by the two values of the x coordinate and the z coordinate of the HMD. The use of the angle relative to the y-axis will be described later. In the Socket communication, information cannot be transmitted from the server unless there is communication from the client, so the procedure is as follow.

1. The PC on the client side transmits three values to the server PC, the x coordinate, the z coordinate of the local HMD and the orientation of the robot relative to the y-axis of the local HMD.
2. When the PC on the server side receive the data from the client, it will send the same information mentioned above of its local workplace to the client.
3. Repeat the above every 0.1 s.

We use Unity to gain the position and rotation and build a Socket communication environment. Also, the robot control program is run in python. Therefore, every time Socket communication is performed, Unity will print out a TXT file which will be read by python program once per 0.1 s. According to this, the robot will move as the remote operator.

4.5   Image in the HMD

In this system, images taken by an omnidirectional camera attached to a remote robot are presented to the operator. As the system design, robot orientation equal to the front of the camera. Owing to this, the front side of the omnidirectional image can be described by the angle relative to y-axis that we mentioned in Sect. 4.2. The data of the front orientation will be sent to the remote PC, so that the remote Unity environment will identify the orientation of the image in its HMD screen (see Fig. 5). For the beginning, the omnidirectional image is attached to a sphere in Unity as Texture, the front side of the camera can be seen as the positive direction of the x axis in Fig. 5. As we can see the front side of the image is not the same as the robot.

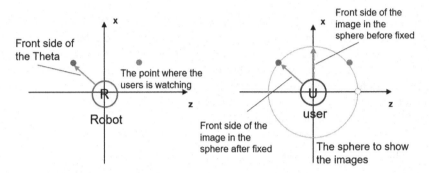

Fig. 5. Display of the video from the omnidirectional camera

Because of the same coordinate system in two PC, sphere which is used to print the image will rotate owing to the angle difference from the remote coordinate system. So that the image will be shown in the correct orientation, which means that the image will always be in a same orientation as the robot's front side.

As described above, the video displayed on the HMD is the first-person view video from the 360° camera installed on the robot. Figure 6 shows how communication is taking place between two workplaces by the proposal system. In this way, the users will see each other through the HMD rather than the robot that is set in the same place. We also use a technology called WebRTC [19] to transfer the video images to one PC to another one. It is also confirmed that there was no lag which would affect communication if the communication environment state was normally displayed stably.

The image displayed on the HMD is the first person's view from the 360° camera attached to the robot synchronously moving with the user at the remote place. For each user, there is a robot in front of the user, but the user can see the opponent because HMD shows the first-person viewpoint from the remote robot, so user cannot see the robot in front of them and seems to be the opponent in front of his/her. The video is transferred from the PC to the remote PC by using the video chat system using WebRTC.

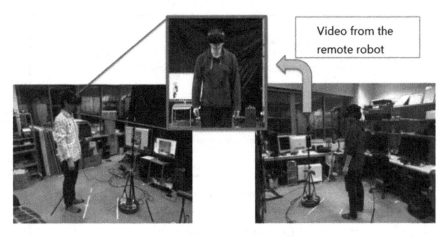

Fig. 6. Prototype system in use

5 Experiment

The user A looks the partner B in the remote site as if B is in the position of B's telepresence robot through the HMD in the implemented system. The experiment was conducted to see how remote physical cooperative movement was affected by the environment.

5.1 Outline of Experiment

In our evaluation experiment, we evaluate that only one side of participant operate the robot as the comparison. The participants contained 12 college students and two of them made up a group. We recorded video and audio during the experiment. It was supposed that two participants passed by each other while they were walking face to face. And owing to this system, we set this situation in two workplace that were apart. In our experiment, the passing-by is that a person is walking on the road when someone comes in the opposite direction and in order not to make a bump they will pass by each other. As we can see, it is necessary for each participant to predict in which direction the opponent will avoid from the preliminary action and select the direction to avoid. Therefore, it is essential to realize the position relationship with opponent and also to predict the where the opponent would go according to the action of the opponent. With this passing-by task, we evaluate whether the participants could forecast the preliminary operation of each other to pass smoothly and the nonverbal information could be shared effective. From the recorded images, we evaluate this system by the participant's behavior during the experiment and the time from task start to the operation start.

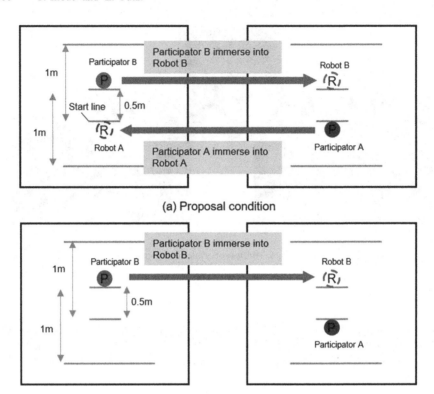

(a) Proposal condition

(b) Control condition

Fig. 7. Experimental conditions

5.2 Conditions of Experiment

We prepared the following two conditions of the experiment. Participants were asked to perform the same tasks under the following two conditions and then compared.

1. Proposal condition (Both the participants used the proposal system)
2. Control condition (One of the participant used the proposal system but the other one did not)

The proposal condition is shown in Fig. 7(a). We set up two workplaces in the same size, the participants stay in each place with a telepresence robot. As we can see, participant A could see the participant B through the images came from the robot A in the far place. While participant B can also directly see participant A from the images transferred by robot B.

In proposal condition, we prepared two workspaces, and the participants were divided into their workspaces. They had their tasks with telepresence robot bi-directionally. For the control condition, one participant operated the robot, the other participant did not use the robot, wore the HMD and watched the image of the camera attached to the HMD. By this, participant who used this system performed work while

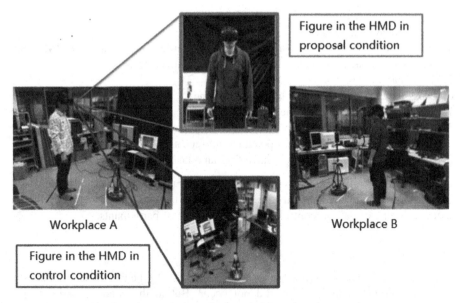

Fig. 8. Video see-through view and the tele-existence view

watching the figure of the opponent in the work space at the remote site, whereas the other participant could just perform tasks against the robot in the same work space. Two lines are provided at a position 0.5 m apart as the start line at the start of the task. Participants stood on the start line, and the tip of the robots were similarly set on the start line. Also, the robot and the participant were set in the opposite direction in one workplace. Finally, as the goal line for the end of the task, it was drawn 1 m ahead from each start line.

The control condition is shown in Fig. 7(b). We used the same start line and goal line in control condition. The difference was that we set only one participant in one workplace, and we set a participant and a robot in another one. We can see that participant B work with the image came from the robot B (We called it Tele-existence), but participant A just saw the sight of his/her workplace which meant that participant A work with seeing the robot (We called it Video see-through).

The participants in Tele-existence state could both see each other during the task by our system, while the participant in Video see-through state could just see the robot and worked with it. In Fig. 8 we show the see sight of both states. Participant A can see participant B in Tele-existence state which is shown in the upper part of the figure. In the bottom of the figure, it shows that participant A can just see the robot in Video-see through state.

5.3   Procedure

We conducted experiments with the following procedure.

1. Explain about the system, let the experimenter become familiar with the system.

2. Explain the experiment.
3. Choose one of the condition of the experiment.
4. Divide two participants into each workplace. Participants wear their HMD and stand face to each other as if they were in the same space.
5. Task starts.
6. Cross by each other without bumping any one.
7. Stop beyond the goal line ahead 1 m.
8. Task stop when both participants exceed the goal line.
9. Have them return to the initial position and repeat (5) to (8) three times in total.
10. Change to another condition to have the same task above.

In the control condition, when one of the participant repeated the task three times, it was time for the other participant to repeat the same task with our system. In all, we gained 6 groups of data in control condition in a pair of participants.

5.4 Result

There were scenes where pairs were about to collide during the experiment. Under the proposed condition, this situation did not occur. But in the control condition, the traveling direction overlapped in 4 pairs of participant pairs, one of them actually collided. In addition, time from task start to operation start is shown as Fig. 9.

As a result of analysis of variance of it, there was no significant difference in each data group. It seems that time from task start to operation start proposed a condition that the proposal condition has a tendency to cost shorter time than the Video see-through state in control condition.

5.5 Discussion

It can be seen that there is a tendency that the time from the start of the task to the operation to avoid in proposal condition is shorter than the two states of the control in Fig. 9. We consider that the using the users can predict the direction of progression of the partner earlier in the proposal condition. Also, it is hard for the participants to predict the action by the motion of the robot in Video see-through state. As a result, it cost more time for participants to avoid the robot in the Video see-through state.

Participants in Video see-through state could just see the robot as they cannot gain the information of the body motion of the robot. With this, the task could not run smoothly. Oppositely, participants who used the proposal system could pass by each other smoothly making the task successfully. We can conclude that this system can do remote support by sharing both the nonverbal information and position relationship during the task.

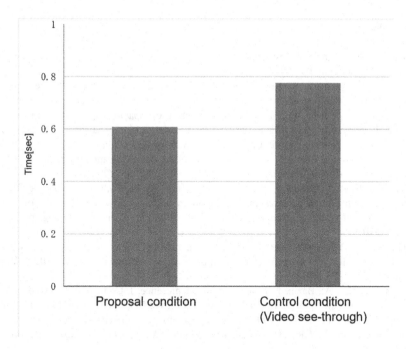

Fig. 9. Time from task start to operation start (s)

6 Conclusion

In collaborative work, workers share various type of information during performing. The same information should be required to achieve remote collaboration in the same quality. This study has focused on spatial collaborative work in which workers perform while moving in a certain space such as theatrical performance, team dancing, team sport, and so forth. A worker chooses his/her action according to the position and moving direction of the partner in such spatial collaborative work. It is very important to grasp positional relation that changes dynamically. Thus we proposed an environment where workers at two remote sites mutually immerse into another site by telepresence robots. The telepresence robot moves according to worker's movement and acquires the first-person view video in the remote site. Worker wears the HMD and sees the video from the telepresence robot. This way workers can share the positional relation while recognizing nonverbal cues.

From the result of the passing-by experiment where a telepresence robot passed by a worker, we found out that the video for conveying nonverbal cues was effective for remote spatial collaborative work including movement.

References

1. Jones, A., et al.: Achieving eye contact in a one-to-many 3D video teleconferencing system. ACM Trans. Graph. **28**(3), 64 (2009)
2. Handberg, L., Gullströ, C., Kort, J., Nyström, J.: Spatial and social connectedness in web-based work collaboration. In: Proceedings of the 19th ACM Conference on Computer Supported Cooperative Work and Social Computing Companion, pp. 45–48 (2016)
3. Inoue, T., Nawahdah, M., Noguchi, Y.: User's communication behavior in a pseudo same-room video conferencing system BHS. Int. J. Inf. Soc. **6**(2), 39–47 (2014)
4. Hirata, K., et al.: t-Room: next generation video communication system. In: Global Telecommunications Conference, pp. 1–4. IEEE GLOBECOM (2008)
5. Pejsa, T., Kantor, J., Benko, H., Ofek, E., Wilson, A.: Room2Room: enabling life-size telepresence in a projected augmented reality environment. In: Proceedings of the 19th ACM Conference on Computer-Supported Cooperative Work & Social Computing, pp. 1716–1725 (2016)
6. Maimone, A., Yang, X., Dierk, N., Dou, M., Fuchs, H.: General-purpose telepresence with head-worn optical see-through displays and projector-based lighting. In: 2013 IEEE Virtual Reality, pp. 23–26 (2013)
7. Fuchs, H., State, A., Bazin, J.: Immersive 3D telepresence. J. Comput. **47**(7), 46–52 (2014)
8. You, B., Kwon, J., Nam, S., Lee, J., Lee, K., Yeom, K.: Coexistent space: toward seamless integration of real, virtual, and remote worlds for 4D+ interpersonal interaction and collaboration. In: SIGGRAPH Asia 2014 Autonomous Virtual Humans and Social Robot for Telepresence, p. 1 (2014)
9. Beck, S., Kunert, A., Kulik, A., Froehlich, B.: Immersive group-to-group telepresence. Visualization and computer graphics. IEEE Trans. Vis. Comput. Graph. **19**(4), 616–625 (2013)
10. Fairchild, A.J., Campion, S.P., García, A.S., Wolff, R., Fernando, T., Roberts, D.J.: A mixed reality telepresence system for collaborative space operation. IEEE Trans. Circuits Syst. Video Technol. **27**(4), 814–827 (2017)
11. Orts-Escolano, S., Rhemann, C., Fanello, S., et al.: Holoportation: virtual 3D teleportation in real-time. In: Proceedings of the 29th Annual Symposium on User Interface Software and Technology, pp. 741–754. ACM, October 2016
12. Adalgeirsson, S.O., Breazeal, C.: MeBot: a robotic platform for socially embodied presence. In: Proceedings of the 5th ACM/IEEE International Conference on Human-Robot Interaction, pp. 15–22. IEEE Press, March 2010
13. Kawanobe, H., Aosaki, Y., Kuzuoka, H., Suzuki, Y.: iRIS: a remote surrogate for mutual reference. In: 2013 8th ACM/IEEE International Conference Human-Robot Interaction (HRI), pp. 403–404. IEEE, March 2013
14. Tachi, S.: Telexistence: enabling humans to be virtually ubiquitous. IEEE Comput. Graph. Appl. **36**(1), 8–14 (2016)
15. Tachi, S., Watanabe, K., Takeshita, K., Minamizawa, K., Yoshida, T., Sato, K.: Mutual telexistence surrogate system: Telesar4-telexistence in real environments using autostereoscopic immersive display. In: 2011 IEEE/RSJ International Conference Intelligent Robots and Systems (IROS), pp. 25–30. IEEE, September 2011
16. Nakanishi, H., Tanaka, K., Wada, Y.: Remote handshaking: touch enhances video-mediated social telepresence. In: Proceedings of the SIGCHI Conference on Human Factors in Computing Systems, pp. 2143–2152. ACM, April 2014
17. Nagendran, A., Steed, A., Kelly, B., Pan, Y.: Symmetric telepresence using robotic humanoid surrogates. Comput. Anim. Virtual Worlds **26**(3–4), 271–280 (2015)
18. Unity. https://unity3d.com/. Accessed 1 Oct 2017
19. WebRTC. https://webrtc.org/. Accessed 10 Nov 2017

Characterization of Public Opinion on Political Events in Brazil Based on Twitter Data

Gabriel Peres Nobre, Kecia Aline Marques Ferreira,
Ismael Santana Silva$^{(\boxtimes)}$, and Glívia Angélica Rodrigues Barbosa

Computer Department, Centro Federal de Educação Tecnológica de Minas Gerais,
Belo Horizonte, Brazil
gabrielpnobre@live.com,
{kecia,ismaelsantana,gliviabarbosa}@decom.cefetmg.br

Abstract. In this work we characterize Brazilian online population sentiment on different political events using data from Twitter and we also discuss the advantages of the usage of this social media as data source. The results demonstrated that the Brazilian population uses Twitter to manifest their political view, expressing both positive and negative sentiments regarding political events. This kind of characterization may contribute to build a critical opinion of Brazilian people, once they would not be limited by what is being divulgated by typical media, such as television and newspapers. Additionally, we reinforced the applicability of social media, as Twitter, to make this kind of characterization.

Keywords: Sentiment analysis · Data characterization · Online social network

1 Introduction

The democratic system is identified by the involvement of population on political events that are fundamental for the development of a nation (e.g. elections, lawmaking and street protests). In this context, characterizing and monitoring the opinion of population about those events are crucial for the democratic process [16].

Traditionally, extracting and analyzing surveys is a way to know public opinion regarding political events and are usually linked to high costs. Moreover, in most cases this kind of survey takes into account just a piece of society sample [8, 16].

Given this scenario, researchers have been exploring other sources to collect and characterize large volume of data which represent the public opinion on political events [8, 16]. Twitter is a promising source for this kind of characterization. This social media has become popular to discuss and to disseminate different kinds of information and knowledge, mainly regarding political issues [8, 10].

Previous studies have demonstrated the Twitter applicability as a source of data to characterize and automatically monitor the online population's opinion related to political scenario in different countries (e.g. The United States and India) [1–3, 8, 10]. Furthermore, they reinforced the argument that the characterization of online population opinion reflects the real sentiment of the society [1–3, 8, 10].

© Springer Nature Switzerland AG 2018
A. Rodrigues et al. (Eds.): CRIWG 2018, LNCS 11001, pp. 105–116, 2018.
https://doi.org/10.1007/978-3-319-99504-5_9

This kind of characterization is important because it may contribute to the reflection and it may guide the decisions and actions of government and society based on the population's opinion [1, 2, 8]. Thus, this paper aims to characterize the Brazilian population's opinion about political events in this country and demonstrate the applicability of social media, such as Twitter, to make this kind of characterization. In particular, we investigate the reaction of society facing one of the most impactful political event in Brazil: the impeachment of Dilma Rousseff [7].

To achieve this goal, we collected and analyzed Twitter data related to the process of impeachment of the former president Dilma Rousseff and the inauguration of Michel Temer as the new Brazil's president. This perspective of characterization in Brazilian scenario is important because the culture may influence both (1) the political position of population and (2) the use of Twitter to express opinion about this subject.

The results indicated that people in Brazil discuss political issues on Twitter and they also stand for these issues positively or negatively. Besides, from a comparative analysis, it was possible to observe that the online public opinion about politic events reflects the real sentiment of the Brazilian population.

The results presented in this paper are relevant because the sentiment characterization using data from Twitter may contribute for the formation of the public opinion regarding political events. Thus, the population would not be limited on what is published by typical media (e.g., television and newspapers). Furthermore, the government and other interested organizations (e.g. unions) could make use of this new source of information to guide their campaigns and projects, aiming a higher public support.

Additionally, the methodology adopted in this work may be used in services which characterize the opinion of society in relation to political issues. This methodology also may be used to conduct other opinion characterization in relation to events which are not limited to the political scenario, such as sports, products and services.

2   Related Works

In this section, we present some previous works that have demonstrated that data collected from Twitter can be used to monitor or predict the real opinion of population on different political scenarios.

The works of Barbosa et al. [2, 3] presented the hashtags effectiveness to perform sentiment analysis in presidential elections in different countries. The results indicated that it is possible to track the sentiment of online population from the hashtags that express sentiment about this content. Wang et al. [20] developed a system for real time sentiment analysis using Twitter data about the candidates for the US presidency in 2012. The system was considered satisfactory because it demonstrated that the content produced by the users of Twitter reflected events and news related to the electoral process.

Some researchers analyzed how the population used the Twitter during elections in regions where the democracy may be considered young and in development [1, 14, 21]. Jaidka and Ahmed [14] studied the variation of the use of Twitter by the political parties in India during the presidential campaign in 2014. Younus et al. [21] analyzed messages related to 2013 elections in Pakistan and concluded that most messages were considered negative and, probably, it happened due to the lack of political maturity of society in this country.

Other researches have used data from Twitter to predict electoral results. Bermingham and Smeaton [8] demonstrated that Twitter could be used to predict the result of elections in Ireland in 2011 with a margin of error between 3.67% and 5.85%. Dokoohaki et al. [10] analyzed the 2014 electoral campaign in Sweden and concluded that the popularity of candidates in Twitter was directly related to the elections results.

The related works showed the applicability of Twitter as a source of data to monitor and predict political events. The reported results allowed us to highlight the following relevant aspects: (1) there were results variation due to the geographic region analyzed and (2) the majority of the political studies focus in electoral results [14, 21]. These aspects have been supporting the demand showed by Barbosa et al. [2] and Wang et al. [20]. According to these authors, it is necessary to consider different regions and political scenarios to characterize the online population's opinion using Twitter data. This kind of characterization would reinforce the applicability of Twitter as a data source to track the online population's opinion about political events.

This research differs from previous work because it presents a characterization of the Brazilian's public opinion on a different political event, which is not limited to federal or regional elections. Therefore, the results of this work complement the previous researches, once our results demonstrate new evidences of Twitter applicability to detect and track the public opinion regarding an uncommon political event in Brazil.

3   Characterization of Twitter Data Related to Political Events

Since the proposed characterization comprises different events related to the political scenario in Brazil, we analyzed the Twitter data stream in different periods. Next, we present the methods and results of the proposed characterization.

3.1   Characterization of Volume of Shared Messages by Brazilian Population

To characterize the volume of Twitter messages concerning to different political events shared by Brazilian population, we collected and analyzed Twitter data related to the process of Dilma Rousseff's impeachment. Figures 1, 2, 3 and 4 show the total volume of tweets collected per hour related to each analyzed event and the number of tweets by keyword searched.

As shown in Fig. 1, the first analysis was related to the initiation of the impeachment process of Dilma in the Senate and the inauguration of Michel Temer as an interim president. This analysis was carried out between May 11 and 13, 2016 and gathered 698,953 Twitter messages. In this stage, the following keywords were used to collect the data: Dilma, Temer, Coup and Impeachment.

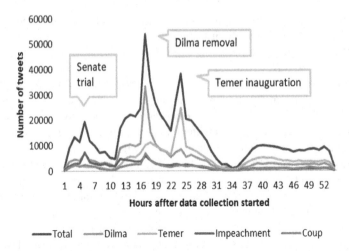

Fig. 1. Tweets per hour related to the initiation of the impeachment process of Dilma in the Senate and the inauguration of Michel Temer as an interim president.

The second event was the repercussion generated by the disclosure of recorded conversations among politicians Romero Jucá, Renan Calheiros, and Sergio Machado. Such conversations were about the impeachment process and the *Car Wash* operation. As shown in Fig. 2, we collected 406,552 messages in the period between May 23 and 28, 2016. In this stage, the following keywords were used to collect the data: Dilma, Temer, Coup and Impeachment as well as Renan, Jucá, and Machado, since these were the main politicians involved in the audios.

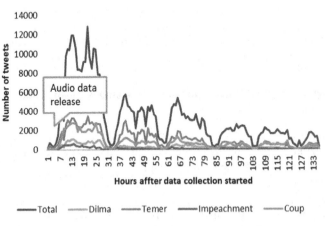

Fig. 2. Tweets per hour related to the recordings involving politicians.

The third event analyzed was the 2016 Olympic Games in Rio de Janeiro (RJ), which took place during the impeachment process of Dilma Rousseff and the presence of the interim president Michel Temer. Once the event was promoted during a historical political event, the goal of this analysis was to verify whether this sport event would cause a change in the focus of the discussions on Twitter. The data was collected during the opening and the first week of Olympic Games, between August 3rd and 10th, 2016. In this stage, the following keywords were used to collect the data: Dilma, Temer, Coup and Impeachment as well as World Cup. As shown in Fig. 3, the collection resulted in 318,469 tweets.

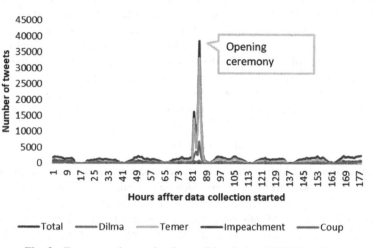

Fig. 3. Tweets per hour related to politics during 2016 Olympics.

The fourth and last political event analyzed refers to the final trial of the impeachment on the Senate and its repercussion. It was collected 1,545,737 tweets in the period between August 25th and September 5th, 2016. In this stage, the following keywords were used to collect the data: Dilma, Temer, Coup and Impeachment.

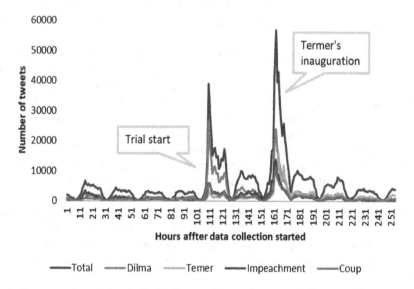

Fig. 4. Tweets per hour during the final judgment of impeachment on the Senate and its repercussion.

The graphs in Figs. 1, 2, 3 and 4 show sudden rises in the volume of messages in moments that something striking happened in the real world. Considering the characteristics presented, it was possible to realize that there was a large volume of messages on Twitter that contained the keywords related to political issues in Brazil. These results allow us to argue that the online population uses this social media to express opinions in reaction to events that occurred during the presidential impeachment process, a milestone in the political and economic scenarios of Brazil [6, 7].

However, according to Barbosa et al. [2], Wang et al. [20], and Almatrafi et al. [1], the characterization of population's opinion by means of Twitter data should consider not only the volume of data but also the sentiment expressed by them. In this sense, in the next stage, this research aimed to carry out the sentiment analysis on data, as well as to verify equivalence between the online population's opinion and public opinion surveys reported by other sources (e.g., television).

3.2 Sentiment Analysis of Collected Data

Sentiment analysis on Twitter data can be performed using different approaches [17]. Among them, it is possible to highlight Machine Learning [17]. The sentiment analysis with Machine Learning algorithms consists in the automatic classification of a set of messages. This type of algorithm receives as input a sample of messages previously labeled with sentiment and this algorithm learns to classify other messages from that input [19].

We characterized Twitter messages related to Michel Temer according to their polarities (i.e., negative or positive). The characterization of sentiment from this perspective is relevant because all the analyzed events were related to impeachment process of Dilma Rousseff and the probable inauguration of Michel Temer without direct elections. According to the BBC News (2016) and BBC Brazil (2016b), understanding the popular position in relation to this possible presidential change could guide the actions after the impeachment process (e.g., to promote new direct elections or not) [6, 7, 16].

The first phase to perform the sentiment analysis was the creation of the training set. In this step, the training set used for automatic classification was generated following the "*most frequent hashtags*" approach presented by Barbosa et al. [2, 3]. We used this approach because Barbosa et al. [2, 3] demonstrated its applicability and effectiveness to generate training sets in similar contexts of classification.

Following this approach, initially, we extracted all hashtags from collected tweets and we ordered these hashtags from the most frequent to the less frequent. The frequency of hashtag is the sum of distinct messages (i.e., tweets) that contain the hashtag [2, 3]. Next, the most frequent hashtags were classified regarding the sentiment that they transmitted. In this process, we extracted the top-100 most frequent hashtags that expressed some feeling. We characterized each hashtag as positive to Michel Temer (e.g., #byeDilma and #continueTemer) or negative (e.g. #byeTemer #DilmaInnocent), when the sentiment was explicit. One author of this study conducted the classification and this process resulted in 32 hashtags categorized as negative and 59 classified as positive.

The top-100 positive and negative hashtags to Michel Temer were mentioned in 172,656 collected tweets. Thus, the last step in this process was to generate a training set from tweets containing the hashtags previously classified. In this step, we categorized all tweets containing negative hashtags as negative messages (e.g., "Leave Temer #byeTemer") and, in turn, the tweets with positive hashtags were categorized as positive messages (e.g., "Not Dilma #NoDilma"). This process resulted in a training set composed by a sample of 102,017 negative tweets and 70,639 positive tweets.

In the second phase of the sentiment analysis, we defined the algorithm to perform the automatic classification of messages that did not contain the most frequent hashtags. We chose Naïve Bayes algorithm, one of the most suitable algorithms for this kind of classification [1, 9, 15, 17].

We conducted an experiment to demonstrate the effectiveness of the classifier in the collected data of this work. We performed this experiment following the 10-fold cross validation technique [17] in the training set previously generated. Initially, we applied traditional text pre-processing steps [17] on the collected data. Specifically, we removed accentuation, punctuation, stop words and the hashtags used to classify the training set, additionally, we converted all letters to lowercase. Next, we used the representation model bag-of-words to transform the messages as an input for the classification algorithm. In this model each tweet was represented as a bag-of-words, disregarding the context and the order of words [17].

Finally, in the last step of the experiment to demonstrate the effectiveness of Naïve Bayes, we selected the attributes that should be used to compose the classification model. To select these attributes, we filtered the words considering a threshold of minimal number of occurrences of each word in the dataset [17]. In this step, we evaluated different thresholds to define the most appropriated threshold for this kind of classification. From Table 1 it is possible to see that the most appropriated threshold was ten, once that the classifier achieved an accuracy of 83.09% using 65,445 attributes.

Table 1. Effectiveness of Naïve Bayes to classify the collected data considering different thresholds.

Threshold	10	50	75	100	200
# Attributes	**65,445**	24,764	19,333	16,122	10,230
Accuracy	**83.09%**	82.96%	82.77%	82.64%	81.54%

Once demonstrated the effectiveness of Naïve Byes, we performed the sentiment analysis of tweets that had not been categorized from hashtags using: (1) Naïve Bayes algorithm; (2) The training set generated; (3) The previously pre-processing described, considering the threshold equal ten. Naive Bayes provides, as results, the categorization as well as the likelihood of successful classification (i.e., confidence) [17, 19].

These results of sentiment analysis of data related to each event are shown in Table 2. In this table, the "General Classification" column indicates the classification for the whole data set, showing the quantity and the percentage of positive and negative messages.

The "*Confidence Classification* > 80%" column shows the number and percentage of messages classified as positive and negative with at least 80% confidence. The classifications with at least 80% confidence were highlighted because they can better reflect the sentiment of the online population in this kind of characterization [19]. Next, we present and discuss the results comparing them with the population sentiment during these political events reported by other sources.

In Table 2 we can see the summarization of the sentiment analysis about Michel Temer in the beginning of the impeachment process in the Senate and in the inauguration of Michel Temer as interim president. This data shows that most of the messages (i.e., approximately 70%) are unfavorable to Michel Temer. When comparing this indicator with other sources that report the sentiment of the population, it is possible to observe some equivalence. For example, according to BBC Brazil [6] in May 2016, the inauguration of Temer as interim president after the impeachment was supported by only 8% of the population. Conversely, 25% of Brazilian people supported Dilma's permanence in the presidency, and 62% of them wanted new presidential elections.

Another survey conducted by Vox Populi in the same period indicated that 11% of Brazilian people supported the inauguration of Michel Temer without direct elections, 25% of them preferred the Dilma permanence, and 61% of population wanted new elections. These surveys help to evidence that the opinion reported in Twitter messages reflects population's opinion.

Table 2. Sentiment about Michel Temer during different events related to the Dilma's impeachment.

Event	Sentiment	General classification		Confidence classification > 80%	
		# messages	% messages	# messages	% messages
Michel Temer at the start of the impeachment process in the Senate and inauguration of Michel Temer as interim president	Negative	481,129	**68.84**	355,022	**73.10**
	Positive	217,822	31.16	130,626	26.90
Michel Temer during the disclosure of recordings involving politicians and *Car Wash* operation	Negative	365,170	**89.92**	314,946	**94.59**
	Positive	41,381	10.18	17,998	5.41
Michel Temer in the first week of the 2016 Olympic Games during the impeachment process	Negative	252,828	**79.39**	215.527	**84.76**
	Positive	65,640	20.61	38.754	15.24
Michel Temer during the final impeachment judgment in the Brazilian Senate	Negative	1,090,656	**70.56**	813.985	**75.97**
	Positive	455,079	29.44	257.497	24.03

Furthermore, Table 2 shows the data that characterizes the sentiment of the online population over the initial days of *Michel Temer as interim president and the disclosure of recordings involving politicians and Car Wash operation*. It is possible to observe that approximately 90% of the messages reflect the negative sentiment to Michel Temer. Comparing the data from Table 2, it is possible to see an increase in the percentage of negative messages related to Michel Temer at the beginning of his acting as interim president in May 2016.

A possible explanation for these results may be related to the fact of Michel Temer mentioned in these recordings subjects as: (1) the impeachment process and (2) the strategies to compromise the *Car Wash* operation [4]. The research published by Iglesias [13], in June 2016, reinforces this explanation, which reported that for at least 40% of the respondents, the recordings disclosed compromised the acceptance of Michel Temer [13].

In relation to the event *Michel Temer in the first week of the 2016 Olympic Games during the impeachment process*, our goal was to verify whether this sports event, promoted during a historical political event in the country, would cause some change in the sentiment of the population over the interim president. Table 2 shows that approximately 80% of messages were negative for Michel Temer, in this period, especially as reported by BBC Brazil [5], this ceremony was highlighted by public demonstrations during the speech of Michel Temer. Complementarily, a survey released in the same period reported that the popular approval of Michel Temer was less than 14%. Furthermore, to 62% of Brazilian population the impeachment process should result in new direct elections [12, 18]. This information evidences equivalence between the opinion expressed in the messages on Twitter and the feeling of the population reported by other sources.

Finally, in Table 2 we can see that the sentiment regarding to *Michel Temer during the final impeachment judgment in the Brazilian Senate* were negative for most messages (approximately 75%). This result is compatible with the surveys released in the same period (i.e., August 2016). According to Fagundez [11], for 87% of Brazilian people, the country was on the wrong track. Additionally, the disapproval rate of president Michel Temer was 68%, and his approval varied from 8% to 19% in the capitals of Brazil [11].

4   Discussion of Results

In this work, we characterized the popular opinion about political events using Twitter data. The results indicated that Brazilian people discuss political issues in this social media, expressing opinion, favorably or not, about these events. Additionally, we showed, by means a comparative analysis, that the opinion of the online population reflects the real positioning of Brazilian population regarding political events.

These results are significant because, as argued by Barbosa et al. [3], Wang et al. [20], and Almatrafi et al. [1], through the perspectives presented here it is possible to report the opinion of the population about the political scenario so that this characterization can guide the decisions and actions of the government and society based on the popular opinion.

Thus, the characterization of the opinion of Brazilian people regarding political events through Twitter data has shown to be a viable alternative to traditional opinion surveys (e.g., questionnaires), since: (1) it allows to analyze a large volume of data using resources that do not require high processing capacity; (2) messages may represent popular opinion distributed in different regions of Brazil, not limited to large capitals; (3) the opinions expressed may reflect different perspectives about a particular event, not limited to the script of a questionnaire; (4) and the methodology for sentiment analysis of messages demanded a low effort, since the set of training was generated following the approach based on hashtags [3].

These presented results complement other initiatives that evidenced the applicability of data extracted from Twitter to characterize popular opinion about political issues considering other countries (e.g., USA [20] and India [14]). In this sense, this work supports the arguments that social media, as Twitter, as well as the adopted methodology, may be used to characterize and to track the opinion of people about political events in perspective of different cultures [8, 10, 14, 20, 21].

As complimentary results, we highlight that this work reinforces the applicability of use of hashtags [2, 3], as a low-cost approach, to generate the training set for automatic classification of data. The experiments showed that using a training set generated from hashtags: (1) the Naïve Byes achieved an accuracy of 83% in a 10-fold cross validation and (2) the results of the automatic classification of sentiment were compatible with the real sentiment of the population. These results are significant because they may contribute to consolidating the use of hashtags as a viable and useful approach to generate a training set to perform sentiment analysis with low cost. To demonstrate the applicability of this kind of approach it is important because one of the biggest challenges of sentiment analysis using Machine Learning is to generate the training set with low cost [2, 3, 19].

5   Conclusions and Future Works

The presented characterization indicated that the Brazilian population discusses political subjects in Twitter and the people express negative or positive feelings about these events. Additionally, in a comparative analysis, we showed that there is equivalence between the opinion of the online population and the real positioning of Brazilian people regarding the political events analyzed. These results complement other related works that discussed the utility of Twitter data to characterize opinion about political issues considering other countries (e.g., USA [20] and India [14]).

Thus, this work also reinforces the arguments that both Twitter and the adopted methodology may be used to track and to report the popular opinion about political issues in the perspective of different countries [8, 10, 14, 20, 21]. These results are relevant because they show the viability of using data of online social networks to track the opinion of people regarding to political issues.

In addition, the methodology proposed in this work can be used in tools that present and make the characterization of the opinion of the population available about political events. This methodology can also be used to conduct other characterizations of opinion about events that are not limited to the political scenario (e.g., products, and services).

Furthermore, the data collection and the training set provided in this work are also significant contributions since they can be used by other researchers interested in applying and evaluating techniques of sentiment analysis (available in: https://goo.gl/FwxWhs). As future work, we aim to evaluate the viability of creating tools to present and to visualize this type of characterization in real time.

References

1. Almatrafi, O., Parack, S., Chavan, B.: Application of location-based sentiment analysis using Twitter for identifying trends towards Indian general elections 2014. In: Proceedings of IMCOM 2015, pp. 1–5 (2015)
2. Barbosa, G.A.R., et al.: Caracterização do uso de hashtags do Twitter para mensurar o sentimento da população online - Um estudo de caso nas Eleições Presidenciais dos EUA em 2012. In: Proceedings of SBBD 2013 (2013)
3. Barbosa, G.A.R., Silva, I.S., Zaki, M., Meira Jr., W., Prates, R.O., Veloso, A.: Characterizing the effectiveness of Twitter hashtags to detect and track online population sentiment. In: Proceedings of CHI 2012 EA, Austin, Texas, USA, pp. 2621–2626 (2012)
4. BBC: Brazil leaked tape forces minister Romero Juca out (2016). https://goo.gl/HxB9cA. Accessed 29 Sept 2017
5. BBC Brasil: Cerimônia emocionante de abertura da Olimpíada dá início oficial à Rio 2016 (2016a). https://goo.gl/4R8n7k. Accessed 29 Sept 2017
6. BBC Brasil: O que as últimas pesquisas revelam sobre apoio ao impeachment e a Temer? (2016b). https://goo.gl/TKTL4U. Accessed 29 Sept 2017
7. BBC News: Brazil's Dilma Rousseff to face impeachment trial (2016). https://goo.gl/v31EQx. Accessed 29 Sept 2017
8. Bermingham, A., Smeaton, A.F.: On using Twitter to monitor political sentiment and predict election results, 2016. In: Proceedings of SAAIP 2011 (2011)
9. Bifet, A., Frank, E.: Sentiment knowledge discovery in Twitter streaming data. In: Pfahringer, B., Holmes, G., Hoffmann, A. (eds.) DS 2010. LNCS (LNAI), vol. 6332, pp. 1–15. Springer, Heidelberg (2010). https://doi.org/10.1007/978-3-642-16184-1_1
10. Dokoohaki, N., Zikou, F., Gillblad, D., Matskin, M.: Predicting swedish elections with Twitter: a case for stochastic link structure analysis. In: Proceedings of ASONAM 2015, pp. 1269–1276 (2015)
11. Fagundez, I.: Para 87% dos brasileiros, país está no rumo errado, mas pessimismo diminui, 29 de Agosto de 2016 (2016). https://goo.gl/657uyo. Accessed 29 Sept 2017
12. Forbes: Latest Brazil Study On Impeachment Unlikely To Save Dilma (2016). https://goo.gl/Yr4U1q. Accessed 29 Sept 2017
13. Iglesias, S.: Governo Temer tem aprovação de 13% dos brasileiros, diz pesquisa CNI/Ibope, Julho de 2016 (2016). https://goo.gl/Xontfp. Accessed 29 Sept 2017
14. Jaidka, K., Ahmed, S.: The 2014 Indian general election on Twitter: an analysis of changing political traditions. In: Proceedings of ICTD 2015 (2015)
15. Le, L., Ferrara, E., Flammini, A.: On predictability of rare events leveraging social media: a machine learning perspective. In: Proceedings of the 2015 ACM on Conference on Online Social Networks, COSN 2015, Estados Unidos, pp. 3–13 (2015)
16. Maciel, C., Cappelli, C., Slaviero, C., Garcia, A.C.B.: Technologies for popular participation: a research agenda. In: Proceedings of dg.o 2016 (2016)
17. Pang, B., Lee, L., Vaithyanathan, S.: Thumbs up? Sentiment classification using machine learning techniques. In: Proceedings of EMNLP 2002, pp. 79–86 (2002)

18. Schreiber, M.: Nem Dilma, nem Temer: maioria da população quer eleição antecipada, aponta nova pesquisa, 26 de Julho de 2016 (2016). https://goo.gl/MWswMt. Accessed 29 Sept 2017
19. Silva, I.S., Gomide, J., Veloso, A., Meira Jr., W., Ferreira, R.: Effective sentiment stream analysis with self-augmenting training and demand-driven projection. In: Proceedings of SIGIR 2011 (2011)
20. Wang, H., Can, D., Kazemzadeh, A., Bar, F., Narayanan, S.: A system for real-time Twitter sentiment analysis of 2012 U.S. presidential election cycle. In: Proceedings of ACL 2012, pp. 115–120 (2012)
21. Younus, A., Qureshi, M.A., Saeed, M., Touheed, N., O'riordan, C., Pasi, G.: Election trolling: analyzing sentiment in tweets during Pakistan elections 2013. In: WWW, pp. 411–412 (2014)

Estimating the Ability of Crowd Workers: An Exploratory Experiment Using the Japanese-English Translation Work

Tsutomu Takamiya[1]([✉]), Kunihiko Higa[1], and Kousaku Igawa[2]

[1] Department of Innovation Science, Tokyo Institute of Technology, Tokyo, Japan
takamiya.t.ac@m.titech.ac.jp, khiga@mot.titech.ac.jp
[2] Graduate School of Innovation Management,
Tokyo Institute of Technology, Tokyo, Japan

Abstract. Crowdsourcing (CS) has its superiority in regards to the quick access to workers throughout the world. On the other hand, when viewed from the prospect of clients who are seeking workers, it is difficult to estimate workers' performance prior to ordering a task in CS. Crowdsourcing service providers (CSP) produce some indices which may be useful in estimating workers' performance, however, the correlation between workers' performance and these indices has not been verified.

In this study, several new indices are proposed and their effectiveness are tested via an exploratory experiment using the Japanese-English translation work. The experimental result indicates some of the proposed indices such as the contribution of consciousness to clients, ambition, the degree of difficulty workers show in the work, awareness of the reward, and the degree of colloquial tone in writing show the correlation with the quality of deliverables. In particular, these trends are more significant for low-performers in terms of the quality of deliverables. Therefore, clients may be able to avoid low-performers by using the proposed indices when they choose workers for CS.

Keywords: Crowdsourcing · Motivation · Text analysis

1 Introduction

1.1 Background

Crowdsourcing (CS) is one of the new styles of teleworking that combines Information Technology (IT) infrastructure with conventional jobs and makes it possible to realize a fair working environments in which the evaluation of workers is based on their ability and not affected by work place and time. Unspecified human resources around the world are potential workers in CS, so it is expected that clients can enjoy benefits by the open innovation, and that further growth is expected in the future [1].

Supported by JSPS KAKENHI Grant Number 15K03647.

© Springer Nature Switzerland AG 2018
A. Rodrigues et al. (Eds.): CRIWG 2018, LNCS 11001, pp. 117–132, 2018.
https://doi.org/10.1007/978-3-319-99504-5_10

The word crowdsourcing was defined by Howe [2], which is characterized as an undefined (and generally large) network of people in the form of an open call. In the case of the platform-type CS, on the side of clients, it is possible to procure human resources more economically and quickly, compared with in-house assignment or outsourcing. Meanwhile, on the side of workers, there is an advantage in that flexible working independent of time and place is possible.

The style of work performed on the crowdsourcing service provider (CSP) is roughly divided into three, according to the type and scale of a task: a competition type, a micro-task type (also simply referred to as a task type), and a project type. Although CS provides merits for both clients and workers as mentioned before, there are some difficulties as well. One of the serious difficulties, which is common to the task type and the project, is the selection of an appropriate worker for the task. Unlike the competition type, clients cannot see deliverables produced by workers before the contract is finalized with these two types. In order to alleviate these difficulties, CSP provide several indices so that clients can judge candidate workers. For example, the evaluation scores from the clients in the past, the number of retained skills, the number of orders received, etc. These seem to be effective indices at a glance, but there are problems for all. It is known that the evaluation scores from past clients tend to be biased to higher end. One of the reasons for this is that when a client wishes to continuously place orders with the worker, he or she may deliberately give a high evaluation score. In addition, many of the workers who have low evaluation scores discard the CSP registration and move on to the other CSPs. Regarding the number of retained skills, it may be exaggerated because it is a self-report by a worker. Furthermore, regarding the number of orders received and the number of evaluations, these can be said to reflect the reputation of the worker, not necessarily the quality of deliverables, that is, the ability of the individual worker is not reflected in them. Also there is a problem that newly registered workers have no historical data in CS. Therefore, CSP provided indices may not be suitable for evaluating workers.

Apart from existing CSP indices, the character and psychological factors of the worker may have influence on the carefulness and performance of the person's work. Also, if we can quantify attitudes towards work, degree of concern, communication skills, etc. in a generalized way, we may find some relations to the ability of the individual worker. As well as numerical indices, unexpected discoveries may be found from differences in more delicate linguistic expressions, such as comments at the time of entry and free text answers by applied workers. At any rate, there are no established indices that can be estimated without directly judging the ability of the worker from deliverables at present, which is the impediment factor in using the CSP not only for clients but also for workers.

1.2   The Objective of This Study

Based on the possibilities and tasks of the CSP mentioned in the previous section, this study aims to propose new indices that can substitute, or at least complement, the existing CSP indices for judging the ability of applied workers in a project type task. The ability here refers how the three baselines attained by a worker in a project, namely the quality of deliverables, the work period, and the cost, satisfy the expectations of the client. It should be understood that the reputation, annual income, and past achievement of the worker are not equal to the ability of the worker. Also, the quality of deliverables can generally be evaluated against the requirements presented by the client, and that evaluation depends on the type of requested work. In order to achieve the objective of this study, an experiment will be conducted. In this experiment, work with a fixed working period and order amount will be ordered in CS, and the effectiveness of the proposed indices will be determined.

The project type is selected because, unlike the task type, it can clarify the period, the cost, and the target of the quality of deliverables beforehand so that it can be widely targeted from a simple skill to a high skill level. Also, compared with the task type, it tends to have a much higher cost. Therefore, the selection of appropriate workers will be more critical for the project type task.

The significance of this study is as follows. If the client can correctly grasp or estimate the ability of the worker, he or she can expect an improvement in the quality of deliverables by requesting the work from the person with more ability, not depending on his or her reputation, etc. At the same time, it is thought that even the worker or applicant can reduce the concern of suffering from disadvantage such as being rejected because of an unfair evaluation of his or her ability.

The composition of the report is as follows. In Sect. 2, related works will be reviewed, and an approach to define new indices will be determined. In Sect. 3, after explaining the hypothesis, the exploratory experiment, contents of acquired data, and survey methods including analytical policy will be described. In Sect. 4, the analysis results will be discussed. In the last section, the conclusion will be described with limitation.

2   Related Studies

Although there are many studies on CS, there are few focusing on the ability of the worker in CS or the effectiveness of the CSP index itself. Therefore, as a reference which can be taken into consideration in view of the purpose of this study, we describe the studies focusing on the relationship between CSP indices and deliverables, the performance of workers, the intrinsic/extrinsic motivation, and the approach concerning natural language processing such as the text analysis.

2.1   Relation Between CSP Indices and Deliverables

Kittur et al. [3] noted that in CS it is one of the important issues to be able to guarantee in advance that work deliverables from workers are of high quality, even from the requesting side. Assemi and Schlagwein [4] classified various indices of workers in the e-service market into the external information such as actual results in the market and number of qualifications, and the internal information by the clients and the workers, such as various evaluation scores, and have shown that there is a significant correlation between the former and the amount of order receipts. However, the amount of order receipts itself merely reflects expectations and reputations viewed from the clients, and does not refer to the quality of deliverables themselves. Igawa et al. [5] verified the relationship between the CSP indices and the quality of deliverables, and found limited correlation with the ability of the worker in CSP.

2.2 Performance Indices

First of all, as a definition of the word here, we say that performance is represented by the magnitude of the ability. A lot of studies can be found to find out about the skill and ability of a person without directly seeing his/her deliverables. Conway [6], for example, examined management works and found that devotion to work contributes to the improvement of its performance, and that interpersonal communication skills are one of the elements of leadership. As a study in the virtual space of the Internet, Bozzon et al. [7] examined how to find experts in Social Networking Service (SNS), and found that they can be found more efficiently by analyzing the user registration information, contents of remarks, and distance to friends connected by the SNS community in addition to the questionnaire provided to candidates.

There are several studies on how to find the high performance talents on CS, among which it is suggested to repeatedly request works to narrow them down [8], to build the special teams of sophisticated technicians to create synergistic effects [9], and to do some work on non-experts to extract a group with expertise by performing a clustering analysis [10]. However, we cannot find a study of estimating the performance of the worker prior to request.

As a study on the performance of workers, Borman and Motowidlo [11] insisted that the capacity to work is composed of the task performance, i.e. ability to work itself, and the contextual performance, i.e. ability to improve the work environment to make work run smoothly, and that the latter is also an important factor as much as the former. In addition, the latter is deeply linked to the personality of a person itself, and they further noted that it is classified into the following five dimensions.

- Persisting with enthusiasm and extra effort as necessary to complete one's own task activities successfully
- Volunteering to carry out task activities that are not formally part of one's own job
- Helping and cooperating with others
- Following organizational rules and procedures
- Endorsing, supporting, and defending organizational objectives.

This study suggests that considering the opponent on a job request with ambiguous content and judging from the surrounding circumstances are affecting the capacity to work, which is no less than the technical capability. In a CS environment where client and worker cannot communicate directly with face to face, these may be more important factors.

Koopmans et al. [12] classified the worker's performance (Individual Work Performance, IWP) into four indicators and developed a simple method that can be quantified by multiple questionnaires with fixed forms.

- Task Performance
- Contextual Performance
- Adaptive Performance
- Counterproductive Work Behavior.

While this can be a powerful tool as an objective indicator as Igawa et al. [5] used it and the Big Five traits [20] to find a moderate correlation to the ability of the worker on CSP, there is a complication in that the worker has to answer many questionnaire items in advance. Also, since the items are fixed in forms, there is concern that it is easy for the worker to understand how to respond if they answer, and that the contents of the response are easily capable of being intentionally manipulated.

2.3   Intrinsic/Extrinsic Motivation

Generally, there seems to be a certain relation between the ability of the worker and the motivation that the person has, that is, the reason for feeling the necessity of work. Deci [13–15] classified the motivation as an extrinsic one and an intrinsic one: The former includes reward and evaluation from others, and the latter includes the sense of ability, self-determination, and acceptance from others who are important for that person. He has shown the importance of the latter by exploratory experiments, and that the degree of motivation as a whole is lowered as the extrinsic motivation is strengthened for those who mainly worked for the intrinsic motivation. In addition, Deci and Ryan [16] developed the concept of intrinsic/extrinsic motivation and presented the self-determination theory that the action motivated by external factors can change into being autonomously motivated through the internalization process. Through a meta-analysis study in psychology, Utman [17] reported that in the case of work which is somewhat complicated, the actual performance is better when setting the goal for learning obtained in the process than for the resultant performance itself.

All of these psychological findings seem to be applicable throughout human activities, and it seems that there is room for discussion in the CS tasks as well. For example, Rogstadius et al. [18] examined the quality of deliverables by manipulating extrinsic motivations for people with different intrinsic motivations under a controlled experimental environment, and found that the intrinsic motivation can improve it. On how to give rewards in a CS task such as a tournament method, Straub et al. [19] has shown that whether to select a competitive type or a micro-task type under the constant total amount affects the withdrawal of workers and that the quality level of deliverables will also be affected.

2.4   Approach to NLP

Studies on natural language processing in CS are also recently being performed from the viewpoint of artificial intelligence (A.I.). Kashima and Kajino [21] pointed out the effectiveness of using CS to gather the information that is the base of machine learning, such as the classification of words for the natural language processing. Also Resnik et al. [22] suggested that the quality of translation on CS can be improved better by asking people who can handle only the language to be translated (monolingual), with expressions of fine nuances which are difficult for machines and the multilingual to translate.

Because the natural language processing by machines is indispensable to have a large amount of data and a database such as a dictionary to distinguish them, in the cases where a sufficient number of words cannot be secured statistically or there is not a highly accurate dictionary, auxiliary work or evaluation by hand is effective in advance of the analysis as described above. Although the problem of the quality of work is often pointed out, [21,22] has shown that it is possible to overcome this problem by simplifying it like a microtask, and by making multiple workers do the same work and matching the results later. In addition, in the case that the evaluation of the CS task depends on the general impression of a person, that evaluation can be requested on CS. Baba et al. [23] additionally asked the general people on CS rather than just machine learning to confirm the works presented on CS as to whether they are inappropriate or not contrary to public order and morals, and succeeded in reducing the number of experts by 25% when combined with them.

This shows that, seemingly CS and artificial intelligence are quite contrasting, but they may actually complement each other.

3   Exploratory Experiment and New Indices

After explaining the hypothesis based on the related studies in the previous section and the objective of this study in Sect. 1.2, we explain the exploratory experiment using the Japanese-English translation work, contents of acquired deliverables and text sentences by questionnaire, and survey methods using their sentences to introduce new indices.

3.1   Hypothesis Setting

As mentioned in Sect. 1.1, the existing CSP indices may not be significantly correlated with the quality of deliverables by the worker, and workers who have just registered with the CS site may not have them, i.e. N/A. So we focus on the discussion in consideration of alternative index candidates, in which we use the text sentences by questionnaire as input. According to the related studies in the previous section the indices such as IWP, Big Five traits can be candidates. But considering the problem of the questionnaires with fixed forms mentioned in the previous section, we exclude them from targets.

Referring to the studies of [21–23] in which they effectively used the microtask on CS for work requiring a relatively complicated judgment, as done by machine learning, regarding the evaluation of deliverables and of the text sentences by the questionnaire, we perform CS tasks separately from the request for deliverables.

In order to examine the indices related to the ability of the workers, we set the hypothesis based on the knowledge obtained from the related studies to understand the relationship between the ability of the workers as input and the quality of deliverables as output. The latter is considered to be expressed as a result of the former, although it is impossible to directly measure the former in advance. The CSP indices seem to be among the candidates presenting it, but there might be no significant correlation with the quality of deliverables or, even if there is, a relatively weak correlation [5].

On the other hand, based on Borman and Motowidlo [11], the ability of the workers consists of two categories of performance. It is seemed that, the task performance has a direct relationship with the CSP indices such as the number of retained skills, but the contextual performance has a weak relationship with them, although it is linked to the character of the worker and has an influence on the quality of deliverables indirectly such as attention to work success and consideration to the client. From the viewpoint of the intrinsic/extrinsic motivation theory, it is also linked to the motivation of the workers themselves, and depending on how questions in the questionnaire are asked, there is a possibility that characteristic keywords correlated to the quality of deliverables can be captured. We describe the above as a hypothesis.

- H1: There are keywords that substitute the CSP indices and have a correlation with the quality of deliverables, which are related with the contextual performance and the intrinsic/extrinsic motivation.

3.2 Outline of the Exploratory Experiment

In order to verify the hypothesis set in the previous section, we requested a Japanese-English translation work at a Japanese CSP site. While translation work is one of the general business categories in CSP, at the present time machine translation is still limited and there is eventually no choice but to rely on human hands, which makes our experiment meaningful to examine the relation between the ability of workers and the quality of deliverables. The deliverables are evaluated on microtask requests on CS in native English.

The exploratory experiment is roughly divided into the steps of obtaining Japanese-English translated deliverables, and questionnaires, and of obtaining the evaluations of deliverables and questionnaires after the work ends, each of which is implemented as an independent CS task.

For the Japanese-English translation work, our order is as follows.

- Contents of work: Japanese-English translation of articles introducing Japanese sake (alcohol)
- Number of characters: 659

- CSP: CrowdWorks
- Recruitment period: 10 days
- Recruitment staff (planned): 30
- Submission deadline of the deliverable: One week after placing an order
- Reward: 6,000 Japanese yen (1 U.S. dollar is nearly 105 yen).

The content of the work that has been set up should be realistic. Although it is a theme familiar to many Japanese people, several unique Japanese expressions are included, and the worker must properly translate these words so that the people in English-speaking countries who are not familiar with Japanese culture can understand them.

If the reward is too low for a worker, sufficient entries will not be expected. On the contrary, if it is too high, the proportion of people who set the reward as the main reason for entry will be high, and the degree of motivation as a whole will be lowered [13–15]. Typically the price of a reward in Japanese-English translation is about 5 to 20 yen per character, and in the case of the documents with high specialty, such as business documents, it tends to be higher. Experimentally, we made a pre-order with the same reward for Japanese-English translation of the sentences containing 605 letters, and within 24 h from the start of ordering, we could have seven applicants which are sufficient numbers for the assumption of our main order. Based on this result, the reward in our main order is set as described above.

3.3   Questionnaire

We examined the content of the questionnaire to the worker before and after work. When asking for text input in a questionnaire, two cases are considered: a case where several keywords are requested and a case where a completely free sentence is requested. Relatively, the former is easy to analyze, and it is possible to avoid the difficulty of classifying ambiguous expressions. However, even if multiple keywords are collected, the number of words collected in this experiment is estimated to be several hundreds at the most as a total number, and it is quantitatively insufficient for natural language processing by machines. On the other hand, in the latter case, the analysis becomes more complicated because it contains ambiguous expressions, but the character of the respondent is expected to be more strongly reflected than the former, and it is qualitatively more suitable as the content of the text. Therefore we adopted requesting the completely free sentences.

Next, we examined the specific content of the question. As also mentioned in Sect. 2.2, it is important to make it as natural as possible and not inductive in order to prevent respondents from predicting what kind of responses will lead to their own high evaluation. On the other hand, it is also important to make content lead to the motivation and the estimation of individual personality, and it is necessary to balance them. As a result, we asked the following questions in the pre-order mentioned in Sect. 3.2.

- Q1 (Pre-work question). Please feel free to write your ambition for conducting this Japanese-English translation in the range of 50 to 100 words.
  - Intention of question: Whether you are looking at work objectively or subjectively (from the perspective of contextual performance), or whether you are conscious of your own improvement (from the perspective of intrinsic motivation)
- Q2 (Pre-work question). Please write concisely your experience in the range of 50 to 100 words, about what you thought was especially difficult in the translation work so far and how it was dealt with.
  - Intention of question: The difference between intrinsic motivation and extrinsic motivation appears or not
- Q3 (Post-work question). Please feel free to write your impressions after completing this translation within 100 words.
  - Intention of question: Whether you perceive it as a personal experience or just as a business (from the perspective of contextual performance)
- Q4 (Post-work question). Please feel free to write the source of motivation to do the translation work (it can be limited to this translation work) within 100 words.
  - Intention of question: Whether you are looking at work objectively or subjectively (from the perspective of contextual performance), or whether you are conscious of your own improvement (from the perspective of intrinsic motivation).

There is an overlap in the content intended by the above questions, which is because the results may be different by the expression of words even for questions of similar contents [23]. In addition, questions that are almost duplicate are set before and after the work, which is to confirm whether there is a difference in response between at the time of application and the time of completion. In fact, in the case of requesting on CS, although workers write many of their skills better at the time of application in order to win orders, it is often seen that the reactions get lost at the time of confirming the situation after winning the orders. From the pre-order it is considered that the expression of the question is appropriate because of the clear difference being seen between high-performers and low-performers. Therefore, we adopt this content for the questionnaire at the time the order is placed.

3.4   New Indices on Questionnaire

As a result of the examination in Sect. 3.3, the same questionnaire as the pre-order one was given to the workers. From text information obtained here, we examined new indices, i.e. keywords and questions used for our analysis. When considering the questions, first we extracted concepts and keywords referred from related studies and made them candidates for questions [STEP. 1]. Then, by comparing and examining the content of the top five performers to that of the bottom five in order to find a characteristic difference, we confirmed the new questions along with the STEP. 1 [STEP. 2]. Finally, as with the evaluation of deliverables, we requested evaluating them as a microtask on CS and converted the results to quantitative evaluations for each deliverable [STEP. 3].

[STEP. 1] Based on the investigation of related studies and the hypothesis, we refer to the concepts and keywords as follows.

– Contextual performance
  • Commitment to success: Attitude to face difficulties, tenacity, high quality work, etc.
  • Voluntary cooperation for work not in charge of yourself: Responding to unexpected workload, etc.
  • Support for other people: Care for users and customers, dealing with sudden requests, etc.
  • Compliance with organization rules and procedures: Honorifics, spoken words, punctuality, etc.
  • Support for organization's goals: Awareness of customer needs, etc.
– Intrinsic/extrinsic motivation
  • Reward: Reward, bonus, etc.
  • Recognition from others: Recognition, etc.
  • Feeling of competence: Self improvement, etc.
  • Sense of self-determination: Your own judgment, etc.
  • Sense of acceptance from others: Appreciation, pleasure, sensation being relied upon, etc.

There are overlapping factors between the contextual performance and the concept of intrinsic/extrinsic motivation, but here we do not seek validity of classification but search candidates for evaluation items from related studies, so that there is no problem in the evaluation process.

[STEP. 2] We compared the content of answers to the four questions between the top five performers and the bottom five, Q1 to Q4, and decided the questionnaire to be requested on the microtask as follows.

– Q1_1. A sense of consciousness and responsibility to the reader of the translated sentence or the work client
– Q1_2. A sense of motivation for self-improvement
– Q1_3. A sense of difficulty more than enjoyment in the work
– Q1_4. Whether the expression is colloquial or not
– Q3_1. A sense of consciousness and responsibility to the reader of the translated sentence or the work client
– Q3_2. A sense of motivation for self-improvement
– Q3_3. A sense of difficulty more than enjoyment in the work
– Q3_4. Whether the expression is colloquial or not
– Q4_1. A sense of consciousness and responsibility to the reader of the translated sentence or the work client
– Q4_2. A sense of motivation for self-improvement
– Q4_3. A sense of consciousness to reward
– Q4_4. Whether the expression is colloquial or not.

We exclude the Q2 because they cite technical issues on translation, such as technical terms and terms with which they do not have knowledge, i.e., task performance, while there are few remarks in terms of motivation and contextual performance. It seems to be because the expression of the question sentence has induced the consciousness of the worker into technical issues.

[STEP. 3] We requested the evaluation by the Likert 5-scale survey to 50 people per each question of one deliverable. In the request, we included a question for confirmation in which evaluators should select the specific answer, and if they make wrong answers then they are judged as malicious users and their answers are excluded from the evaluation. Also, the data whose standard deviation is larger than 1 is excluded. The evaluation scores in average and the standard deviation are obtained for each of one deliverable by using the answers of the evaluators that eventually remain.

4   Results and Discussion

The exploratory experiment started on December 1, 2015, and 38 people were adopted in order of application. One was canceled on the way due to the reasons of the worker side, and one was unable to contact on the way, so finally we got deliverables from 36 people. We are able to confirm for all of 36 people their sex, age, CSP indices, and evaluation scores of deliverables. The summary of the workers including their occupations are shown in Table 1.

4.1   Evaluation of Deliverables

The translations as deliverables are evaluated following three viewpoints that Goto et al. [24] used for evaluating machine translation. While they originally evaluated them with two scales, Yes/No, here we evaluate them by the Likert 5-scale survey.

1. Is it grammatically correct?
2. Is it easy to understand the contents?
3. Does it look like English written by a native speaker?

We requested evaluating them as a microtask on Microworkers, the CS in the United States, and adopted 50 people for each deliverable. Applicants (evaluators) were restricted to those who live only in the English speaking countries in North America and Europe, excluding those who live in Asian countries where English is the official language. The evaluators evaluated the above three viewpoints in five scales, and we used the total scores as the evaluation scores of deliverables. We included questions for confirmation in the questionnaire and those which are clearly judged as malicious users were deleted from the subject of evaluation. We also asked two native speakers who can understand Japanese to evaluate all the deliverables on Upwork and confirmed that there is no difference in general between their evaluations and those by the microtask, and that they convey the important information and the content of the source sentence. The summary of the evaluation scores is shown in Table 2.

Table 1. Summary of the crowd workers

Characteristics	Class	N	%
Age	20–29	8	22.2%
	30–39	13	36.1%
	40–49	9	25.0%
	50–59	5	13.9%
	60–69	1	2.8%
Sex	Male	9	25.0%
	Female	27	75.0%
Occupation	Part-time	2	5.6%
	Student	2	5.6%
	Company employee	9	25.0%
	Self-employed	9	25.0%
	House wife or husband	6	16.7%
	Other	8	22.2%

Table 2. Summary of the evaluation

	Mean	Min	Max	SD
Grammatically correct	3.95	3.30	4.24	0.20
Easy to understand	3.41	2.46	3.93	0.33
Native level	3.32	2.25	3.91	0.34
Total score (output quality)	10.67	8.00	12.07	0.84

4.2 Relation Between the Results of Questionnaire and Deliverables

In Table 3, we describe the correlation matrix between the evaluation of deliverables and the results of questionnaire of Q1_1 to Q4_4, twelve questions, for the text information of the workers. The correlation coefficients are significant in five cases of Q1_3, Q3_1, Q3_2, Q3_4, and Q4_3. On the other hand, the number of samples is insufficient due to an increase in the missing value, for example, the number of data of Q1_4 is 9, and Q3_4 is 16, which is less than the half of original data. In addition, since many of the questions have similarities, such as Q1_3 and Q1_4, Q3_4 and Q4_4, many cases show a strong correlation, so in cases such as the multiple regression analysis with CSP indices it must be necessary to remove the effect of multiple collinearity.

Consciousness and Responsibility to the Reader of the Translated Sentence or the Work Client. For Q1_1, Q3_1, Q4_1 which evaluated the consciousness of the worker for the end user and the client, Q3_1 is showing only a moderately positive correlation with the evaluation of deliverables, but two

Table 3. The correlation matrix of the questionnaire and the evaluation

	Mean	SD	N	Q1_1	Q1_2	Q1_3	Q1_4	Q3_1	Q3_2	Q3_3	Q3_4	Q4_1	Q4_2	Q4_3	Q4_4	Evaluation
Q1_1	4.24	0.38	34	1												
Q1_2	4.02	0.48	33	0.201	1											
Q1_3	2.53	0.35	32	-0.19	-0.3	1										
Q1_4	3.11	0.21	9	-0.59	-0.05	.967**	1									
Q3_1	3.81	0.49	32	0.249	-0.1	0.192	0.453	1								
Q3_2	3.72	0.51	31	.450*	-0.08	0.244	-0.28	.698**	1							
Q3_3	2.91	0.83	29	0.036	-0.24	.491*	-0.02	0.178	0.116	1						
Q3_4	3.35	0.52	16	-0.21	-0.02	-0.14	0.46	-.820**	-.648*	-0.51	1					
Q4_1	3.82	0.68	27	-0.04	-0.29	-0.15	-0.51	-0.24	0.156	-0.1	-0.2	1				
Q4_2	4.07	0.51	32	0.048	0.306	-0.3	-0.65	-0.15	-0.24	0.183	-.564*	.473*	1			
Q4_3	2.71	1.01	30	-0.35	-0.07	0.099	0.184	-0.11	-0.18	-0.12	.647*	-.502*	-.533**	1		
Q4_4	3.27	0.44	14	-0.1	-0.07	0.318	0.791	-0.02	-0.14	-0.32	.865**	-.749*	-.688**	0.503	1	
Evaluation	10.67	0.84	36	0.178	0.154	.355*	0.377	.461**	.360*	-0.03	-.536*	-0.2	0.002	-.388*	-0.31	1

*$p < 0.05$ **$p < 0.01$

outliers are somewhat influential. These outliers are 35th and 36th, and it can be said that the tendency of low-performers is remarkable. Also, since it shows a positive correlation, there is a tendency that the ability of the worker who is strongly conscious of the end user and the client tends to be high, which is also consistent with the contextual performance of the support to others.

Motivation for Self-improvement. For Q1_2, Q3_2, Q4_2 which evaluated the motivation for self-improvement, only a weak positive correlation is shown for Q3_2 on the evaluation of deliverables. Since a positive correlation is shown, it can be interpreted that there is a tendency of the worker with higher ability to perform a job to have the internalized motivation.

Consciousness to Reward. For Q4_3, which evaluated the consciousness to reward as a basis of motivation to work, a weak negative correlation is shown on the evaluation of deliverables. It is distinctive to be divided into two groups, one with little consciousness to reward and one with relatively clear consciousness. Although it should be noted that the rank of deliverables of the worker who shows the most clear consciousness is 12th place and that not all members with it clearly are in low ranks, this suggests the possibility that the overall motivation may be reduced with the strength of the extrinsic motivation.

Attitude to Work. For Q1_3 and Q3_3, which evaluated the sense of difficulty on the work, a weak positive correlation is shown only for Q1_3 on the evaluation of deliverables. It is interesting that the group with lower sense, i.e., optimistic attitude, includes both the top and the bottom in ranking. It seems to be because the workers with high ability are so confident that they can afford to have fun before starting the work, and those with low ability tend to be optimistic in nature. On the other hand, the workers who anticipate difficulties tend to converge in a relatively high ranking, although not at the top.

Literary Style. For Q1_4, Q3_4 and Q4_4, which evaluated whether the text described by the worker is colloquial or not, a moderate negative correlation is found for Q3_4 on the evaluation of deliverables, which is most notable among all question items. Although Q1_4 shows a positive and non-significant correlation, this is mainly due to the lack of samples and it should not be referred to the result.

For the interpretation that Q3_4 shows a negative correlation, workers who use informal words even in formal situations may lack the ability to engage, i.e., task performance, in the task of Japanese-English translation. Moreover, it may be connected to the finding of Sect. 4.2 from the viewpoint of the degree of respect for clients. It is interesting if we can see such a tendency between the informal words and the ability of workers not only for our experiment but also for other studies.

The reasons why there is no correlation between Q1_4 or Q4_4 and the evaluation of deliverables are seems to be as follows.

- Since Q1 is a question before the work, the worker is considered to be consciously or unconsciously in a situation that a relative formal description is aimed at compared with Q3.
- Since Q4 is a specific question focused on with the keyword "motivation," there is a possibility that a colloquial expression could be suppressed as compared with Q3, which makes it the completely free comment.

4.3   Evaluation of the Hypothesis

Following the discussion up to the previous section, we evaluate the hypothesis H1 in Sect. 3.1. There exists a concept that correlates with the quality of deliverables from the viewpoint of the contextual performance and the intrinsic/extrinsic motivation. Specific keywords confirmed this time are "consciousness to users/clients," "motivation for self-improvement," "sense of difficulty on the work," "consciousness to reward," and "colloquial expression."

5   Conclusion

In seeking the substituting indices and keywords of the existing CSP indices which are correlated with the quality of deliverables and related with the contextual performance and the intrinsic/extrinsic motivation, we performed an exploratory experiment using the Japanese-English translation work as an example. As a result, from the analysis of the text information by a questionnaire to the worker, the quality of deliverables was positively correlated with the consciousness to users and clients, the motivation for self-improvement, and the sense of difficulty in the work, while it was negatively correlated with the consciousness to reward and the colloquial expressions. These trends are more significant for low-performers in terms of the quality of deliverables, therefore, clients may be able to avoid low-performers by using the proposed indices when they choose workers for CS. Since these keywords are not unique to the translation work in this time, it is expected that similar features can be seen in other types of work as well.

Limited conditions in this study are listed below:

1. Possibility of specific results in the Japanese-English translation work. As a cultural background of a worker seems to have strong influence on all five keywords in Sect. 4.3, the correlation may be only seen in this study. Also, the work of translation is sensitive to the words, so workers' wording may have influenced the quality of deliverables. We need to do additional experiments as to whether this result can be applied to other kind of work or culture. Even though the content of specific correlation is different, we can take the same approach as this study.
2. Necessity of more samples. Considering the possibility of the necessity of performing multiple regression analysis, it is more desirable that the number of workers should be at least 100 or more. Also, when dealing with words mechanically in the natural language processing, it is desirable that the number of words is about several hundreds of thousands to several million, and it seems necessary to collect the data using SNS.
3. Necessity of obtaining a questionnaire before starting work. There is no point in the post-work questionnaire for our purpose. Although some findings were obtained on valid keywords when creating questionnaires from this experiment, the information on the worker needs to be acquired before work, and it should be common to any task.
4. Comparison of effectiveness with other indicators, such as the CSP indices and the Big Five traits. Although it was excluded this time, we may discover the keywords that can reinforce each other.

References

1. Afuah, A., Tucci, L.C.: Crowdsourcing as a solution to distant search. Acad. Manag. Rev. **37**(3), 355–375 (2012)
2. Howe, J.: The rise of crowdsourcing. Wired Mag. **14**(6), 1–4 (2006)
3. Kittur, A., et al.: The future of crowd work. In: CSCW 2013, San Antonio, Texas, USA, 23–27 February 2013
4. Assemi, B., Schlagwein, D.: Profile information and business outcomes of providers in electronic service marketplaces: an empirical investigation. In: Proceedings of the 23rd Australasian Conference on Information Systems (2012)
5. Igawa, K., Higa, K., Takamiya, T.: An exploratory study on estimating the ability of high skilled crowd workers. In: Proceedings of the 5th IIAI International Congress on Advanced Applied Informatics (2016)
6. Conway, J.M.: Distinguishing contextual performance from task performance for managerial jobs. J. Appl. Psychol. **84**(1), 3–13 (1999)

7. Bozzon, A., Brambilla, M., Ceri, S., Silvestri, M., Vesci, G.: Choosing the right crowd: expert finding in social networks. In: EDBT/ICDT 2013, Genoa, Italy, 18–22 March 2013
8. Gottlieb, L., Friedland, G., Choi, J., Kelm, P., Sikora, T.: Creating experts from the crowd: techniques for finding workers for difficult tasks. IEEE Trans. Multimed. **16**(7), 2075–2079 (2014)
9. Retelny, D., et al.: Expert crowdsourcing with flash teams. In: ACM Symposium on User Interface Software and Technology, UIST (2014)
10. Burnap, A., Ren, Y., Gerth, R., Papazoglou, G., Gonzalez, R., Papalambros, P.Y.: When crowdsourcing fails: a study of expertise on crowdsourced design evaluation. J. Mech. Des. **137**(3), 031101 (2015)
11. Borman, W.C., Motowidlo, S.J.: Expanding the criterion domain to include elements of contextual performance. In: Schmitt, N., Borman, W.C. (eds.) Personnel Selection in Organizations, pp. 71–98. Jossey-Bass, San Francisco (1993)
12. Koopmans, L., Bernaards, C.M., Hildebrandt, V.H., van Buuren, S., van der Beek, A.J., de Vet, H.C.: Improving the individual work performance questionnaire using Rasch analysis. J. Appl. Meas. **15**(2), 160–175 (2014)
13. Deci, E.L.: Effects of externally mediated rewards on intrinsic motivation. J. Pers. Soc. Psychol. **18**(1), 105–115 (1971)
14. Deci, E.L.: Intrinsic motivation, extrinsic reinforcement, and inequity. J. Pers. Soc. Psychol. **22**(1), 113–120 (1972)
15. Deci, E.L.: The effects of contingent and noncontingent rewards and controls on intrinsic motivation. Org. Behav. Hum. Perform. **8**, 217–229 (1972)
16. Deci, E.L., Ryan, R.M.: Intrinsic Motivation and Self-determination in Human Behavior. Plenum, New York (1985)
17. Utman, C.H.: Performance effects of motivational state: a meta-analysis. Pers. Soc. Psychol. Rev. **1**(2), 170–182 (1997)
18. Rogstadius, J., Kostakos, V., Kittur, A., Smus, B., Laredo, J., Vukovic, V.: An assessment of intrinsic and extrinsic motivation on task performance in crowdsourcing markets. In: Proceedings of the Fifth International AAAI Conference on Weblogs and Social Media (2011)
19. Straub, T., Gimpel, H., Teschner, F., Weinhardt, C.: How (not) to incent crowd workers: payment schemes and feedback in crowdsourcing. Bus. Inf. Syst. Eng. **57**(3), 167–179 (2015)
20. McCrae, R.R., John, O.P.: An introduction to the five factor model and its applications. J. Pers. **60**(2), 175–215 (1992)
21. Kashima, H., Kajino, H.: Crowdsourcing and machine learning. J. Jpn. Soc. Artif. Intell. **27**(4), 381–388 (2012)
22. Resnik, P., Buzek, O., Kronrod, Y., Hu, C., Quinn, A.J., Bederson, B.B.: Using targeted paraphrasing and monolingual crowdsourcing to improve translation. ACM Trans. Intell. Syst. Technol. **4**(3), 38 (2013)
23. Baba, Y., Kashima, H., Kinoshita, K., Yamaguchi, G., Akiyoshi, Y.: Leveraging non-expert crowdsourcing workers for improper task detection in crowdsourcing marketplaces. Expert Syst. Appl. **41**, 2678–2687 (2014)
24. Goto, I., Chow, K.-P., Lu, B., Sumita, E., Tsou, B.K.: Overview of the patent machine translation task at the NTCIR-10 workshop. In: Proceedings of the 10th NTCIR Conference, Tokyo, Japan, 18–21 June 2013

Crowdsourcing and Massively Collaborative Science: A Systematic Literature Review and Mapping Study

António Correia[1,2(✉)], Daniel Schneider[3], Benjamim Fonseca[1,2], and Hugo Paredes[1,2]

[1] University of Trás-os-Montes e Alto Douro, UTAD, Vila Real, Portugal
ajcorreia1987@gmail.com, {benjaf,hparedes}@utad.pt
[2] INESC TEC, Porto, Portugal
[3] Tércio Pacitti Institute of Computer Applications and Research (NCE),
Federal University of Rio de Janeiro, Rio de Janeiro, Brazil
schneider@cos.ufrj.br

Abstract. Current times are denoting unprecedented indicators of scientific data production, and the involvement of the wider public (the crowd) on research has attracted increasing attention. Drawing on review of extant literature, this paper outlines some ways in which crowdsourcing and mass collaboration can leverage the design of intelligent systems to keep pace with the rapid transformation of scientific work. A systematic literature review was performed following the guidelines of evidence-based software engineering and a total of 148 papers were identified as primary after querying digital libraries. From our review, a lack of methodological frameworks and algorithms for enhancing interactive intelligent systems by combining machine and crowd intelligence is clearly manifested and we will need more technical support in the future. We lay out a vision for a cyberinfrastructure that comprises crowd behavior, task features, platform facilities, and integration of human inputs into AI systems.

Keywords: AI · Crowdsourcing · Distributed scientific collaboration
Human computation · Human-machine hybrid computation
Massively collaborative science · Systematic literature review

1 Introduction

Increasing amounts of scientific data are being produced at an exponential rate, fueled by the development of high-throughput technology and the rapid growth of research capacity [1]. Thus, data discovery and reuse can be extremely difficult for a researcher working alone. Such processes have been highly individualized, labor-intensive, and error-prone and are not well supported by existing systems since automated reasoning approaches do not encompass the cognitive abilities of a human brain for tasks such as characterizing a field or discipline [2]. To address these challenges, scientists have

© Springer Nature Switzerland AG 2018
A. Rodrigues et al. (Eds.): CRIWG 2018, LNCS 11001, pp. 133–154, 2018.
https://doi.org/10.1007/978-3-319-99504-5_11

leveraged the power of crowds and large communities of volunteers to perform tasks that no known efficient algorithms can yet solve. Crowdsourcing has been established as a computing paradigm intended to bridge the gap between machine and human computation [3]. When applied to tackle scientific problems, crowdsourcing can be characterized by openness to a large pool of researchers and citizen scientists and their respective interactions within or outside their institutions [5]. As mentioned by Ranard and colleagues [6], the use of "crowdsourcing can improve the quality, cost, and speed of a research project while engaging large segments of the public and creating novel science". However, researchers are often reluctant to adopt crowdsourcing for creating, treating, and analyzing research data and there was little discussion on the difficulties associated with crowdsourcing research endeavors and how we might make progress in this area [7].

It is worth noting that there is a lack of systematic studies "investigating the applicability of crowdsourcing in not-for-profit fundamental research (as conducted in traditional universities)" [5]. In addition, few studies have already characterized how the synergies between mechanical and cognitive operators work and how to use them effectively for knowledge discovery and acquisition in scientific work scenarios [3]. Our aim is to describe how research might benefit from crowd computing based on literature found. While numerous areas of literature can illuminate this topic of inquiry, the actual contribution is closer to a survey paper and tries to explore the interplay between technology and the crowd in scientific settings.

In the ensuing section of this work, we try to revisit the theoretical background on crowd-computing hybrids by outlining in detail prior contributions. Section 3 explains the method followed for performing the systematic review presented here. Section 4 describes the main results of our study and discusses some challenges and open issues for further improvement. Section 5 provides some concluding remarks.

2 Background

All science is a social system in its own nature, being characterized by challenges of massive scale [8]. As reported before, the collective wisdom of a crowd can be leveraged as a source of intellectual labor since "humans understand language, inference, implication, abstraction and concepts better than computers" [10]. However, harnessing crowdsourcing and human computation at large scale faces challenges that range from the difficult to scale up complexity and low quality responses [11] to the limited expertise or attention to cope with high-dimensional and ill-structured data [12], lack of motivation for participation [13], and worker honesty [14]. In the literature there are several examples of studies on crowdsourcing scientific tasks using Amazon Mechanical Turk (AMT)[1]. For instance, Good et al. [15] recruited non-scientists to

---

[1] https://www.mturk.com/.

recognize disease concepts in biomedical paper abstracts. In addition, Brown and Allison [16] showed a high accuracy rate when using AMT to systematically evaluate scientific publications by distributing groups of Human Intelligence Tasks (HITs). Experiments on massive authorship of academic papers reported some challenges related to coordination mechanisms, tool design, content handling, and task differences [17]. There are also examples of leveraging an academic crowd for organizing conference sessions while extracting categories and clusters from high-dimensional data through crowd synthesis [12]. Some thematic reviews have already been performed to help identify parallels between crowd computing classes, descriptions, and systems while revealing gaps in the existing work as opportunities for new research (e.g., [19–21]).

As we enter an age of steadily larger and noisier data, a combination of both machine and human intelligence is required [22]. AI can help make the crowd more efficient and accurate through machine intelligence. On the other hand, "crowd intelligence can help train, supervise, and supplement automation" [23]. Most studies agree on the use of crowdsourcing as a reliable method for supervised and semi-supervised machine learning (e.g., active learning), from feature generation to prediction, deeper analysis, and classification of mass volumes of data [16]. Active learning and crowd-based human computation can be used to enhance the performance of automatic data classification and minimize the impact of possible erroneous or abusive feedback. Hybrid crowd-machine computation and mixed-initiative systems have been introduced as interactive, intelligent approaches that combine the strengths of human interaction with the algorithmic power of machine learning in order to solve problems that could not be solved by either computers or humans alone [24]. Examples of mixed-initiative systems in scientific discovery include PANDA [25] and Apolo [26]. Furthermore, Higgins [27] integrates automatic information extraction and human computation for crowdsourced knowledge acquisition. This kind of approach can be particularly fruitful in scientific contexts to refine machine-extracted metadata while providing evidence on demand using automatic classification techniques enabled by human crowd workers who can filter, process, and verify the information [3].

3   Method

Systematic mapping is a process established on the identification, categorization, and analysis of scientific data concerning a certain research topic. The result is a structured summary that portrays the relationship between literature and categories [28]. SLR represents a critical part of research in evidence-based software engineering. Cruzes and Dybå [29] go even further by describing a SLR as "a concise summary of the best available evidence that uses explicit and rigorous methods to identify, critically appraise, and synthesize relevant studies on a particular topic". The systematic review and mapping study described here follows published guidelines from works on software engineering (e.g., [30]). This section discusses the review protocol, formulate the research questions that the review intends to answer, and describes the strategy used to search for primary studies, study selection criteria and procedures, sources of studies, data extraction and synthesis strategies, and mapping procedures.

3.1   Study Aims and Research Questions

Our aim is to identify and describe conceptual dimensions behind crowdsourcing and mass collaboration in science towards the creation of a theoretical framework. In order to do this, we undertook a systematic review of publications discussing concepts and techniques related to crowdsourcing and human computation in scientific settings. The rationale is established on understanding the key characteristics of crowds and the social-technical infrastructure of crowd computing in scientific research.

The work presented here addresses the following research questions:

RQ1. Which forms of crowdsourcing and human computation have been discussed in the literature? Are they suitable for use in scientific discovery and thus generalized for several disciplines?

RQ2. What techniques have been proposed for performing research activities using crowd computing and what is the strength of evidence supporting them?

RQ3. To what extent has research examined crowd-computing hybrids concerning the integration of human inputs into AI systems for data-driven scientific discovery?

3.2   Search and Selection Processes

The authors performed searches on central scientific literature databases and followed the references in the resulting papers by means of a snowballing strategy for gathering new research studies that were then recorded in a spreadsheet. During the initial phase of the study, search engines (Google Scholar, ISI Web of Knowledge, Scopus) and traditional digital libraries (ACM Digital Library, IEEE Xplore, Springer Link, ScienceDirect, PLoS One, PubMed, BioMed Central, arXiv, etc.) were queried using a string sufficiently comprehensive for including research from multiple disciplines and research domains. Google Scholar was chosen as the primary search engine since it covers multivariate types of documents, while including papers from several fields of research. The following search strings were used to build the queries:

> (crowd **OR** crowdsourcing **OR** human computation **OR** collective intelligence **OR** mass collaboration **OR** citizen science) **AND** (artificial intelligence **OR** machine learning **OR** machine intelligence **OR** natural language processing **OR** mixed-initiative systems **OR** computing) **AND** (qualitative **OR** survey **OR** taxonomy **OR** systematic literature review **OR** science **OR** scientific discovery **OR** research)

Instead of searching for specific sources, which would not be so efficient due to the lack of perspectives spread across disciplines, reference lists of the publications found were recorded and examined towards identifying relevant studies. Furthermore, direct searches for related publications, prolific authors, and research groups were also performed. The search process was assessed for completeness by acquiring a large corpus of studies based on manual search of relevant sources. Snowballing enlarged the scope of this examination by considering aspects not previously addressed in the initial study. Thus, some limitations concerned with the use of a specific set of search terms, publication sources, and electronic databases were partially overtaken.

3.3   Inclusion/Exclusion Criteria and Primary Study Selection

The studies were screened according to various criteria pertinent to the research questions (Table 1). We established the following criteria for the inclusion of primary studies. Regarding a paper, it must be available as a full paper, written in English, and published in a peer-reviewed venue. Some exceptional documents (i.e., technical reports) were included due to the relevance of their content to the present study. As for the studies informed by the papers, they must report empirical evidence on conceptual dimensions behind crowd computing. The exclusion criteria consisted of eliminating duplicate studies that were not within the scope of this research. Publications that were clearly duplicated or for which we found newer and more complete versions (extensions) were excluded. In cases when articles present high levels of similarity, the most comprehensive study prevails. The database searches resulted in an extensive list of 3996 potential papers gathered after evaluation and deduplication.

Table 1. Inclusion and exclusion criteria (adapted from Kitchenham [30])

Inclusion criteria	Exclusion criteria
- Papers that survey or describe features and models related with the ability of leveraging crowd-based human computation and collective intelligence for scientific purposes - Papers about the integration of human inputs into AI systems - Surveys, systematic reviews and mapping studies, case studies, experience reports, meta-analyses, and conceptual/taxonomic studies - Studies published between 2006 and 2017	- Not written in English - Duplicate (when several reports of a study exist in different sources the most complete version of the study was included in the review) - Full paper not available (lack of access to full text documents through the database or other means) - Invalid type (e.g., the study is just published as an abstract) - Editorials, keynotes, tutorials, panel discussions, introductions to special issues, theses and dissertations - Not related to the topics under research - Studies published before 2006 - Highly technical papers presenting no relevant conceptual dimensions

The title, abstract, and keywords were used to remove any studies not related to the research focus. From this sample, certain types of documents (e.g., theses and dissertations) were excluded. The SLR only included studies that were published between 2006 and 2017 and the key criterion required by a publication to be included was the relevance of the paper towards answering the research questions defined in this study. Afterwards, the remaining papers were read in order to remove any that do not fulfill the inclusion criteria. From the remaining entries, only 148 papers[2] were selected after

---

[2] In Appendix A will be found a list of all publications included in the final review.

full paper reading, where the initial and closing sections of each study were evaluated regarding their objectives. Journal and conference papers constitute the largest part of the sample, followed by workshop papers, book chapters, and symposium papers.

3.4 Data Extraction and Synthesis

The papers returned in the searching phase were stored using a data extraction form developed to gather all relevant data from the primary studies (Table 2). This registry supported the classification and analysis procedures. Only one researcher reviewed all papers and extracted metadata according to the data collection form for consistency.

Table 2. Data extraction form (adapted from Cruzes and Dybå [29])

Data items	Description
Identifier	Unique identifier for the paper (same as the reference number of the paper considered for study)
Year	The year of the publication
Title	The title of the publication
Author(s)	The author(s) of the paper
Type of publication	Journal, conference, symposium, congress, workshop, book chapter, technical report
Venue	Publication venue in which the study was published (e.g., Information Systems Frontiers)
Citation count	Impact of a publication measured by the number of times that was cited by other works
Status	Included, excluded (according to the quality assessment strategy)
Main themes	Principal conceptual dimensions/categories extracted from qualitative data analysis
Levels of analysis	Different categories under the banner of the main categories (i.e., taxonomic units)
Additional notes	Complementary observations supporting the qualitative study

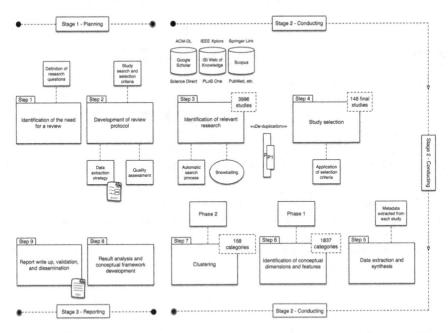

Fig. 1. Stages of the systematic review and mapping (adapted from Kitchenham [30])

A list of 1837 categories identified from primary studies was gathered and organized by their unique themes. Decisions on including or excluding features were made after reading the primary studies and the data were then grouped into meaningful clusters for synthesising qualitative evidence. Deduplication and aggregation were also performed in the clustering process, resulting in 158 themes/categories. Figure 1 summarizes all the steps followed in this review.

4 Results and Discussion

In any review of the literature, placing the individual results within a larger framework is important to help build understanding of the larger pattern. A total of 8 clusters (#) emerged from the systematic review. A deeper insight into the key aspects and forms of crowdsourcing and massively collaborative science (RQ1) led us to explore distinguishing factors, dimensions and sample values as a starting point for academics who are interested in following up the extant literature on this topic. The *time-space matrix* (#1) was initially proposed by Johansen [31] to classify groupware by when participants are working at the same time (synchronous), same space (co-located), different time (asynchronous), or different places (remote). Schneider and colleagues [19] adopted the original version of this scheme to explain how time and space affect crowdware and crowd work settings. The contribution time (engagement profile) of each user is a relevant aspect of distributed human computation systems and crowd workers can be recruited and made available quickly [32]. As pointed out by Ponciano and co-workers [33], the level of engagement of each volunteer can be measured by relative activity duration, daily devoted time, and variation in periodicity. Uchoa et al. [34] go even further by claiming that "volunteers can assist researchers collecting and/or analyzing massive amounts of data that cover long periods of time or large geographic areas or employing some human cognitive ability in large scale". As the authors put it, crowdware can reshape scientific work through crowd collaboration without temporal and spatial barriers.

Different *forms of digital participation and public engagement* (#2) can be established in scientific projects involving human crowds. For example, citizen science relies on getting ordinary citizens to voluntarily contribute toward scientific research [35]. Other forms of participation in crowdsourcing ecosystems include but are not limited to crowd funding (e.g., Experiment[3]), free and open source software development, altruistic crowdsourcing, and idea generation. Contributions can be individual or collaborative [20, 21]. In the latter case, we adopted the original Ellis et al.'s [36] 3C collaboration model to cluster the various ways and means of interacting by crowd

---

[3] https://experiment.com/.

Table 3. Temporal/spatial issues and modes of digital participation in crowd science.

#	Main theme	Reference(s)
1	Time/temporal factors (e.g., tenure in project, latency)	P9, P14, P18, P70, P80, P106, P118, P141, P145
	Same time/synchronous	P66, P81, P103
	Different times/asynchronous	P81, P103
	Space/campaign channel (physical, virtual, hybrid)	P18, P28, P70, P79, P81, P92, P107, P114, P146
	Same place/collocated	P81
	Different place/remote	P81
2	Collaboration (e.g., degree, setting, conflict, awareness)	P11, P20, P22, P16, P18, P28, P38, P48, P55, P57, P58, P66, P69, P71, P81, P84, P113, P121, P136, P143, P147, P148
	Cooperation	P5, P136, P143
	Coordination (implicit, explicit)	P11, P14, P28, P33, P35, P44, P54, P57, P60, P99, P123
	Communication	P35, P101, P113, P144
	Macrotasking	P6, P40, P101, P124
	Microtasking	P6, P8, P13, P28, P39, P40, P46, P60, P101, P105, P124
	Human computation and distributed HITs	P9, P17, P19, P29, P37, P45, P55, P59, P62, P76, P80, P95, P98, P114, P126, P139, P142
	Games with a scientific purpose	P95
	Collective intelligence	P8, P11, P26, P34, P44, P61, P68, P80, P81, P99, P101, P102, P113, P118, P125, P136, P143, P147
	Citizen science	P5, P8, P9, P12, P16, P19, P26, P32, P35, P52, P89, P104, P115, P130, P134, P140, P144
	Free and open source software	P8, P19, P40
	Managerial control	P48
	Altruistic crowdsourcing	P64, P94
	Competition/contest	P5, P18, P35, P40, P64, P101, P113, P129, P136, P143
	Idea generation	P14, P19, P40
	Knowledge production and information sharing	P5, P17, P18, P28, P31, P117, P119, P136
	Dissemination and feedback	P8, P16, P22, P28, P71, P103, P133, P134, P135, P137
	Planning and scheduling	P33
	Crowd voting and rating	P8, P48, P81, P91, P101, P117, P118, P136, P143
	Crowd processing	P30, P35, P80, P91, P139
	Crowd funding	P14, P18, P40, P81, P101
	Wikis	P40, P44

Table 4. Key characteristics of crowds.

#	Main theme	Reference(s)
3	Size and nature of the crowd engaged	P1, P7, P10, P22, P23, P24, P28, P34, P54, P75, P76, P78, P81, P96, P118
	Diversity of the crowd (e.g., spatial, gender, age)	P7, P8, P10, P20, P22, P28, P36, P46, P50, P70, P79, P90, P99, P106, P107, P109, P114, P146
	Crowd performance	P4, P7, P52, P85
	Crowd interest and preferences	P29, P30, P32, P65, P70, P112
	Crowd intention/goals (e.g., scientific knowledge)	P22, P30, P32, P35, P101, P136
	Crowd skills (e.g., visual recognition, judgement)	P8, P23, P27, P28, P30, P43, P70, P82, P99, P136, P137
	Crowd value	P92
	Crowd bias	P2, P4, P22, P37, P99
	Crowd management (e.g., profiling the crowd)	P7, P14, P22, P23, P29, P40, P61, P69, P73, P90, P124
	Motivation for participation (intrinsic/hedonistic, extrinsic)	P1, P8, P10, P20, P22, P28, P29, P49, P51, P52, P60, P64, P65, P69, P70, P71, P80, P81, P89, P90, P99, P112, P115, P124, P132, P133, P134, P137, P139, P143, P144, P145, P147
	Level of expertise (e.g., novice, beer-mat knowledge)	P5, P53, P119
	Cognitive system (e.g., cognitive diversity, distributed memory)	P29, P80, P87, P99, P125
	Demographics and worker identities	P58, P64, P70, P100, P119, P144
	Intelligence	P99
	Attention	P99
	Emotion	P29, P139
	Satisfaction	P10, P144, P147
	Trust and reliability	P20, P22, P28, P32, P48, P63, P99, P104, P132, P137, P140, P141
	Individual emergent states (commitment, roles)	P144
	Source of human workers (e.g., general crowd volunteers, specific group)	P137, P143
	Behavior of crowd workers (social behavior)	P13, P20, P22, P29, P99
	Behavioral typology of (un)trustworthy crowd workers	P13
	Crowd task selection behavior	P22
	Crowd's attitude toward participation and system functions	P22
	Crowd connection schemes (e.g., virtual proximity)	P119
	Social structure of online crowds (e.g., hierarchy, strength of ties)	P40, P66, P81, P99, P101, P119
	Crowd worker roles (e.g., coordinator, researcher, amateur scientist)	P5, P6, P26, P30, P31, P100, P121, P138, P144
	Volunteers' engagement profiles (e.g., hardworking, spasmodic)	P4, P9
	Type of crowd (e.g., unskilled, locally trained, specialized)	P8, P21, P58, P90
	Social transparency (anonymous, demographic information revealed)	P64
	Social factors (team affiliation)	P145
	Suitability	P10
	Degree of manual effort (activity ratio)	P9, P16, P121

Table 5. Motivational factors and reward schemes in crowdsourcing.

#	Main theme	Reference(s)
4	Enjoyment	P101, P133, P137, P139, P145
	Fun	P8, P28, P51, P65, P80, P86, P89, P93, P101, P102, P106, P110, P112, P118, P119, P129, P131, P146
	Economic and monetary incentives (e.g., money, profit, pay, remuneration)	P4, P8, P28, P37, P47, P50, P80, P86, P93, P96, P101, P108, P109, P112, P118, P119, P129, P133, P137, P139, P143, P147
	Curiosity and discovery	P106, P147
	Information seeking	P11, P147
	Ambition	P65
	Social incentives (social connection, social status within a community, respect from others)	P49, P51, P90, P102, P110, P112, P115
	Community (e.g., community reputation, social contact, sense of belonging to a community)	P28, P32, P52, P60, P89, P99, P115, P129, P133
	Contribute to a large project of common interest	P52, P86, P89
	Personal incentives (e.g., personal skill development, self-value, mental satisfaction, learning)	P10, P28, P32, P49, P86, P89, P90, P101, P112, P137, P145, P147
	Social motivation (e.g., indirect feedback from the job)	P133
	Recognition and reputation	P8, P28, P32, P41, P101, P102, P108, P123, P129, P134, P139, P145
	Science	P89
	Initial motivations (prior interest in science, pro-citizen science)	P52
	Continued engagement (e.g., gaming elements)	P52
	Desired improvements (e.g., explaining the science, progress updates)	P52
	Political and mandatory incentives (e.g, rules, regulations, laws, activism)	P32, P112
	Altruism and meaningful contribution	P8, P18, P64, P80, P88, P93, P94, P101, P112, P118, P139
	Usefulness	P118
	Help(fulness)	P65, P89
	Empathy	P65
	Duty	P65, P102
	Challenge	P86, P102
	Knowledge	P51, P119, P127, P132
	Teaching and mentorship	P32, P108
	Ease of entry and participation	P89, P129
	Feedback and impression of change	P8
	Social responsability	P8
	Love and glory	P28, P60, P32, P143
	Competition	P18, P35, P64, P101, P129
	Reciprocity and expectancy	P88, P129
	Volunteering	P28, P36, P46, P47, P90
	Career	P102, P134

members. Table 3 summarizes some evidence on the temporal/spatial issues and the participation modes in crowdsourcing and massively collaborative science.

Overlapping definitions describe a *crowd* (#3) as a large group of undefined, dispersed individuals showing varying work patterns, expertise, heterogeneity and performance, with little or no control imposed on them [37]. A crowd can read, classify and vote in a varied set of ways, providing supplementary observations and thus adding value to the findings obtained by researchers and small research teams [5]. As shown in the Table 4, a crowd is characterized by aspects like size, skills, social behavior, diversity, cultural differences, and motivation. Prior studies on quality control in crowdsourcing have addressed techniques like filtering out untrustworthy crowd workers for reducing bias [38]. Crowds are also represented by virtual proximity [39], social transparency [40], and social structure [23]. They can be hierarchy-neutral or hierarchical, being formed by strong/weak/absent ties [19]. Researchers' roles vary in a crowdsourcing scenario. For instance, they can act as requestors, leaders (researchers design projects for which volunteers contribute data), collaborators, co-creators, and colleagues (volunteers that conduct research independently) [7].

The success of a crowd-powered system is directly influenced by the involvement of a large number of contributors. It is worth noting that the *motivation for participation* (#4) is considered a central unit in almost all crowdsourcing studies. Motivating crowd members to contribute is complex by nature due to their individual and social differences [13]. The Self-Determination Theory [41] splits motivation constructs into two types: intrinsic/hedonistic (e.g., enjoyment) and extrinsic (e.g., payment). Sometimes, motivational factors overlap and are difficult to distinguish. As pointed out by Freitag and Pfeffer [42], many projects "have additional goals of engaging people in science and motivating them to incorporate scientific thought, hence the process of engaging citizen scientists can in itself also be a measure of success". In a previous study with citizen scientists, Nov and colleagues [13] drew attention to the need for further analysis on the effects of motivation in scientific projects since the factors that improve participation may not lead to enhanced contribution quality. Table 5 summarizes some of the main motivational factors extracted from literature.

Crowd work is usually decomposed into small *tasks* (#5) taking into account the particular needs and characteristics of each group of workers. Such independent and homogeneous tasks "may be structured through multistage workflows in which workers may collaborate either synchronously or asynchronously" using quality control mechanisms [23]. For instance, massively distributed authorship (e.g., writing an academic paper) involves a strong coordination effort to produce a high-quality output [17, 23]. On the other hand, crowd voting by means of critic reviews (e.g., Rotten Tomatoes[4]) comprises simple deskilled tasks (particular views/opinions). Such crowd-generated training data can be also incorporated into AI systems for informing future

---

[4] https://www.rottentomatoes.com/.

Table 6. Crowdsourcing tasks and processes.

#	Main theme	Reference(s)
5	Typology and nature of the task crowdsourced to the crowd (e.g., divisible to microtasks)	P6, P8, P13, P27, P28, P39, P40, P41, P46, P60, P69, P82, P90, P93, P96, P100, P105, P106, P111, P119, P127, P148
	Characteristics of the crowdsourced task	P3, P28, P73, P111, P128
	Variety	P22, P101
	Specificity	P12, P101
	Context	P1
	Length	P1
	Interdependence	P1, P27
	Complexity/difficulty	P10, P22, P27, P28, P34, P58, P60, P90, P105, P110, P111, P120, P132
	Automation characteristics (difficult and/or expensive to automate)	P10, P28, P146
	Task-request cardinality (e.g., one-to-one, many-to-many)	P139
	Process order (computer ↔ worker ↔ requester)	P139
	Problem solving	P28, P60, P110, P142
	Provide task broadcast	P28
	Expertise demands/required skills for executing a task	P1, P101, P28, P63, P106
	Task assignment and recommendation	P28, P29, P36, P40, P41, P56, P58, P66, P67, P69, P106
	Task design (e.g., compensation policy)	P4, P12, P19, P37, P41, P43, P80, P139, P144
	Specialized and complex task support	P37, P43, P52, P58
	Impact of task features on participants' outputs	P22
	Workflow design and optimization (e.g., task decomposition, result aggregation)	P22, P29, P30, P33, P37, P43, P66, P69, P120, P123
	HITs primitives as simple task interfaces used by workers	P17, P19, P42, P72, P95
	Individual processes (joining, contributing)	P144
	Organizational processes (scientific research, volunteer management, data management)	P144
	Models to depict human computation processes (iterative, parallel)	P126
	Decision making (distributed, decentralized)	P99, P123, P136

Table 7. Crowdsourcing platform features (facilities).

#	Main theme	Reference(s)
6	Computing platform (internal, external)	P3, P18, P61, P73, P74
	Type of platform	P14, P69
	Distinguishing features/facilities	P28, P58
	Crowd-related interactions (e.g., result submission)	P10, P28, P36, P56, P63, P67, P97, P106
	Crowdsourcer-related interactions (e.g., result verification, feedback loops)	P10, P20, P28, P36, P63, P78, P97, P106, P116, P131, P135
	Task-related facilities (e.g., aggregate results)	P10, P20, P28, P42, P49, P54, P60, P63, P76
	Platform-related facilities (e.g., manage platform misuse)	P10, P28, P38, P49, P54, P63, P75, P78, P106, P116, P131
	System and technology issues (e.g., architecture)	P20, P22, P29, P61, P69, P118, P121, P144
	Common design patterns (e.g., gamification)	P8
	Openness (closed, internally open, externally open)	P14, P18
	Ownership (public, private)	P101, P143
	Technology access and proficiency of potential participants	P70

behavior. At the highest level, distributed scientific collaboration implicates several constraints on task design taking into account some aspects like training, supervision, and retention of crowd members for non-profit, scientific goals [35]. Table 6 presents some of the main issues related to crowdsouring tasks and process.

To investigate RQ2, we analyzed papers discussing the *functional attributes of crowd computing systems* (#6). Crowdsourcing platforms are required for supporting interactions between crowd members and requestors while managing taks and outputs within an interactive working environment [23]. Hosseini et al. [21] provided a review of crowdsourcing platform features. According to the authors, a crowdsourcing system must be able to support enrolment, authentication, skill declaration, task assignment, assistance, result submission, coordination, supervision, and feedback loops when considering crowd-related interactions. Extrapolating the crowdsourcer domain, task broadcast and time/price negotiation must be also taken into account. Task-related features include result aggregation, history of completed tasks, quality and quantity threshold. Last but not least, a crowd-powered system must provide an interactive, ease to use interface while managing platform misuse and supporting payment, attraction, and interaction. The technology proficiency of participants [34] is another kind of aspect that must be also carefully considered when designing crowdsourcing systems for scientific purposes. Table 7 summarizes some crowdsourcing platform facilities identified in this literature review.

A closer inspection on the combination of both crowdsourcing and machine intelligence (RQ3) revealed a gap between automated reasoning and human cognition when performing complex tasks. Hybrid, *crowd-machine interaction* (#7) can close this gap by putting humans "into the loop" to overcome the failures of AI systems [22]. Nevertheless, some problems arise "when a disruptive shift like crowdsourcing crosses the traditional artificial boundaries we have constructed between knowledge areas" [18]. Reasoning abilities for hybrid intelligence allow better decisions towards the success of the collaborative activity [22]. Quinn and colleagues [9] addressed the different types of tradeoffs resulting from human labor, supervised learning, automated reasoning with human inputs, and mixed initiative systems. The authors presented a framework in which machines are leveraged by human-generated training data, while crowd workers can benefit from having automated reasoning results for which are necessary only simple actions for correcting them instead of doing all the work. It is also worth mentioning the introduction of hybrid algorithmic-crowdsourcing approaches for academic knowledge acquisition [25]. Table 8 presents some concepts related with crowd-computing hybrids with applicability for scientific research.

The contextual settings within which crowd science may occur must be considered with caution [4]. Crowdsourcing schemes vary in the degree of control afforded to the crowd and the outputs provided by crowd members must be validated and aggregated

Table 8. Crowd-computing hybrids and mixed-initiative approaches.

#	Main theme	Reference(s)
7	Methods for integrating human inputs into AI systems (e.g., training strategies)	P4
	Reasoning capabilities for hybrid intelligence	P37
	Flow for hybrid inteligent systems (e.g., self-assessment model trained from human input)	P37, P122
	Tradeoffs resulting from different kinds of systems (speed, cost, quality)	P138
	Human labor only	P138
	Supervised learning using human-created training data	P138
	Automated machine methods with human correction	P138
	Mixed-initiative systems	P138
	Hybrid algorithmic-crowdsourcing methods for academic knowledge acquisition	P41
	Management of knowledge within scientific literature (digital indexing, digital curation)	P41
	Automatic information extraction from scientific literature	P41
	Crowdsourcing as a tool for knowledge acquisition	P41
	Task-oriented crowdsourcing	P41
	Crowdsourcing task and workflow	P41
	Answers aggregation	P41
	Quality control	P41
	Machine learning implications (e.g., labeled data, rapid evaluation, relative cost of researcher time)	P122
	Crowd parting for annotation and classification tasks (e.g., clustering annotations)	P2
	Output of crowdsourcing multi-label classification	P72
	Hierarchy of skills in crowd-computing annotation (i.e., expert, crowd, machine learning)	P83
	Impact of crowdsourcing on NLP research (e.g., diversification of research, inferring bias, filtering)	P2, P93, P94
	Intersection of information retrieval and crowdsourcing (e.g., clustering, classification, stemming)	P77
	Crowdsourcing for data mining (question design, mining data from crowdsourcing)	P25, P37
	Automated task algorithms	P58
	Micro-human computation algorithms (skill, parallelism, cost)	P98
	Key observations for labels in real world applications (correlation, hierarchy, sparsity)	P24

Table 9. General dimensions of crowdsourcing.

#	Main theme	Reference(s)
8	Environmental/contextual and organizational issues	P15, P137, P147
	Environment (log of current grants, field/discipline, number of collaborators)	P147
	Contextual influences (cultural, linguistic, regional)	P15, P137
	Organization (e.g., crowdsourcing adoption and implementation)	P20, P69, P124, P136, P144
	Crowd control	P1, P106, P141
	Quality control and assurance (e.g., gold standard, reputation system)	P25, P37, P40, P43, P45, P46, P62, P80, P94, P98, P118, P122, P139
	Worker perception of quality assurance	P25, P45, P62, P80, P124
	Error detection and correction	P124
	Fault detection and tolerance	P118
	Elicitation and aggregation (e.g., collection/knowledge base, genetic algorithm, active learning)	P2, P8, P28, P29, P42, P60, P68, P69, P76, P94, P99, P109, P119, P121, P41, P80, P128, P136, P139, P143
	Crowdsourcer type (government, private organizations, individuals)	P18, P90
	Requestor purpose (fund initiatives, share knowledge, perform tasks, change behavior)	P18
	Design space for crowd feedback (e.g., ratio)	P22, P103
	Contribution to science (e.g., size and type of contribution, data value)	P16, P136
	Assistance provenance (transparent, opaque, obfuscated)	P137
	Ubiquity	P81
	Centrality	P8
	Principles (e.g., recursion and reflectivity, participation along all research phases)	P31, P148
	Persuasion	P81
	Concurrency	P81
	Information properties in crowdsourcing (quality, trust, utility)	P99, P104, P137, P140
	Level of information disclosure	P100
	Governance and management issues (maturity, resources, focus)	P14, P69, P74, P99, P123, P128, P130
	Governance structures and mechanisms (e.g., membership management)	P123, P130
	Crowdsourcing expertise/experience (e.g., risk, budget, expertise profiling and assessment)	P6, P14, P29, P59, P66, P73
	Emergence	P125
	Robustness and redundancy	P125
	Sources of crowdworker disagreement (e.g., clarity of annotation labels)	P2
	Targeted disability	P33
	Legal and ethical issues	P10, P22, P66, P94, P119
	Confidentiality, privacy, and anonymity	P10, P61, P64, P70, P90, P106, P137, P139

in a coherent way. There are distinct forms of quality control and assurance in crowd-enabled settings [3]. Previous work has addressed the use of machine learning strategies for assessing worker quality while detecting lurkers, "spammers", and other types of bad workers. Governance and management instruments are critical for crowdsourcing success. According to Hosseini and colleagues [21], "ethical issues are not fully and duly investigated in crowdsourcing activities", and issues such as confidentiality, privacy and anonymity must be also considered when designing crowd-enabled systems. Table 9 shows *general crowdsourcing aspects* (#8) extracted from literature.

5   Concluding Remarks

This paper presented a review of earlier contributions towards a reference model on the components that should be considered in crowd computing for data-driven scientific discovery. Such work shed a light to the theory and practice of innovative interactive systems, and the results achieved act as a foundation for more complex evaluation exercises to be undertaken. Scientific collaboration requires more than technology and there is little knowledge about theoretical frameworks for helping institutions and researchers analyzing concrete situations and identifying requirements before designing crowdsourcing systems. Crowd science can be particularly fruitful for making scientific work more accessible while enriching educational programs and disseminating results. A possible benefit of crowdsourcing is on a closer integration between human and machine intelligence and we need to deal with the question of what parts of scientific work to crowdsource and how to support these processes with AI. Putting AI on guiding (and be guided by) crowds enlarges the design space for application developers [23] and there is a large path of further improvement towards hybrid classifiers embedding crowds inside of machine learning architectures.

Acknowledgements. This work is financed by the ERDF – European Regional Development Fund through the Operational Programme for Competitiveness and Internationalisation - COMPETE 2020 Programme within project «POCI-01-0145-FEDER-006961», and by National Funds through the Portuguese funding agency, FCT - Fundação para a Ciência e a Tecnologia as part of project «UID/EEA/50014/2013».

Appendix A

See Table 10.

Table 10. Publications included in the final review (adapted from Cruzes & Dybå [29])

ID	Year	Author(s)	Title
P1	2016	LaToza & van der Hoek	Crowdsourcing in Software Engineering: Models, Opportunities, and Challenges
P2	2016	Kairam & Heer	Parting Crowds: Characterizing Divergent Interpretations in Crowdsourced Annotation Tasks
P3	2016	Aris & Din	Crowdsourcing Evolution: Towards a Taxonomy of Crowdsourcing Initiatives
P4	2016	Kamar	Directions in Hybrid Intelligence: Complementing AI Systems with Human Intelligence
P5	2016	Dickel & Franzen	The "Problem of Extension" Revisited: New Modes of Digital Participation in Science
P6	2015	Dragan et al.	A-posteriori Provenance-enabled Linking of Publications and Datasets via Crowdsourcing
P7	2015	Robert & Romero	Crowd Size, Diversity and Performance
P8	2015	Organisciak & Twidale	Design Facets of Crowdsourcing
P9	2015	Ponciano & Brasileiro	Finding Volunteers' Engagement Profiles in Human Computation for Citizen Science Projects
P10	2015	Hosseini et al.	Crowdsourcing: A Taxonomy and Systematic Mapping Study
P11	2015	Bigham et al.	Human-Computer Interaction and Collective Intelligence
P12	2015	Tinati et al.	Designing for Citizen Data Analysis: A Cross-sectional Case Study of a Multi-domain Citizen Science Platform
P13	2015	Gadiraju et al.	Human Beyond the Machine: Challenges and Opportunities of Microtask Crowdsourcing
P14	2015	Sivula & Kantola	Ontology Focused Crowdsourcing Management
P15	2015	Klippel et al.	Pitfalls and Potentials of Crowd Science: A Meta-analysis of Contextual Influences
P16	2015	Graham et al.	How is Success Defined and Measured in Online Citizen Science? A Case Study of Zooniverse Projects
P17	2015	Benedek et al.	Practices of Crowdsourcing in Relation to Big Data Analysis and Education Methods
P18	2015	AlShehry & Ferguson	A Taxonomy of Crowdsourcing Campaigns
P19	2015	Hossain & Kauranen	Crowdsourcing: A Comprehensive Literature Review
P20	2014	Zhao & Zhu	Evaluation on Crowdsourcing Research: Current Status and Future Direction
P21	2014	Lasecki et al.	Information Extraction and Manipulation Threats in Crowd-Powered Systems
P22	2014	Chiu et al.	What Can Crowdsourcing Do for Decision Support?
P23	2014	Prpic & Shukla	The Contours of Crowd Capability
P24	2014	Noriega & d'Inverno	Crowd-based Socio-cognitive Systems
P25	2014	Xintong et al.	Brief Survey of Crowdsourcing for Data Mining
P26	2014	Tinati et al.	Collective Intelligence in Citizen Science - A Study of Performers and Talkers
P27	2014	Franzoni & Sauermann	Crowd Science: The Organization of Scientific Research in Open Collaborative Projects
P28	2014	Hosseini et al.	Crowdsourcing Definitions and Its Features: An Academic Technical Report
P29	2014	Ponciano et al.	Considering Human Aspects on Strategies for Designing and Managing Distributed Human Computation
P30	2017	Law et al.	Crowdsourcing as a Tool for Research:Implications of Uncertainty
P31	2014	Wechsler	Crowdsourcing as a Method of Transdisciplinary Research - Tapping the Full Potential of Participants
P32	2014	Rotman et al.	Motivations Affecting Initial and Long-term Participation in Citizen Science Projects in Three Countries
P33	2014	Stol & Fitzgerald	Researching Crowdsourcing Software Development: Perspectives and Concerns
P34	2014	Wagner & Suh	The Wisdom of Crowds: Impact of Collective Size and Expertise Transfer on Collective Performance
P35	2014	Wiggins & Crowston	Surveying the Citizen Science Landscape
P36	2013	Ho et al.	Adaptive Task Assignment for Crowdsourced Classification
P37	2017	Kamar & Manikonda	Complementing the Execution of AI Systems with Human Computation
P38	2013	O'Neill et al.	Form Digitization in BPO: From Outsourcing to Crowdsourcing?
P39	2013	Larson et al.	Activating the Crowd: Exploiting User-Item Reciprocity for Recommendation
P40	2017	Moayedikia et al.	Framework and Literature Analysis for Crowdsourcing's Answer Aggregation
P41	2017	Dong et al.	Using Hybrid Algorithmic-Crowdsourcing Methods for Academic Knowledge Acquisition
P42	2013	Abraham et al.	Crowdsourcing Gold-HIT Creation at Scale: Challenges and Adaptive Exploration Approaches
P43	2013	Allahbakhsh et al.	Quality Control in Crowdsourcing Systems: Issues and Directions
P44	2008	Kittur & Kraut	Harnessing the Wisdom of Crowds in Wikipedia: Quality through Coordination
P45	2013	Huang & Fu	Enhancing Reliability Using Peer Consistency Evaluation in Human Computation
P46	2013	Hansen et al.	Quality Control Mechanisms for Crowdsourcing: Peer Review, Arbitration, & Expertise at FamilySearch Indexing
P47	2013	Mao et al.	Volunteering Versus Work for Pay: Incentives and Tradeoffs in Crowdsourcing
P48	2013	Saxton et al.	Rules of Crowdsourcing: Models, Issues, and Systems of Control
P49	2008	Brabham	Moving the Crowd at iStockphoto: The Composition of the Crowd and Motivations for Participation in a Crowdsourcing Application

ID	Author	Year	Title
P50	Seltzer & Mahmoudi	2013	Citizen Participation, Open Innovation, and Crowdsourcing: Challenges and Opportunities for Planning
P51	Bozzon et al.	2013	Reactive Crowdsourcing
P52	Iacovides et al.	2013	Do Games Attract or Sustain Engagement in Citizen Science?: A Study of Volunteer Motivations
P53	Law et al.	2013	Curio: A Platform for Supporting Mixed-expertise Crowdsourcing
P54	Alonso et al.	2008	Crowdsourcing for Relevance Evaluation
P55	Rettberg	2013	Human Computation in Electronic Literature
P56	Crescenzi et al.	2013	Wrapper Generation Supervised by a Noisy Crowd
P57	Wu et al.	2013	An Evaluation Framework for Software Crowdsourcing
P58	Vakharia & Lease	2013	Beyond AMT: An Analysis of Crowd Work Platforms
P59	Ul Hassan et al.	2013	Effects of Expertise Assessment on the Quality of Task Routing in Human Computation
P60	Goncalves et al.	2013	Crowdsourcing on the Spot: Altruistic Use of Public Displays, Feasibility, Performance, and Behaviours
P61	Parshotam	2013	Crowd Computing: A Literature Review and Definition
P62	Schulze et al.	2013	Workers' Task Choice in Crowdsourcing and Human Computation Markets
P63	Vukovic	2009	Crowdsourcing for Enterprises
P64	Huang & Fu	2013	Don't Hide in the Crowd!: Increasing Social Transparency Between Peer Workers Improves Crowdsourcing Outcomes
P65	Schultheiss et al.	2013	How to Encourage the Crowd? A Study about User Typologies and Motivations on Crowdsourcing Platforms
P66	Kittur et al.	2013	The Future of Crowd Work
P67	Whitla	2009	Crowdsourcing and its Application in Marketing Activities
P68	Lyon & Pacuit	2013	The Wisdom of Crowds: Methods of Human Judgement Aggregation
P69	Thuan	2013	Crowdsourcing Design Reference: A Preliminary Model
P70	Uchoa et al.	2013	Mix4Crowds - Toward a Framework to Design Crowd Collaboration with Science
P71	MacLean et al.	2013	Crowdsourcing Genomic Analyses of Ash and Ash Dieback - Power to the People
P72	Chilton et al.	2013	Cascade: Crowdsourcing Taxonomy Creation
P73	Thuan et al.	2013	Factors Influencing the Decision to Crowdsource
P74	Pederson et al.	2013	Conceptual Foundations of Crowdsourcing: A Review of IS Research
P75	Baba & Kashima	2013	Statistical Quality Estimation for General Crowdsourcing Tasks
P76	Lehman & Miikkulainen	2013	Leveraging Human Computation Markets for Interactive Evolution
P77	Lease & Yilmaz	2013	Crowdsourcing for Information Retrieval: Introduction to the Special Issue
P78	Adeptu et al.	2012	CrowdREquire: A Requirements Engineering Crowdsourcing Platform
P79	Kern et al.	2012	Dynamic and Goal-based Quality Management for Human-based Electronic Services
P80	Quinn & Bederson	2009	A Taxonomy of Distributed Human Computation
P81	Schneider et al.	2012	CSCWD: Five Characters in Search of Crowds
P82	Schall et al.	2012	Crowdsourcing Tasks to Social Networks in BPEL4People
P83	Nallapati et al.	2012	Skierarchy: Extending the Power of Crowdsourcing Using a Hierarchy of Domain Experts, Crowd and Machine Learning
P84	Tomlinson et al.	2012	Massively Distributed Authorship of Academic Papers
P85	Yuen et al.	2012	Task Recommendation in Crowdsourcing Systems
P86	Bernstein et al.	2012	Programming the Global Brain
P87	Rotman et al.	2012	Dynamic Changes in Motivation in Collaborative Citizen-Science Projects
P88	Raddick et al.	2013	Galaxy Zoo: Motivations of Citizen Scientists
P89	Estellés-Arolas & González-Ladrón-de-Guevara	2012	Towards an Integrated Crowdsourcing Definition
P90	Geiger et al.	2012	Crowdsourcing Information Systems - Definition, Typology, and Design
P91	Erickson et al.	2012	Hanging with the Right Crowd: Matching Crowdsourcing Need to Crowd Characteristics
P92	Wang et al.	2012	CrowdER: Crowdsourcing Entity Resolution
P93	Sabou et al.	2012	Crowdsourcing Research Opportunities: Lessons from Natural Language Processing
P94	Yuen et al.	2009	A Survey of Human Computation Systems
P95	Corney et al.	2009	Outsourcing Labour to the Cloud
P96	Lofi et al.	2012	Information Extraction Meets Crowdsourcing: A Promising Couple
P97	Gingold et al.	2012	Micro Perceptual Human Computation for Visual Tasks
P98	Salminen	2012	Collective Intelligence in Humans: A Literature Review
P99	Otterbacher & Hemphill	2012	Is the Crowd Biased? Understanding Binary Value Judgments on User-Contributed Content

ID	Author	Year	Title
P101	Tokarchuk et al.	2012	A Framework to Analyze Crowd Labor and Design a Proper Set of Incentives for Humans in the Loop
P102	Maher et al.	2012	Motivating Collective Intelligence in Design: Is Social Intelligence Relevant?
P103	Dow et al.	2012	Shepherding the Crowd Yields Better Work
P104	Antelio et al.	2012	Qualitocracy: A Data Quality Collaborative Framework Applied to Citizen Science
P105	Difallah et al.	2012	Mechanical Cheat: Spamming Schemes and Adversarial Techniques on Crowdsourcing Platforms
P106	Fraternali et al.	2012	Putting Humans in the Loop: Social Computing for Water Resources Management
P107	Grier	2011	Not for All Markets
P108	Kazai	2011	In Search of Quality in Crowdsourcing for Search Engine Evaluation
P109	Geiger et al.	2011	Managing the Crowd: Towards a Taxonomy of Crowdsourcing Processes
P110	Ross et al.	2010	Who are the Crowdworkers?: Shifting Demographics in Mechanical Turk
P111	Schenk & Guittard	2011	Towards a Characterization of Crowdsourcing Practices
P112	Pan & Blevis	2011	A Survey of Crowdsourcing as a Means of Collaboration and the Implications of Crowdsourcing for Interaction Design
P113	Lykourentzou et al.	2011	Collective Intelligence Systems: Classification and Modeling
P114	Heymann & Garcia-Molina	2011	Turkalytics: Analytics for Human Computation
P115	Nov et al.	2011	Dusting for Science: Motivation and Participation of Digital Citizen Science Volunteers
P116	Ambati et al.	2011	Towards Task Recommendation in Micro-Task Markets
P117	Yuen et al.	2011	A Survey of Crowdsourcing Systems
P118	Müller et al.	2010	Crowdsourcing with Semantic Differentials: A Game to Investigate the Meaning of Form
P119	Sakamoto et al.	2011	The Crowdsourcing Design Space
P120	Treiber et al.	2011	Tweetflows: Flexible Workflows with Twitter
P121	Doan et al.	2011	Crowdsourcing Systems on the World-Wide Web
P122	Lease	2011	On Quality Control and Machine Learning in Crowdsourcing
P123	Jain	2010	Investigation of Governance Mechanisms for Crowdsourcing Initiatives
P124	Grier	2011	Foundational Issues in Human Computing and Crowdsourcing
P125	Schut	2010	On Model Design for Simulation of Collective Intelligence
P126	Little et al.	2010	Exploring Iterative and Parallel Human Computation Processes
P127	Rouse	2010	A Preliminary Taxonomy of Crowdsourcing
P128	Zwass	2010	Co-creation: Toward a Taxonomy and an Integrated Research Perspective
P129	Siorpaes & Simperl	2010	Human Intelligence in the Process of Semantic Content Creation
P130	Conrad & Hilchey	2011	A Review of Citizen Science and Community-based Environmental Monitoring: Issues and Opportunities
P131	Bederson & Quinn	2011	Web Workers, Unite! Addressing Challenges of Online Laborers
P132	Gao et al.	2011	Harnessing the Crowdsourcing Power of Social Media for Disaster Relief
P133	Kaufmann et al.	2011	More than Fun and Money. Worker Motivation in Crowdsourcing - A Study on Mechanical Turk
P134	Nov et al.	2010	Scientists@Home and in the Backyard: Understanding the Motivations of Contributors to Digital Citizen Science
P135	Oleson et al.	2011	Programmatic Gold: Targeted and Scalable Quality Assurance in Crowdsourcing
P136	Georgi & Jung	2011	Collective Intelligence Model: How to Describe Collective Intelligence
P137	Bigham et al.	2011	The Design of Human-powered Access Technology
P138	Quinn et al.	2010	CrowdFlow: Integrating Machine Learning with Mechanical Turk for Speed-cost-quality Flexibility
P139	Quinn & Bederson	2011	Human Computation: A Survey and Taxonomy of a Growing Field
P140	Alabri & Hunter	2010	Enhancing the Quality and Trust of Citizen Science Data
P141	Lasecki et al.	2011	Real-time Crowd Control of Existing Interfaces
P142	Das & Vukovic	2011	Emerging Theories and Models of Human Computation Systems: A Brief Survey
P143	Malone et al.	2010	The Collective Intelligence Genome
P144	Wiggins & Crowston	2010	Distributed Scientific Collaboration: Research Opportunities in Citizen Science
P145	Nov et al.	2010	Volunteer Computing: A Model of the Factors Determining Contribution to Community-based Scientific Research
P146	Heipke	2010	Crowdsourcing Geospatial Data
P147	Buecheler et al.	2010	Crowdsourcing, Open Innovation and Collective Intelligence in the Scientific Method: A Research Agenda and Operational Framework
P148	Piller et al.	2010	A Typology of Customer Co-Creation in the Innovation Process

References

1. Jirotka, M., Lee, C.P., Olson, G.M.: Supporting scientific collaboration: methods, tools and concepts. Comput. Support. Coop. Work **22**(4–6), 667–715 (2013)
2. Gil, Y., Greaves, M., Hendler, J., Hirsh, H.: Amplify scientific discovery with artificial intelligence. Science **346**(6206), 171–172 (2014)
3. Quinn, A.J., Bederson, B.B.: Human computation: a survey and taxonomy of a growing field. In: Proceedings of the ACM SIGCHI Conference on Human Factors in Computing Systems, pp. 1403–1412 (2011)
4. Klippel, A., Sparks, K., Wallgrün, J.O.: Pitfalls and potentials of crowd science: a meta-analysis of contextual influences. In: ISPRS Annals (2015)
5. Buecheler, T., Sieg, J.H., Füchslin, R.M., Pfeifer, R.: Crowdsourcing, open innovation and collective intelligence in the scientific method – a research agenda and operational framework. In: ALIFE, pp. 679–686 (2010)
6. Ranard, B.L., et al.: Crowdsourcing – harnessing the masses to advance health and medicine, a systematic review. J. Gen. Intern. Med. **29**(1), 187–203 (2014)
7. Law, E., Gajos, K.Z., Wiggins, A., Gray, M.L., Williams, A.C.: Crowdsourcing as a tool for research: implications of uncertainty. In: ACM CSCW, pp. 1544–1561 (2017)
8. Good, B.M., Su, A.I.: Games with a scientific purpose. Genome Biol. **12**(12), 135 (2011)
9. Quinn, A.J., Bederson, B.B., Yeh, T., Lin, J.: Crowdflow: integrating machine learning with mechanical turk for speed-cost-quality flexibility. Technical report HCIL-2010-09, University of Maryland (2010)
10. Absalom, R., Luczak-Rosch, M., Hartmann, D., Plaat, A.: Crowd-sourcing fuzzy and faceted classification for concept search. arXiv preprint arXiv:1406.7749 (2014)
11. Barowy, D.W., Curtsinger, C., Berger, E.D., McGregor, A.: Automan: a platform for integrating human-based and digital computation. ACM Sigplan Not. **47**(10), 639–654 (2012)
12. André, P., Zhang, H., Kim, J., Chilton, L., Dow, S.P., Miller, R.C.: Community clustering: leveraging an academic crowd to form coherent conference sessions. In: Proceedings of the First AAAI Conference on Human Computation and Crowdsourcing (2013)
13. Nov, O., Arazy, O., Anderson, D.: Scientists@home: what drives the quantity and quality of online citizen science participation. PLoS ONE **9**(4), e90375 (2014)
14. Chandler, J., Paolacci, G., Mueller, P.: Risks and rewards of crowdsourcing marketplaces. In: Michelucci, P. (ed.) Handbook of Human Computation, pp. 377–392. Springer, New York (2013). https://doi.org/10.1007/978-1-4614-8806-4_30
15. Good, B.M., Nanis, M., Wu, C., Su, A.I.: Microtask crowdsourcing for disease mention annotation in PubMed abstracts. In: Pacific Symposium on Biocomputing, pp. 282–293 (2014)
16. Brown, A.W., Allison, D.B.: Using crowdsourcing to evaluate published scientific literature: methods and example. PLoS ONE **9**(7), e100647 (2014)
17. Tomlinson, B., et al.: Massively distributed authorship of academic papers. In: CHI EA, pp. 11–20 (2012)
18. Lease, M.: On quality control and machine learning in crowdsourcing. In: Proceedings of the 11th AAAI Conference on Human Computation, pp. 97–102 (2011)
19. Schneider, D., Moraes, K., de Souza, J.M., Esteves, M.G.P.: CSCWD: five characters in search of crowds. In: CSCWD, pp. 634–641 (2012)
20. Zhao, Y., Zhu, Q.: Evaluation on crowdsourcing research: current status and future direction. Inf. Syst. Front. **16**(3), 417–434 (2014)

21. Hosseini, M., Shahri, A., Phalp, K., Taylor, J., Ali, R.: Crowdsourcing: a taxonomy and systematic mapping study. Comput. Sci. Rev. **17**, 43–69 (2015)
22. Kamar, E.: Directions in hybrid intelligence: complementing AI systems with human intelligence. In: IJCAI, pp. 4070–4073 (2016)
23. Kittur, A., et al.: The future of crowd work. In: ACM CSCW, pp. 1301–1318 (2013)
24. Horvitz, E.: Principles of mixed-initiative user interfaces. In: CHI, pp. 159–166 (1999)
25. Dong, Z., Lu, J., Ling, T.W., Fan, J., Chen, Y.: Using hybrid algorithmic-crowdsourcing methods for academic knowledge acquisition. Clust. Comput. **20**(4), 3629–3641 (2017)
26. Chau, D.H., Kittur, A., Hong, J.I., Faloutsos, C.: Apolo: making sense of large network data by combining rich user interaction and machine learning. In: CHI, pp. 167–176 (2011)
27. Kondreddi, S.K., Triantafillou, P., Weikum, G.: Combining information extraction and human computing for crowdsourced knowledge acquisition. In: ICDE, pp. 988–999 (2014)
28. Petersen, K., Feldt, R., Mujtaba, S., Mattsson, M.: Systematic mapping studies in software engineering. EASE **8**, 68–77 (2008)
29. Cruzes, D.S., Dybå, T.: Research synthesis in software engineering: a tertiary study. Inf. Softw. Technol. **53**(5), 440–455 (2011)
30. Kitchenham, B.: Procedures for performing systematic reviews. Keele University, Keele, UK, vol. 33, pp. 1–26 (2004)
31. Johansen, R.: Groupware: computer support for business teams. The Free Press (1988)
32. Lasecki, W.S., Murray, K.I., White, S., Miller, R.C., Bigham, J.P.: Real-time crowd control of existing interfaces. In: UIST, pp. 23–32 (2011)
33. Ponciano, L., Brasileiro, F., Simpson, R., Smith, A.: Volunteers' engagement in human computation for astronomy projects. CiSE **16**(6), 52–59 (2014)
34. Uchoa, A.P., Esteves, M.G.P., de Souza, J.M.: Mix4Crowds – toward a framework to design crowd collaboration with science. In: CSCWD, pp. 61–66 (2013)
35. Wiggins, A., Crowston, K.: Distributed scientific collaboration: research opportunities in citizen science. In: ACM CSCW 2010 Workshop on Changing Dynamics of Scientific Collaboration (2010)
36. Ellis, C.A., Gibbs, S.J., Rein, G.: Groupware: some issues and experiences. Commun. ACM **34**(1), 39–58 (1991)
37. Estellés-Arolas, E., González-Ladrón-de-Guevara, F.: Towards an integrated crowdsourcing definition. J. Inf. Sci. **38**(2), 189–200 (2012)
38. Gadiraju, U., Demartini, G., Kawase, R., Dietze, S.: Human beyond the machine: challenges and opportunities of microtask crowdsourcing. IEEE Intell. Syst. **30**(4), 81–85 (2015)
39. Sakamoto, Y., Tanaka, Y., Yu, L., Nickerson, J.V.: The crowdsourcing design space. In: Schmorrow, Dylan D., Fidopiastis, Cali M. (eds.) FAC 2011. LNCS (LNAI), vol. 6780, pp. 346–355. Springer, Heidelberg (2011). https://doi.org/10.1007/978-3-642-21852-1_41
40. Huang, S.W., Fu, W.T.: Don't hide in the crowd!: increasing social transparency between peer workers improves crowdsourcing outcomes. In: CHI, pp. 621–630 (2013)
41. Deci, E.L., Ryan, R.M.: The general causality orientations scale: self-determination in personality. J. Res. Pers. **19**(2), 109–134 (1985)
42. Freitag, A., Pfeffer, M.J.: Process, not product: investigating recommendations for improving citizen science "success". PLoS ONE **8**(5), e64079 (2013)

A New Study of Conversational Commerce in Thai Urban Office Employees

Tantham Rungvithu and Chutisant Kerdvibulvech[✉]

Graduate School of Communication Arts and Innovation
and Management Innovation, National Institute of Development Administration,
118 SeriThai Rd., Klong-Chan, Bangkapi, Bangkok 10240, Thailand
Tantham.rungvithu@gmail.com, chutisant.ker@nida.ac.th

Abstract. Conversational commerce has become an emerging global marketing communication trend in the past few years. Recent studies suggested some beneficial aspects of conversational commerce in customer satisfaction, while some claimed different areas that conventional (traditional) commerce still excels in. Therefore, this research examined and compared conversational commerce with conventional commerce in terms of customer satisfaction towards Thai urban office employees, which helped to determine areas of improvement for conversational commerce sellers. Accordingly, a convenient sampling quantitative and qualitative surveys were conducted with the sample size of 50 (n = 50), on Thai office employees aged 22–60 years. Nine different customer satisfaction factors and commentary session were employed to determine the effectiveness and winner of each commerce type via vertically designed ordinal Likert Scales. Mode scores were utilised as an average comparison tool for customer satisfaction of both commerces.

Results suggested that the two commerces rate competitively in terms of customer satisfaction, with the Likert level of 4 (satisfied) in all factors. However, they excelled in different aspects. Accordingly, conversational commerce rates higher in terms of product cost, keeping customers in touch, and product/brand image, while conventional commerce rated higher in terms of meeting customer needs, point-of-purchase condition, and delivery time.

Although both commerces rated close in terms of seller credibility and product expectancy, conventional commerce tended to be more preferred in customers' minds. Additionally, the areas of chatbot and cryptocurrency are briefly discussed as a forthcoming conversational commerce trend.

Keywords: Conversational commerce · Conventional commerce
Customer satisfaction · Chatbot · Likert scales

1 Introduction

Conversational commerce has recently become a vital aspect in merchandising and marketing communication in the modern world [12]. This type of commerce allows humans to communicate [6] via artificial chatting robots, texting programs, and simulating cyber helpers. Large innovative firms have assigned large budgets for the development of robots with Deep Learning and Natural Language Processing in order

© Springer Nature Switzerland AG 2018
A. Rodrigues et al. (Eds.): CRIWG 2018, LNCS 11001, pp. 155–168, 2018.
https://doi.org/10.1007/978-3-319-99504-5_12

to allow the devices to deliver data and services in a convenient and two-way communication manner [11]. Conversational commerce sellers are found to be more effective in terms of digitized connectivity, high virtual interaction, and seller credibility when compared with regular e-commerce sellers. Recently, there have been several studies on the pros and cons of e-commerce and face-to-face commerce, but there is still a limited amount of findings when it comes to the new area of conversational commerce. In fact, conversational commerce has grown rapidly in recent years. Additionally, there have been different foreign publications claiming the advantages of either conversational commerce or conventional commerce such as [10, 15, 16]. However, in Thailand, there are still no comparative findings between conversational commerce and conventional commerce in terms of customer satisfaction benefits.

In this paper, our research examines the differences between conversational commerce and conventional commerce by using nine customer satisfaction factors from literature reviews to determine different areas in which conversational commerce and conventional commerce excel in. In addition to a statistical comparison, this research can be utilized by marketing communicators, digital-era sales specialists, and those that study communication arts in order to acquire the potentialities of conversational commerce in terms of sales promotion, daily-life online marketing, SME product, and startup services. At the same time, areas of improvement for conversational commerce are provided for modern marketers to perform competitively with conventional off-line vendors. Figure 1 shows our conceptual framework for conversational commerce and conventional commerce. Independent variables include product cost, meeting customer needs, seller friendliness, keeping customers in touch, deserving expected products, delivery time, Point-of-Purchase condition, seller credibility and product/brand image.

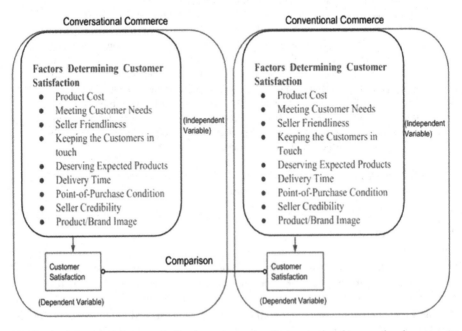

Fig. 1. Our conceptual framework showing conversational commerce and conventional commerce

2 Literature Review

2.1 Factors Contributing to Customer Satisfaction

Customer satisfaction in this research refers to the extent to which the quality of a product or service reaches the buyer's expectations. In order to measure customer satisfaction, some of the contributing factors in this research were gathered from the following articles.

2.1.1 Customer Satisfaction with Conventional Commerce

According to Surbhi's work [17], one noticeable advantage of conventional (traditional) commerce is that the buyers can tangibly examine the products before proceeding to payment. Another advantage is that conventional commerce can provide the product right after the purchase is made, while the online method still requires delivery time. Therefore, the survey questions in this research will also determine if the product's physical expectancy and delivery time in conventional commerce still play a significant role over those in conversational commerce.

One of the related aspects of conversational commerce (also considered as a governed field of conversational commerce) is e-commerce, which seems to be one of the most popular marketing platforms for Thai office employees. One related article on the factors determining e-satisfaction on the part of American customers concluded that higher satisfaction with e-commerce results in more purchases. Additionally, when determined by the amount of money spent in e-commerce, e-service quality, e-satisfaction, and e-royalty have strong relationships with one another. Yet, the area in which face-to-face commerce still dominates is the ability to allow buyers to physically test the goods before paying in order to get what they are actually looking for [14].

In addition, a study of a Chinese researcher also found significant elements leading to customer satisfaction. Li [7] concluded that image, price, reliability, tangibles, empathy (understanding the customer's needs), seller responsiveness, assurance, and perceived value (brand images) have a significant impact on customer satisfaction and customer loyalty in a Chinese shoe company. These factors, in turn, create more customers and expand the market further.

2.1.2 Customer Satisfaction in Conversational Commerce (C-Commerce)

Recent studies have determined the factors that could relatively influence customer satisfaction in conversational commerce. A study on social commerce which refers to business activity derived from social media platforms examined Instagram users. The results suggest that fame and product cost attributes greatly determine the credibility of the electronic vendors, while comfort, electronic point-of-purchase quality, and motivation also have a positive impact on the purchase decision. Yet, the interaction with the sellers results in negative outcomes in terms of credibility [20].

In 2016, Piyush et al. [14] suggested five areas that can generate positive interaction with buyers in conversational commerce, which are identifying the buyers to match their needs, making cordial and modest greetings (friendliness), questioning the buyers to prove that they actually "get into" the product concept, hearing from buyers to understand their situation, and maintaining concise but friendly responses. Accordingly, these five points were summarized and adapted for the survey questions in this research.

Buyer comforts and social exchanges are also strong determinants of buyer satisfaction. A survey was conducted with 480 respondents (n = 480), Indian shoppers aged over 18 years. Four factors were determined; namely, social interaction, convenience, customer satisfaction, and customer experience. The outcomes indicated that the level of "convenience" and "social interaction" had a positive effect on both buyers' experience and satisfaction [18].

Despite credibility challenges in e-commerce, a subset of conversational commerce, or buying through social media, can be used to overcome the problem of e-commerce in terms of elevating the physical interaction in the virtual community. Additionally, the present of social commerce can bring about a higher level of credibility that the buyers have on regular digital marketplaces [1].

However, more recently in 2018, Lin et al. [8] claimed that conversational commerce could bring about risks in self-service payment activities such as fraud, time consumption, and personal data infringement. Accordingly, a research on 1,024 customers summarized that when realizing the risks of payment activities, the perceived usefulness (PU) of e-commerce providers and the customer's willingness to buy decrease. The findings of this research can be applied to E- Commerce activities in the time of social commerce, which is closely related to conversational commerce.

In addition in 2018, Hyun [4] suggests that the buyer's feeling for social commerce (conversational commerce) platforms is determined by usefulness, comfort, fun shopping, and financial security. The research also claims that the positive feelings towards digital vendors greatly determine electronic social sharing, the chance of re-visiting the store, and digital payment [10].

2.2 Customer Satisfaction Measurement

In order to measure the level of customer satisfaction, a Discussion Paper on Scales for Measuring Customer Satisfaction (n.d.) [2] suggests that a Likert scale is a tool that can, overall, transform qualitative measurements into quantitative measurements regarding customer satisfaction, and the scale normally contains five important options, which are "strongly agree, agree, neutral, disagree, and strongly disagree." The scoring from each option briefly allows researchers to calculate the average scores for all related questions (Fig. 2).

Unlike the above typical Likert method, Maeda's work [9] states in "response option configuration of online administered Likert scales" that a Likert scale could be employed in a top-down axis in order to avoid respondent bias toward the left or right side, but would also consume more survey space, as shown in Fig. 3.

By combining both scale design approaches, this research proposes a 5-option nominal Likert scale in a vertical manner. However, the scale will incorporate the term "satisfied" used by the first approach as it conveys clearer access in the customer satisfaction context.

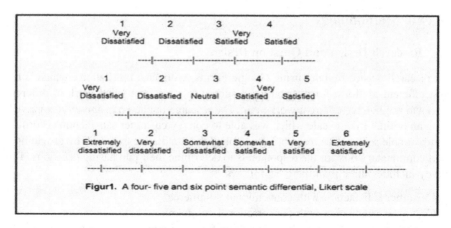

Fig. 2. A four- five- and six-point semantic differential, Likert scale (Source: Discussion Paper on Scales for Measuring Customer Satisfaction (n.d.) [2])

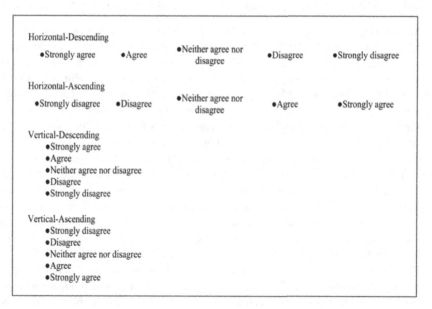

Fig. 3. Vertically Aligned Likert Scales, as Compared to Their Horizontal Counterparts (Source: Maeda's work [9])

2.3 Hypotheses

Hypothesis 1: Conversational commerce rates competitively with conventional commerce in terms of cost, meeting the customer's needs, seller friendliness, keeping the customers in touch, point-of-purchase condition, and product/brand Image.
Hypothesis 2: Conversational commerce rates lower than conventional commerce in terms of delivery time, product expectancy, and seller credibility.

3 Our Methodology

3.1 Research Design and Question Design

The research was carried out using Google Forms (with Thai translation), which is the most efficient platform for distributing a survey to participants that work in different areas and might have different work hours The research applied a quantitative approach using an ordinal Likert scale which was able to convey customer satisfaction according to measurable scores. The research also applied the qualitative approach by providing a short commentary box for the respondents to determine their purchasing decisions. The survey includes three main parts as follows:

1. Customer satisfaction with conventional commerce
2. Customer satisfaction with conversational commerce
3. Commentary Box: a commentary opinion box was provided in the final part of the survey in order to gain better insight into the respondents' purchasing ideology, which was used for the analysis in the discussion. The question asks: What would you prefer, buying via digital chats or via physical vendors? Why?

Accordingly, each of the first two parts had exactly the same nine customer satisfaction factors summarized from the literature review, which were product cost, meeting customer needs, seller friendliness, keeping customers in touch, deserving expected services or products, delivery time, point-of-purchase condition (comfort), seller credibility, and product/brand image. These determinant were measured using a vertically-aligned Likert scale from strongly satisfied (score of five) to satisfied (score of four), neither satisfied nor dissatisfied (score of three), not satisfied (score of two) and strongly dissatisfied (score of one). Figure 4 shows some examples of survey questions for measured on Likert scales. After gaining the results, the means and modes of the Likert scores were compared. Accordingly, the focused average scores were determined by mode, as this is the most standard type of measurement when determining discrete categorical or ordinal data. This mode is preferred in this situation because the greatest frequency of responses is significant for describing categorical variables. However, the mean score was also calculated to further analyze the data in parallel with the mode scores.

The commerce type with a higher value of mode score was considered to be the winner of each customer satisfaction factor. In the case of a similar mode score value, the number of respondents (n) of each mode score was compared. In the case of similar number of respondents (n), both commerce types had the same level of customer satisfaction.

3.2 Recruiting of Participants

The participant recruitment process employed convenient sampling, where various individuals of both genders were invited to participate in the study. They were aged between 22–60 years and had graduated with a bachelor to a doctoral degree. The recruitment criteria were broken down into three parts, demographic and psychographic design, establishing sampling size, and respondent qualification.

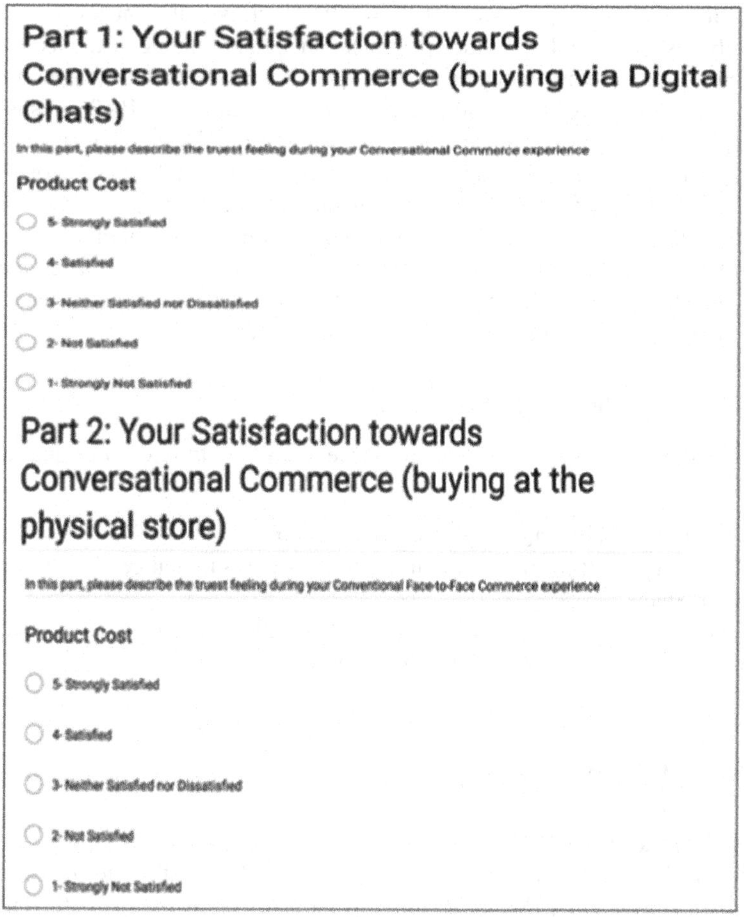

Part 1: Your Satisfaction towards Conversational Commerce (buying via Digital Chats)

In this part, please describe the truest feeling during your Conversational Commerce experience

Product Cost

○ 5- Strongly Satisfied

○ 4- Satisfied

○ 3- Neither Satisfied nor Dissatisfied

○ 2- Not Satisfied

○ 1- Strongly Not Satisfied

Part 2: Your Satisfaction towards Conversational Commerce (buying at the physical store)

In this part, please describe the truest feeling during your Conventional Face-to-Face Commerce experience

Product Cost

○ 5- Strongly Satisfied

○ 4- Satisfied

○ 3- Neither Satisfied nor Dissatisfied

○ 2- Not Satisfied

○ 1- Strongly Not Satisfied

Fig. 4. Sample survey questions in part 1 and part 2 (measured on Likert scales)

Although young adults tend to be more connected to conversational commerce, these versatile demographic ranges (22–60) were set to ensure that the total outlook of the office population, which included first jobbers and those with high managerial positions and that were both males and females, was covered in this pilot study on urban office employees. In addition, demographic segmentation could be studied in further research. The participants were randomly selected from some researchers' TNN news broadcast company, some electronic device sales offices, some university offices, some aviation outsourcing companies, social networks, as well as those that work in an office-format company in urban area, mainly Bangkok. These samples from such companies effectively represent the majority of office employees, because all of them work in urban areas, live in a technologically-friendly environment, absorb word-of-mouth and recommendations from colleagues through social interaction and social media, have high online spending power, and, most importantly, have first-hand experience with conversational commerce.

The number of participant was 50 (N = 50), which is sufficient for a small-sized initial study case and would provide enough sufficient and reliable data to compare the mode score for each commerce type. According to Isaac and Michale [5], the sufficient number of respondents for a pilot project is the range of 10–30 respondents. Accordingly, this range was sufficient to examine the null hypothesis, while capable of disregarding insignificant affecting data. However, this research added more respondents to reach 50 (N = 50), as this number yielded a lower margin of error. It is to be noticed that the sampling size of 50 was based on convenient sampling of a limited number of networking companies due to time constraints and the pilot research conditions. Therefore, the results gained might be represented differently when utilizing research samples from different companies or departments.

3.3 Respondent Qualifications

Before providing a response, the participants were required to have three qualifications as follows:

1. Be a full-time worker in a respected urban company
2. To have been involved in a minimum of three conversational commerce purchases of any products
3. To have bought products worth no more than 1,000 baht in order to establish a common standard for both commerce methods.

4 Result Summary

Factor 1 (Product Cost)
According to the results, the mode for this factor was 4 (Satisfied) for conversational commerce (n = 31), and 4 (Satisfied) for conventional commerce (n = 30). Therefore, the winning commerce type for this factor was conventional commerce. Additionally, the mean score for this factor was 3.94 or conversational commerce, 3.82 for conventional commerce.

Factor 2 (Meeting Customer Needs)
According to the results, the mode for this factor was 4 (Satisfied) for conversational commerce (n = 35), and 4 (Satisfied) for conventional commerce (n = 31). Therefore, the winning commerce type for this factor was conversational commerce. Additionally, the mean score for this factor was 4.02 for conversational commerce, 3.98 for conventional commerce.

Factor 3 (Seller Friendliness)
According to the results, the mode for this factor was 4 (Satisfied) for conversational commerce (n = 27), and 4 (Satisfied) for conventional commerce (n = 27). Therefore, both commerce types had equal customer satisfaction scores for this factor. Additionally, the mean score for this factor was 3.68 for conversational commerce, 3.74 for conventional commerce.

Factor 4, Keeping Customers In-Touch in Conversational Commerce
According to the results, the mode for this factor was 4 (satisfied) for conversational commerce (n = 23), and 4 (Satisfied) for conventional commerce (n = 27). Therefore, the winning commerce type for this factor was conventional commerce. Additionally, the mean score for this factor was 3.60 for conversational commerce, 3.62 for conventional commerce.

Factor 5 (Deserving Expected Products)
According to the results, the mode for this factor was 4 (Satisfied) for conversational commerce (n = 27), and 4 (Satisfied) for conventional commerce (n = 27). Therefore, both commerce types had the same customer satisfaction score for this factor. Additionally, the mean score for this factor was 3.58 for conversational commerce, 4.14 for conventional commerce.

Factor 6 (Delivery Time)
According to the results, the mode for this factor was 4 (Satisfied) for conversational commerce (n = 23), and 4 (Satisfied) for conventional commerce (n = 24). Therefore, the winning commerce type for this factor was conventional commerce. Additionally, the mean score for this factor was 3.76 for conversational commerce, while 3.92 for conventional commerce.

Factor 7 (Point-of-Purchase Condition)
According to the results, the mode for this factor was 4 (Satisfied) for conversational commerce (n = 31), and 4 (Satisfied) for conventional commerce (n = 29). Therefore, the winning commerce type for this factor was conversational commerce. Additionally, the mean score for this factor was 3.82 for conversational commerce, while reading 3.90 for conventional commerce.

Factor 8 (Seller Credibility)
According to the results, the mode for this factor was 4 (Satisfied) for conversational commerce (n = 26), and 4 (Satisfied) for conventional commerce (n = 26). Therefore, both commerce types had the same customer satisfaction score for this factor. Additionally, the mean score for this factor was 3.66 for conversational commerce, 3.82 for conventional commerce.

Factor 9 (Product/Brand Image)
According to the results, the mode for this factor was 4 (Satisfied) for conversational commerce (n = 37), and 4 (Satisfied) for conventional commerce (n = 28). Therefore, the winning commerce type for this factor was conversational commerce. Additionally, the mean score for this factor was 3.92 for conversational commerce, 4.18 for conventional commerce.

Overall Results
Overall, both conversational commerce and conventional commerce were rated similar to one another (Fig. 5). Accordingly, conversational commerce rated higher in three factors, which were product cost, keeping the customer in touch, and product/brand image. Conventional commerce dominates three factors, which are meeting customer needs, point-of-purchase condition, and delivery time. Meanwhile, both conversational commerce and conventional commerce had similar customer satisfaction rate in three factors, which were seller friendliness, deserving expected products, and seller credibility.

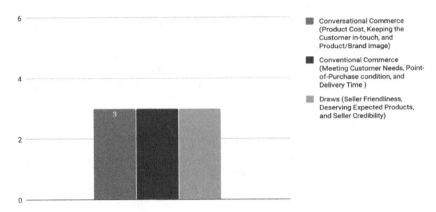

Fig. 5. Overall results of factors excelled by each commerce type

5   Result Discussions

5.1   Point-of-Purchase Condition and Purchase Condition

The overall results implied that conversational commerce had become a competitive player with, or even outperformed, its conventional counterpart. For example, the results for point-of-purchase condition suggested that conversational commerce was less likely to encounter point-of-purchase challenges. In fact, it even performed better than with conventional commerce. In addition, the seller friendliness factor also rated highly for both commerce types.

5.2   Brand Image

Even though both conversational commerce and conventional commerce rated "4" for all factors, there was a significant indication of brand image in Factor 9 (product/brand image). Accordingly, 37 respondents rated 4 for conversational commerce while only 28 respondents rated 4 for conventional commerce. This difference suggests that the new conversational commerce trend does not exert much challenge related to the brand image of the product, given that the prices are lower than 1,000 baht. In fact, it even rates higher than conventional commerce. This result indicates an increasing image acceptance for conversational commerce in daily usage products. However, the two commerce types were not very distinguished in terms of mean score. In fact, the mean score for conventional commerce rated higher than that for conversational commerce. This could be a result of the fact that more than 32% of the respondents rated 5 (strongly satisfied) for conventional commerce, while only 10% did so for conversational commerce, so it can be inferred that the product image acceptance of the product was high for both commerce types when determining the mode score; however, those that were "strongly satisfied" with the brand/product image still belonged to conventional commerce, as suggested by the mean score. Consequently, a modern marketing communicator can apply this idea to promote and increase the brand image for a product with low prices or daily usage products, not only to make the audience become satisfied, but become "strongly satisfied," in order to compete with the traditional face-to-face vendors. This development could be done in two ways: recruiting a larger crew and determining the value-added content. For example, conversational commerce sellers can invest more in hiring content creators, photographers, models, or image editors. Meanwhile, they might also need to create a suitable value-added theme on videos, banners, or ads in social media and conversational platforms, such as Facebook or Line.

5.3 Delivery Time

Another interesting Likert score for conversational commerce was the Delivery Time factor. Interestingly, conversational commerce performs were seen to be almost just as good as conventional commerce. Both commerce types scored almost the same, with the mode of 4 (n = 23) for conversational commerce and mode of 4 (n = 24) for conventional commerce. This little margin implies that delivery time creates less trouble for Thai office employees, and therefore delivery time is less likely to be a hindrance for them when it comes to purchase decisions. Therefore, conversational commerce sellers could utilize more motorbike hailing delivery services in city areas such as Bangkok not only to enhance their stance with conventional commerce sellers, but also to guarantee the receiving time within the same date of the order, provided that the buyer's address is in the same city.

5.4 Keeping the Customer in Touch

However, there were some areas that conventional commerce excelled. Despite the development of chat applications, which allows for convenient conversations between buyers and sellers, it was evident that conventional commerce still performs better in terms of keeping the customer in touch. According to the comments, "keeping the customer in touch" not only refers to the respondents as the act of caring alone, but also to the building of a similar understanding of products. One respondent claimed that face-to-face chatting allows both parties to embrace similar viewpoints of the products in terms of seller advice and comparison, which could hardly be done in chatting applications. Another respondent also claimed that he could ask the seller more "specifically" than talking in chats, which could solve their purchasing problems in detail. This fact implies that, contrary to Yahia et al. [18] presented in 2018, the interaction with sellers is crucial for the seller's credibility when it comes to conversational commerce. Hence, in addition to texting, conversational commerce sellers could open more channels to get in touch with their customers with voice or video calls to explain and to provide their insights into the products so that the buyer will have the same understanding of the products. Moreover, thanks to chatbot technology [3], which demands less investment in human sales representatives; however, the present chatbots are capable of handling basic texting responses. Therefore, more chatbots could be developed in order to handle the complex questions that a specific buyer might come up with [19].

5.5 Cost

Focusing on the cost factor, interestingly, the majority of respondents still prefer the face-to-face method as it provides more financial advantages for them. One respondent claimed that the price bargaining process was enabled when it comes to conventional commerce. However, the number of respondents (n) in terms of mode score was very close between the two commerce types (30 for conversational commerce and 31 for conventional commerce). From this fact it can be inferred that the pricing problem has become smaller and that the pricing in conversational commerce is becoming very competitive with its face-to-face counterparts. Therefore, in addition to the online promotion method, price bargaining strategies in conversational commerce might be considered in order to increase the seller's flexibility. For example, a seller could tailor make a promotion for a particular segment of buyers, including unique discounts or free giveaways. However, this strategy must be done with high caution to avoid seller bias.

5.6 Meeting Customer Needs, Seller Credibility, and Product Expectancy

Technically, from the Likert results, the factors meeting customer needs, Seller credibility, and Product Expectancy seemed to yield similar results for both commerce types. However, when examining the respondents' viewpoints, conventional commerce played a crucial role for them. Most of the respondents that supported conventional commerce claimed that this method allows them to physically try the product before actually being satisfied with it. Therefore, conventional commerce sellers could improve their services by increasing more image angles and details as much as possible regarding the product description.

5.7 Cryptocurrency Interviews

For the cryptocurrency interviews, cryptocurrency, such as Bitcoin, can be utilized hand-in-hand with conversational commerce as one of its payment methods. With Blockchain technology, cryptocurrency can be helpful in terms of increasing customer satisfaction in terms of such factors as transaction time, saving middleman fees in translation, and long-term investment. These advantages would, in turn, enhance the competitiveness of cost and time, which were found to rate competitively between conversational commerce and conventional commerce.

For small-sized conversational commerce businesses, cryptocurrency might be reliable and promptly transferred at one point; however, since cryptocurrency is currently not a legal tender in Thailand, nor is the transfer traceable due to a lack of middlemen, its usage for large companies should be done with high concern regarding anonymity, which in turn would have an impact on their branding and credibility and yield an advantage to conventional commerce vendors. More cryptocurrency access points and platforms in office or city areas could also be provided by large corporations in major city areas in order to generate more cryptocurrency transactions, provided that the broker's system is highly liquidized, secure, and capable of handling the transfer traffic. Additionally, a pilot project on Thai cryptocurrency on the part of the Bank of Thailand could be considered in order to further establish credibility of product quality among the buyers and sellers.

6 Conclusions and Recommendations

To sum up, Hypothesis 1 was confirmed for all factors. However, Hypothesis 2 was confirmed only for the delivery time factor and the seller credibility factor, while a null hypothesis was found for the deserving expected Product factor. Nevertheless, both the conversational and conventional commerce rates were very close for all factors, with a satisfaction mode of 4 (satisfied). The two commerce types were excelled in different areas. Some of the areas in conversational commerce showed very competitive outcomes or even surpassed the face-to-face routines, such as delivery time, seller friendliness, point-of purchase condition, and product costs. Despite having close Likert results, when it comes to seller credibility and product expectancy, conventional commerce is still largely preferred in the customers' mindset. Keeping customers in-touch does not only refers to the act of caring, but also to having a chance to test real products and to get succinct advice from sellers.

In terms of recommendations, since this research primarily aimed to determine the overall comparison of customer satisfaction between conversational commerce and conventional commerce, future studies might incorporate the use of nominal demographic factors (age, gender, income, chatting platform, product price range, product category, etc.) as determining variables. These factors would allow for a more elaborate comparison and insight into the subgroup level, which could yield different detailed results from the main findings in this research. However, balance sampling approaches and calculations should be taken seriously in order to obtain a fair representation of each demographic factor.

In addition, it is to be noted that this research only aimed to ascertain overall customer satisfaction; therefore, the results from the participants represent their overall feelings towards one or multiple vendors/brands, which does not reflect the specific satisfaction rate for a particular vendor and which could be different from the overall average. Therefore, it is recommended that future studies or tests scope down the research area into one vendor and focus on the comparison between the conversational and conventional platforms that the vendor provides in order to obtain a more accurate view of the same vendor. However, the studied vendors should be publically well-known for both commerce types so that the participant recruitment is practical and so that the research scope is not overly specified.

References

1. Baozhou, L., Weiguo, F., Mi, Z.: Social presence, trust, and social commerce purchase intention: an empirical research. Comput. Hum. Behav. **56**, 225–237 (2016)
2. Discussion Paper on Scales for Measuring Customer Satisfaction (n.d.). Market Directions'. http://marketdirectionsmr.com/wp-content/uploads/2017/07/survey-scales.pdf. Accessed 16 Dec 2017
3. Gracia, K., Carr, T., Costa, R.: Conversational Commerce 2017: Chatbots and Virtual Assistants (2017). Accessed 16 Dec 2017
4. Hyun, U.N.: Antecedents and consequences of consumers' attitude toward social commerce sites. J. Promot. Manag. (2018)

5. Isaac, S., Michael, W.B.: Handbook in Research and Evaluation: Collection of Principles, Methods, and Strategies Useful in the Planning, Design, and Evaluation of Studies in Education and the Behavioral Sciences. EdITS, San Diego (1995)
6. Kerdvibulvech, C.: An innovative use of multidisciplinary applications between information technology and socially digital media for connecting people. In: Wang, L., Uesugi, S., Ting, I.-H., Okuhara, K., Wang, K. (eds.) MISNC 2015. CCIS, vol. 540, pp. 60–69. Springer, Heidelberg (2015). https://doi.org/10.1007/978-3-662-48319-0_5
7. Li, J.: Factors affecting customer satisfaction and customer loyalty towards Belle Footwear Company in Lanzhou City, Gansu Province of the People's Republic of China. IOSR J. Bus. Manag. 14(2), 41–48 (2013). https://doi.org/10.9790/487x-1424148
8. Lin, X., Featherman, M., Brooks, S.L., Hajli, N.: Exploring gender differences in online consumer purchase decision making: an online product presentation perspective. Inf. Syst. Front. 20, 1–15 (2018)
9. Maeda, H.: Response option configuration of online administered Likert scales. Int. J. Soc. Res. Methodol. 18(1), 15–26 (2014). https://doi.org/10.1080/13645579.2014.885159
10. Martínez, R.C., Mckee, J.: Bots and payments: closing the conversational commerce loop. Database Netw. J. 46(6), article no. 9. (2016). http://eds.b.ebscohost.com/ehost/pdfviewer/pdfviewer?vid=1&sid=b19addc9-d201-4e63-bcb6-eacd7336af99%40sessionmgr104. Accessed 18 Dec 2017
11. McTear, M.F.: The rise of the conversational interface: a new kid on the block? In: Quesada, J.F., Martín Mateos, F.J., López-Soto, T. (eds.) FETLT 2016. LNCS (LNAI), vol. 10341, pp. 38–49. Springer, Cham (2017). https://doi.org/10.1007/978-3-319-69365-1_3
12. Messina, C.: Conversational commerce – Medium, 15 January 2015. https://medium.com/chris-messina/conversational-commerce-92e0bccfc3ff. 16 Dec 2017
13. Momoh, O.: Chatbot, 30 Oct 2016. https://www.investopedia.com/terms/c/chatbot.asp. Accessed 16 Dec 2017
14. Nisar, T.M., Prabhakar, G.: What factors determine e-satisfaction and consumer spending in e-commerce retailing? J. Retail. Consum. Serv. 39, 135–144 (2017). https://doi.org/10.1016/j.jretconser.2017.07.010
15. Piyush, N., Choudhury, T., Kumar, P.: Conversational commerce a new era of e-business. In: 2016 International Conference System Modeling & Advancement in Research Trends (SMART) (2016). https://doi.org/10.1109/sysmart.2016.7894543
16. Song Feng, R., Gunasekara, C., Shashidhara, S., Fadnis, K.P., Polymenakos, L.C.: A unified implicit dialog framework for conversational commerce. In: AAAI Conference on Artificial Intelligence (AAAI), 2–7 February 2018, New Orleans, Louisiana, United States (2018)
17. Surbhi, S.: Difference Between Traditional Commerce and e-Commerce (with Comparison Chart) 15 September 2016. https://keydifferences.com/difference-between-traditional-commerce-and-e-commerce.html#ComparisonChart. Accessed 16 May 2018
18. Srivastava, M., Kaul, D.: Social interaction, convenience and customer satisfaction: the mediating effect of customer experience. J. Retail. Consum. Serv. 21(6), 1028–1037 (2014). https://doi.org/10.1016/j.jretconser.2014.04.007
19. Xu, A., Liu, Z., Guo, Y., Sinha, V., Akkiraju, R.: A New Chatbot for customer service on social media. In: Conference on Human Factors in Computing Systems (CHI), 6–11 May 2017, Denver, Colorado, United States, pp. 3506–3510 (2017)
20. Yahia, I.B., Al-Neama, N., Kerbache, L.: Investigating the drivers for social commerce in social media platforms: importance of trust, social support and the platform perceived usage. J. Retail. Consum. Serv. 41, 11–19 (2018). https://doi.org/10.1016/j.jretconser.2017.10.021

Quantitative Analysis and Visualization of Children's Group Behavior from the Perspective of Development of Spontaneity and Sociality

Jun Ichikawa[1]([⊠]), Keisuke Fujii[2], Takayuki Nagai[3], Takashi Omori[4], and Natsuki Oka[1]

[1] Kyoto Institute of Technology, Kyoto, Japan
{j-ichikawa, nat}@kit.ac.jp
[2] RIKEN Center for Advanced Intelligence Project, Osaka, Japan
keisuke.fujii.zh@riken.jp
[3] The University of Electro-Communications, Tokyo, Japan
tnagai@ee.uec.ac.jp
[4] Tamagawa University, Tokyo, Japan
omori@lab.tamagawa.ac.jp

Abstract. Spontaneity, which is an attitude of voluntarily participating in activities, and sociality, which is the tendency to interact with others and to keep good relationships with others, are developed during childhood and are the fundamental attitudes in social life. To investigate the development of spontaneity and sociality, several researchers have used Learning Stories, in which on-site observers elaborately describe behaviors of each child. However, Learning Stories would need too much labor cost for monitoring and qualitatively evaluating many children. This study proposed a new method of quantitative analysis and visualization to evaluate children's group behavior related to both spontaneity and sociality during eurhythmics, in which children move in tune with music. It used position data of children for the analysis and visualization. The results showed that children in the 6-year-old class got to work closely with other children in a short time compared to those in the 5-year-old class. Such group behavior would include the actions to spontaneously make a good relationship with others. We hope that this study will be meaningful in creating practical and useful curricula and support methods for children at nurseries.

Keywords: Group behavior · Visualization · Development · Spontaneity
Sociality · Eurhythmics

1 Introduction

Spontaneity, which is an attitude of voluntarily participating in activities, and sociality, which is the tendency to interact with others and to keep good relationships with others, are developed during childhood [1]. They are the fundamental attitudes in social life and are related to important themes of developmental psychology and cognitive science

© Springer Nature Switzerland AG 2018
A. Rodrigues et al. (Eds.): CRIWG 2018, LNCS 11001, pp. 169–176, 2018.
https://doi.org/10.1007/978-3-319-99504-5_13

such as prosocial behaviors [2] and theory of mind [3]. Several behaviors related to spontaneity and sociality are observed at nurseries. In this paper, we classify them into the following three types: (1) *Spontaneous behavior* like doing what children want to do without consideration to other children; (2) *Instructed social behavior* that makes a good relationship with others, such as holding hands of others and cooperating with others in accordance with the instructions of nursery teachers; (3) *Spontaneous social behavior* that makes a good relationship voluntarily with others rather than being instructed. The third one is more difficult and important than the others because children need to achieve a balance between spontaneity and sociality. Quantitative analysis and visualization of these behaviors would hence be meaningful in creating practical and useful curricula and support methods for children at nurseries.

In education and developmental psychology, several researchers have used Learning Stories to observe various activities at nurseries and investigate the development of spontaneity and sociality [1]. They do not grasp the development of children from the perspective of whether they can do some activities, but rather focus on attitudes underlying the activities. In Learning Stories, on-site observers elaborately describe the behaviors of each child who interacts with the environment and others and discuss how the child has developed. The qualitative analysis that shows the development with the same viewpoint as a childcare professional who closely observes the behaviors of each child, would give useful insights to nurseries [1]. However, when some researchers monitor and qualitatively evaluate many children, Learning Stories would need too much labor cost. Considering the opinions that body movements are related to the states of mind [4] and that the relationship with others is reflected in the inter-distance called personal space [5, 6], spontaneous diffusion and aggregation of children should be complicated group behaviors related to spontaneity and sociality. If researchers evaluate the group behaviors using Learning Stories, they need to define diffusion and aggregation. It would be difficult to explain the individual behavioral mechanisms. Then, quantitative analysis and visualization of children's group behavior are needed.

We therefore proposed a new method of quantitative analysis and visualization to evaluate children's group behavior related to both spontaneity and sociality. Our approach was consisted of three steps. The first was to annotate the video on *Spontaneous social behaviors* of each child. The second was to hypothesize the group behavior related to both spontaneity and sociality according to the results of the first step. The third was to validate the hypotheses through the analysis and visualization of the group behavior in each age using the position data of children.

2 Related Work

Recently, group behaviors have been analyzed and visualized in many academic fields of such as biology (e.g., animal group movements of birds [7] and fish [8]) and human science (e.g., cooperative behaviors in sports [9]). They use the position data of agents for the analysis and evaluation of group behaviors and calculate distances between agents or orientation vectors of each agent.

However, there are few studies for children. Although Nakamae et al. [10] analyzed and visualized where, with whom, and what was a child playing, details of how the child played with others were not fully indicated. Most of previous studies on animal group movements and human sports behaviors including simulation studies (e.g., [8]) suppose that individual agents move based on simple rules and regulations. However, children do not always move based on such rules, but often act on an impulse. It will therefore be more difficult for researchers to analyze and visualize the group behavior of children than those of animals and sports players.

3 Activity in Eurhythmics

Music promotes good relationships with others [11]. Recently, for the development of spontaneity and sociality, educational institutions have paid attention to eurhythmics whereby children move in tune with music. Eurhythmics is therefore an appropriate environment for this study. In eurhythmics, there are various activities, for example throwing a ball and swinging a scarf.

This study focused on the running activity, which was the simplest one in eurhythmics. Children ran freely when the instructor played a piano (Fig. 1). The running activity was determined as an object of analysis by the following two reasons. First, it was usually carried out as the warm-up of eurhythmics, although the instructor often changed the overall program of eurhythmics on the day according to the responses of children. Second, it had more degrees of freedom compared to other activities because the instructor did not give explicit instructions such as who to run with nor where to run unlike other activities in eurhythmics. We therefore expected that there were many opportunities to observe *Spontaneous social behavior* while running, which was the point of focus for this study.

Fig. 1. Running activity in eurhythmics

4   Date, Participants, and Running Time of Video Recording

A nursery school in Tokyo, Japan, cooperated with our study. We explained the processes of video recording and collecting data of children to the concerned persons in advance. Approval for this study was given by the ethics and safety committee of Kyoto Institute of Technology, The University of Electro-Communications, and Tamagawa University. Considering the nursery schedule and the hall usage (Size: 10 m × 8.5 m), we periodically took a video of eurhythmics for the two classes in October 2016, January, May, August, November 2017, and February 2018. In October 2016, the ages of males and females ranged from 46 to 49 months and from 43 to 53 months in class A, and from 63 to 66 months and from 56 to 63 months in class B respectively[1]. Class B was the upper grade. The mean numbers of males and females participating in the running activities were 5.67 (SD = 0.47) and 6.50 (SD = 0.96) in class A, and 4.00 (SD = 0.63) and 7.00 (SD = 0.63) in class B. The means when the instructor played a piano were 64.7 s (SD = 22.4) in class A and 47.3 s (SD = 5.61) in class B.

5   Video Annotation

5.1   Procedure and Result

This study focused on *Spontaneous social behaviors* of each child in the group. To ensure the objectivity of analysis as much as possible, we subjectively annotated the explicit behaviors to spontaneously make a good relationship with other children while running, using the software ELAN[2].

This paper reports only a summary of results due to page limitation. The annotated *Spontaneous social behaviors* were four types: (1) Holding hands of others and placing hands on others' shoulders, (2) Hugging others, (3) Giving "hi-fives", and (4) Stopping aggressive behaviors like pushing strongly to guard others. Since children reached six years old (72 months), for the upper grade of class B in May 2017 and later, the frequency of *Spontaneous social behaviors* per minute increased and then the constant frequency level, which was about three times as high as before May 2017, was maintained. However, the duration time of *Spontaneous social behavior* per child did not show a characteristic change and fluctuated with the high coefficient of variance of about 0.50 in the recordings since May 2017.

5.2   Hypothesizing Group Behavior

According to the results of the video annotation, when the attitude of spontaneously participating in an activity without consideration to other children was stronger, the

---

[1] We administered the questionnaire about birth dates of children to their parents. However, we could not get the information of one male and three females in class A, and one female in class B. In addition, one female in class A quit the nursery on the way. The ranges of age were therefore calculated after excluding these children.

[2] Software ELAN URL: https://tla.mpi.nl/tools/tla-tools/elan/.

"running" emerged as its main activity. Meanwhile, when the attitude of spontaneously making a good relationship with others was stronger, the four types of behaviors mentioned above emerged. When children reach six years old, the latter attitude may become clear.

We hypothesized that; when reaching six years old, the two types of *Spontaneous social behaviors* will emerge in children's group behavior: #1 Being a distance that one can touch others, #2 Running toward the direction of another one for touching.

6   Analysis and Visualization of Group Behavior

6.1   Procedure

The hypotheses were validated through the quantitative analysis and visualization using the position data of children. The video images at 20 fps recorded from the bird's-eye view at about 3 m in height (Fig. 1) were digitized using the motion analysis software to capture the positions of children in two-dimension (DITECT Co. Ltd., Tokyo, Japan, Dipp-Motion V/2D). In this study, the position data could be acquired only in November 2017 and February 2018.

We analyzed three indexes shown in Fig. 2 from (1) to (3) to validate the hypotheses. The first index (1) was the distance between a pair of children. We calculated the distances between all pairs of children in each time frame. The second index (2) was $\theta_{other\,child}$, which represented the angle between the velocity vector of a child and the vector composed of positions of a pair of children at the current time, t. If $\theta_{other\,child}$ is close to 0-degree, it indicates that the child runs toward the direction of another one. We calculated $\theta_{other\,child}$ for all pairs of children. The third index (3) was $\theta_{center\,of\,children}$, which represented the angle between the velocity vector of a child and the vector composed of the present position of the child and the static center of children. We calculated the mean position through the running activity of all children as the static center of children. $\theta_{center\,of\,children}$ indicates the direction toward which each child runs based on the static center of children. The data of all children for every index were averaged in the normalized frequency of histogram, and the differences of normalized frequencies between the two classes were compared. The t-tests were conducted for each bin of the histograms at the 5% level.

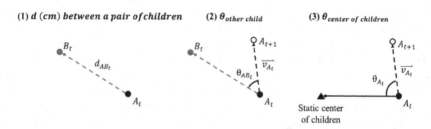

Fig. 2. Three indexes of children's group behavior. A and B are a pair of children. t represents the current time of video frame. Time interval is 0.05 s.

6.2   Result

Figure 3 shows the comparisons of the indexes between classes A and B. The running activity was not conducted in class B in February 2018. This study therefore compared the normalized frequencies between class A in November 2017 and class B in November 2017, and between class A in February 2018 and class B in November 2017. The left-side graphs (a, c, and e) of Fig. 3 indicate the results of the former, meanwhile the right-side graphs (b, d, and f) indicate those of the latter.

Regarding the comparisons in the graphs (a) and (b) of Fig. 3, the t-tests in the bin of 50 cm-distance between the children revealed that the frequencies of the upper grade, class B, were significantly higher than those of the lower grade, class A ($ps < .01$). Considering the results of video annotation, the group behavior in which the distance narrowed less than 50 cm, would include *Spontaneous social behaviors*. This finding supported the hypothesis #1. However, the hypothesis #2 was not supported because the t-tests in most of bins of $\theta_{other\,child}$ did not reveal significant differences between the classes. Accordingly, we made the following additional analysis. When the distance between the children was less than 50 cm, we analyzed the approaching angle during the periods from 0 to 1 s before the approach, from 1 to 2 s before, and from 2 to 3 s before, respectively. During each period, if the distance was 100 cm or more and less than 200 cm, $\theta_{other\,child}$ was calculated. Figure 3 (c) and (d) show the normalized histogram of $\theta_{other\,child}$ during the period from 0 to 1 s before. The t-tests in the bin of 20-degree revealed that the frequencies of class B were significantly higher than those of class A, and the effect sizes were large ((c): $t(21) = -3.80$, $p < .005$, Cohen's $d = 1.59$; (d): $t(21) = -3.18$, $p < .005$, Cohen's $d = 1.33$). It supported the hypothesis #2 because 20-degree at which the significant differences were confirmed was close to 0-degree. However, regarding both comparisons, the t-tests in the bins of $\theta_{other\,child}$ during other periods before did not indicate the results that were consistent with the hypothesis #2.

In the graphs (e) and (f) of Fig. 3, the t-tests in the bins of 80, 90, and 100-degrees of $\theta_{center\,of\,children}$ revealed that the frequencies of class A were significantly higher than those of class B ($ps < .05$). This result indicated that each child in class A tended to run on circles based on the static center of children. It might relate to the attitude of spontaneously participating in the running activity without consideration to others.

7   Discussion

The quantitative analysis of children's group behavior supported our hypotheses. In regard to the distance representing *Spontaneous social behaviors*, the previous studies on personal space [5, 6] suggest that the value of 50 cm is the distance at which children can touch others, and the distance between 100 cm and 200 cm is the distance required to communicate with others. In spite of no explicit instructions by nursery teachers such as who to run with nor where to run, the group behavior in class B had clear *Spontaneous social behaviors* that approached other children in a short time of 1 s. However, we need to consider the possibility that such behaviors of approaching others also included the aggressive actions. Theory of mind is developed during childhood [3]. Its development has increased interests in others, which may have produced the behaviors to spontaneously make a good relationship with others.

Moreover, Fig. 4 shows the heat map of normalized frequency of the bin of 20-degree at which C_1 approached C_2 during the period from 0 to 1 s before. For both classes A and B, the frequencies of the particular pairs tended to higher than those of others (e.g., Pair of children 8 and 6 of class B in November 2017). This might suggest the relationships between the children that nursery teachers were not aware of.

In conclusion, we aimed to clarify children's group behavior from the perspective of development of spontaneity and sociality using quantitative analysis and visualization, and revealed the characteristic events showing *Spontaneous social behaviors*. In the future, we will periodically take a video and discuss the changes in children's group behavior with age. We will also conduct an interview survey with nursery teachers and examine to what extent it agrees with the result of Fig. 4.

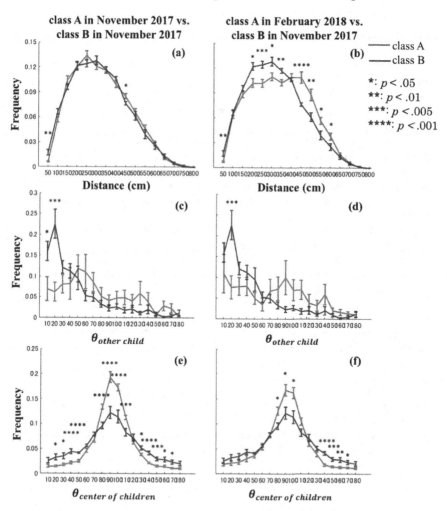

Fig. 3. Normalized histograms of the indexes of children's group behavior. The horizontal axes represent the bins of distance (cm) or θ. The vertical axes represent the normalized frequencies. The error bars present the standard errors.

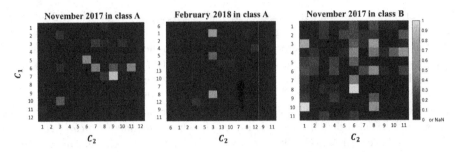

Fig. 4. Heat map of normalized frequency of the bin of 20-degree at which C_1 approached C_2 during the period from 0 to 1 s before

Acknowledgment. This study was supported by JSPS KAKENHI Grant Number 26118003.

References

1. Carr, M.: Assessment in Early Childhood Settings: Learning Stories. SAGE Publication, Thousand Oaks (2001)
2. Eisenberg, N., Miller, P.A.: The relation of empathy to prosocial and related behaviors. Psychol. Bull. **101**(1), 91–119 (1987)
3. Wellman, H.M., Cross, D., Watson, J.: Meta-analysis of theory-of-mind development: the truth about false belief. Child Dev. **72**(3), 655–684 (2001)
4. Nieman, P.: Psychosocial aspects of physical activity. Paediatr. Child Health **7**(5), 309–312 (2002)
5. Gifford, R., Price, J.: Personal space in nursery school children. Can. J. Behav. Sci./Revue canadienne des sciences du comportement **11**(4), 318–326 (1979)
6. Hall, E.T.: The Hidden Dimension. Doubleday and Co., New York (1966)
7. Bialek, W., et al.: Statistical mechanics for natural flocks of birds. Proc. Nat. Acad. Sci. **109** (13), 4786–4791 (2012). https://doi.org/10.1073/pnas.1118633109
8. Couzin, I.D., Krause, J., James, R., Ruxton, G.D., Franks, N.R.: Collective memory and spatial sorting in animal groups. J. Theor. Biol. **218**(1), 1–11 (2002)
9. Fujii, K., Yokoyama, K., Koyama, T., Rikukawa, A., Yamada, H., Yamamoto, Y.: Resilient help to switch and overlap hierarchical subsystems in a small human group. Sci. Rep. **6**, 23911 (2016). https://doi.org/10.1038/srep23911
10. Nakamae, S., et al.: Children's social behavior analysis system using BLE and accelerometer. In: Yoshino, T., Yuizono, T., Zurita, G., Vassileva, J. (eds.) CollabTech 2017, LNCS, vol. 10397, pp. 153–167. Springer, Heidelberg (2017). https://doi.org/10.1007/978-3-319-63088-5_14
11. Kirschner, S., Tomasello, M.: Joint music making promotes prosocial behavior in 4-year-old children. Evol. Hum. Behav. **31**(5), 354–364 (2010)

A New Platform for Question-Based Sharing of Supervision Competencies in Problem-Based Learning

Hans Hüttel[2(✉)], Dorina Gnaur[1], Andreas Hairing Klostergaard[2], and Gideon Blegmand[2]

[1] Department of Learning and Philosophy, Aalborg University, Aalborg, Denmark
dg@learning.aau.dk
[2] Department of Computer Science, Aalborg University, Aalborg, Denmark
hans@cs.aau.dk, {aklost11,gblegm13}@student.aau.dk

Abstract. PBL Exchange is a new web-based, open source platform implemented in Python using the Django framework for sharing competencies among teaching staff at Aalborg University concerning the supervision of problem-based learning (PBL) projects. PBL Exchange uses a crowdsourcing strategy where users ask questions about PBL and answer questions posed by other users. We describe the structure of PBL Exchange and analyze the challenges of building an active user community for the system. A particular challenge has been that of dealing with the highly heterogeneous teaching environments that exist across departments and faculties.

1 Introduction

The main pedagogical model used in all degree programmes at Aalborg University is a project-organized form of problem-based learning (PBL) where students collaborate in groups on a project supervised by a member of the teaching staff. While this model has proved to be successful, it is also a model that is not widely used. It is often a particular challenge for new members of the teaching staff to develop the competences necessary to act as supervisors in this setting.

Since 1993, there have been concrete activities to introduce PBL supervision practice to teaching staff at Aalborg University, and these activities have become mandatory. Recently, there have been efforts underway to use web-based approaches for aiding the ongoing development of PBL supervision competences.

Work by Gnaur et al. [5] describes initial work on sharing reflections on practice among PBL supervisors by using a web-based platform for asking and answering questions about PBL supervision. Our hypothesis is that this approach to sharing and building knowledge about PBL competences can indeed transform professional development of PBL practice in a way that has not previously been possible. However, this also requires a significant effort of building

---

The work reported here has been funded by a PBL Development Project Grant from Aalborg University.

A. Rodrigues et al. (Eds.): CRIWG 2018, LNCS 11001, pp. 177–184, 2018.
https://doi.org/10.1007/978-3-319-99504-5_14

a community of active users of a web-based platform for crowdsourcing. Moreover, it requires that we are able to both extend already existing practices and go beyond them, when necessary, such that one does not simply reproduce the existing community of practice. In particular, crowdsourcing using the Internet makes it possible to reach a much larger community of colleagues, something that previous approaches could not easily accommodate.

In this paper we describe a new web-based platform for sharing PBL competencies which extends and replaces the system described in [5], how this platform is structured and implemented and how it is currently being disseminated to the teaching staff at Aalborg University. We also provide an analysis of the challenges that arise when dealing with the diversity that exists even within the setting of a single university.

The rest of the paper is organized as follows. In Sect. 3 we describe the PBL Exchange system as implemented in the Django framework [2]. The resulting system is released under the GPLv2 license [8] and is publicly available at https://github.com/PBLExchange/PBLExchange. We also report on experiences obtained from introducing PBL Exchange to colleagues at Aalborg University, how this has helped shape PBL Exchange and how this will affect upcoming community building efforts.

2   The Design Intentions Behind PBL Exchange

2.1   Professional Development of PBL Practice

Collegial supervision has been promoted as a way of developing teaching practice. Following work by Lauvås and Handal [10], the notion of colleagues that challenge each other and help each other develop their competences within teaching has been espoused in educational research in the Nordic countries.

However, a practical challenge with the approach of collegial supervision is that systematic efforts of this kind can be time-consuming. Moreover, at universities such as Aalborg University there is now a large throughput of teaching staff and it is often not realistic that experienced staff members in longer-term positions will be able to carry out this kind of supervision.

Finally, and importantly, the practice of collegial supervision as described in the Nordic tradition does not imply that the experience obtained gets preserved for posterity or gets shared with a wider community.

2.2   Crowdsourcing for Building a Community of Practice

PBL Exchange uses a form of *crowdsourcing* to build a community of practice. The collection of questions and answers is a searchable knowledge base built by the interactions by the teaching staff.

Attempts have been made to develop an integrated definition of crowdsourcing by indicating certain characteristics, such as the presence of a task with a clear goal; the recompense received by the crowd; the crowdsourcer and the benefit it receives; the participative nature of the task; and the existence of an open call [4]. When confined to a single institution, the term 'crowd' can be debated as per how many active participants it should involve. However, it has been argued that crowdsourcing is increasingly associated with certain forms of participatory activities that tap into collective intelligence and is widely applied to almost any Internet-based collaborative activity [4].

It is important to understand what generates the motivation for this type of participation and how it can be stimulated when initiating projects such as ours. We reckon that PBL Exchange relies upon social engagement, as a way of making individuals work collaboratively to achieve a common goal, which is here an understanding of PBL practice.

The fundamental form of contributing to PBL Exchange is that of *asking questions and providing answers and comments*. A screenshot of PBL Exchange showing this can be seen in Fig. 1. Any member of the teaching staff can ask a question, and any of their colleagues at the university can then contribute with answers to the question. This is directly inspired by StackExchange [1, 9]. StackExchange fora are open and expert-based and cover a wide variety of topics. Since its inception, StackExchange has become increasingly popular with students in higher education as well as with professionals [9].

Moreover, PBL Exchange makes explicit use of gamification: Questions and answers can receive upvotes and downvotes from users, and in this way the users accumulate points.

In this sense, the system will be self-regulating: Content judged to be of high quality will become prominent, while content that the community consider to be of low quality will sink to the bottom. However, for this to be a viable model, the user base must be sufficiently large and sufficiently active. It is therefore very important to build and maintain the community of users.

Fig. 1. Screenshot of the PBL Exchange platform

The PBL Exchange platform is therefore intended to extend and supplement collegial supervision by using interactive, written format that enables insights to be preserved and structured. Moreover, and importantly, because of the nature of a web platform that can be shared by the entire teaching staff, this makes it possible to share experience across departments and degree programmes in a way that collegial supervision often does not allow for.

3   The System Architecture of **PBL Exchange**

In the following we will describe the design choices and implementation issues that have arisen in the development of PBL Exchange. Many of these have been affected by our interaction with the community and they in turn point towards further challenges for building a large and stable community of users.

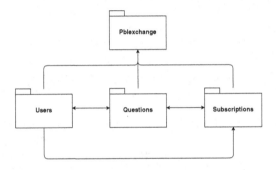

Fig. 2. The architecture of the PBL Exchange platform

3.1   Modularity Issues

A main motivation behind the development of PBL Exchange version 2 was that of creating an extendable platform. The original system described in [5] uses Question2Answer [11], an open source system implemented in PHP and using a mySQL database. However, the codebase of Question2Answer is poorly structured and uses programming styles that are at best dubious. As a result, it is very difficult to re-use the existing work on Question2Answer in new settings, where extendability is necessary.

An early prototype of the system based on Question2Answer has been operational since September 2016 with a small user base of 40 members of the teaching staff across campus. In February 2017 a survey was conducted of this initial user base, and other extensions were suggested by the participants – notably that of mail notifications (see Sect. 3.4).

As a consequence, we have re-implemented PBL Exchange in the Django framework [2] in order to create a modular system that can be easily extended and that can support further features. The Django framework is written in Python and uses Python throughout; the framework was chosen because it can help ensure plugability and ease of reuseability of code.

Using the Django framework allowed us to build the structure around modules, where we for modules such as the authentication (see Sect. 3.2), could use existing modules that has already been tested. We implement four modules as seen in Fig. 2. The four modules are written to be independent; some functionality of each module may require another module to be active, but is not required. An example of this can be found in the Questions module, which only activates the scoring system if the Users module is present. The Pblexchange module serves as the base of the site, defining the front page, and the base layout which the other modules extend.

3.2   The Need for Authentication

The intention of PBL Exchange is that teaching staff can discuss their practice (including person-sensitive issues) without interference from students. One of the challenges has therefore been that of setting up authentication. Most web services provided at Aalborg University rely on a Central Authentication Service (CAS), and in order to make PBL Exchange easily accessible to new users and to enable integration with other, already existing services, we chose to use CAS.

PBL Exchange uses the CAS of Aalborg University together with the default Django user model. By using CAS in conjunction with the default Django user model we attain a high degree of extensibility. A custom user model can easily be implemented by inheriting from the Django user model. Furthermore, any custom user model will interact flawlessly with the rest of the PBL Exchange implementation as long as it inherits from the Django user model. To accommodate the information used in the Users module, we extended the user model by adding the extension as a separate model referencing a user model, thus allowing for any custom user class that inherits from the original Django user model. Another benefit from using CAS is that a user's information, such as the user's name or alias, is consistent with other institutional web services also using CAS. Moreover, CAS can be replaced without affecting the functionality of PBL Exchange.

Consequently, the authentication module ensures that the site is inaccessible to students. This has been implemented by using the information provided in the CAS SAML response, specifically the email address of the user. When a user attempts to log in, her/his email address is checked against two lists, namely disallowed domains and exempt users; if the user's email is in the disallowed domains list and not in the exempt users list, access to PBL Exchange is denied. The two lists can simply be modified to fit the CAS setup for a given institution.

3.3   Supporting Diversity

Another important requirement of PBL Exchange has been that it should address the diversity at Aalborg University and in particular accommodate the large number of non-Danish speaking members of the teaching staff. As these colleagues have an academic background that is almost always from outside Aalborg University, this means that they are a particularly important target group. At the same time, there is a well-established Danish terminology within local PBL practice, and most degree programmes are taught mostly (or wholly) in Danish.

For these reasons, it is important that PBL Exchange can support multiple languages and allow the user to view the content in her language of change. Original content is shown in the chosen language whenever possible, while all other content is translated using the Google Translate API [6]. However, this service is not free, costing 100 $ for the translation of a million words. Moreover, efficiency is also in issue. For these reasons, PBL Exchange uses a local cache to store local copies of the translations of both questions, answers, and comments; the translation cache is only updated if answers are updated or a translation that did not previously exist is requested by a user.

3.4 Mail Notifications

The Question2Answer system used for the initial prototype of PBL Exchange supports a simple form of mail notification: users that have asked a question will be alerted to any further activity (answers or comments) for this particular question. However, social media allow for a much more fine-grained form of mail notifications that can be used to alert users to activity of any kind that matches the profile of the individual user. This is an important technique for cultivating the user base.

As a consequence, PBL Exchange supports mail notifications in the form of weekly digests of new content as well as specialized digests.

The mail notifications functionality is in PBL Exchange version 2 encapsulated in the Subscriptions module seen in Fig. 2. The Subscriptions module independently provides functionality for a user to alter their subscription settings, and methods to send mail notifications and digests. In order to provide fully functional mail notifications and digests the Subscription module depends on both the Users and Questions module. In the Questions module we have implemented methods that register new mail digests and which, by using Django signals [3], are invoked whenever a new question is posted. The Users module is used in order to determine which users should receive email notifications and digests, and at what intervals.

From initial prototype of PBL Exchange we preserved both email notifications and digests, while extending the customisability of the emailing feature such that a user can decide if she/he wants to receive notifications and/or digests, and what specific users, categories and tags to receive digests from.

4   Taking the System to the Local Users

It has been an unexpected challenge to take PBL Exchange to a larger community, and in particular to get potential users interested and ensure that they remain active.

In the setting of the general Internet, there is now a growing understanding of the importance of community building and of cultivating digital communities. However, much less appears to be known about community building and community maintenance in the setting of professional development within a smaller, well-defined community. In [7], Hur and Hara analyze the challenges faced when developing an online community for professionel development among K-12 teachers in Korea. They found that internal factors including a sense of ownership and autonomy among users and that of acknowledging the value of participating in the community were important.

In 2017 and early 2018 we have tried to address these issues by presenting PBL Exchange to the individual departments at Aalborg University. One obstacle that has been pointed out by colleagues attending these presentations is that PBL Exchange runs the risk of being seen as "yet another system". At Aalborg University there is already a plethora of web services, and while most of the services rely on the same authentication (cf. Section 3.2), the lack of interoperability has become a common complaint: while most of the services use the same authentication front-end, most of the existing services are not well-integrated with each other and have very different user interfaces.

An obstacle often mentioned by those attending our presentations is that there is already a tradition among some members of staff for asking colleagues, whenever one is faced with problems concerning PBL supervision. The reluctance to get use PBL Exchange may also stem from the fact that the adoption of question-based fora has been largely confined to certain academic disciplines. Our visit to the departments revealed that StackExchange is widely used in computer science, mathematics, physics and electrical engineering but is completely unknown in other branches of engineering, not to mention in the health and social sciences and in the humanities.

Since the motivational factors are non-commercial, participation must be driven intrinsically by personal interests, or by inherently engaging tasks. When it comes to professional competence development in the context of PBL pedagogy, we may well be able to identify intrinsically motivated people, driven by the PBL philosophy as such. Their presence is presumably consistent throughout the university settings and they act in many ways, both formally and informally. The task is then to expand their engagement spectrum to include digital activism. As for the nature of the tasks, we count on participants' need for clarifying and refining PBL practice for novices as well as experts.

5   Conclusions and Ideas for Further Work

In this paper, we have introduced the new open-source platform PBL Exchange, that is now used as a forum for project supervisors at Aalborg University. We have outlined the design principles behind the system and the central features of its implementation.

Our work points to some challenges to be faced when introducing a system for developing professional competencies to a highly heterogeneous organization such as a modern university In particular, it has turned out that the settings are highly heterogeneous in unexpected ways.

Our experience points towards the need for further efforts in building a stable community around PBL Exchange. The integration with Moodle was meant to help nurturing a new community of users but turned out to be a stumbling block because of the many different set-ups used across the university.

Moreover, in the quest to build a community, one should be careful as not to undermine existing informal traditions for pedagogical discussions.

In a forthcoming paper we will specifically address the challenges associated with community building and how one can best exploit the informal traditions that already exist in an academic community of teaching staff.

One of the coming developments is that of a community wiki that can be used to systematize content in the system. The use of a wiki may provide a new incentive to use the field for users reluctant to use a question-based format.

References

1. StackExchange. http://www.stackexchange.com
2. Django: The web framework for perfectionists with deadlines. https://www.djangoproject.com
3. Django signals. https://docs.djangoproject.com/en/1.11/topics/signals/
4. Estellés-Arolas, E., González-Ladrón-De-Guevara, F.: Towards an integrated crowdsourcing definition. J. Inf. Sci. **38**(2), 189–200 (2012)
5. Gnaur, D., Hüttel, H.: A platform for developing and maintaining competences in PBL supervision. In: Huang, T.-C., Lau, R., Huang, Y.-M., Spaniol, M., Yuen, C.-H. (eds.) SETE 2017. LNCS, vol. 10676, pp. 297–303. Springer, Cham (2017). https://doi.org/10.1007/978-3-319-71084-6_33
6. Cloud Translation API. https://cloud.google.com/translate/
7. Hur, J.W., Hara, N.: Factors cultivating sustainable online communities for K-12 teacher professional development. J. Educ. Comput. Res. **36**(3), 245–268 (2007)
8. Free Software Foundation Inc. GPLv2. https://www.gnu.org/licenses/old-licenses/gpl-2.0.html (1991). Accessed 28 Mar 2018
9. Keller, J.: Stack Overflow's crowdsourcing model guarantees success. The Atlantic, 18 November 2010
10. Lauvås, P., Lycke, K.H., Handal, G.: Kollegaveiledning i skolen (Professional guidance in schools). Cappelen Akademisk Forlag, Oslo (2004). (in Norwegian)
11. Question2answer - free open source Q&A software for PHP. http://www.question2answer.org/

Using Eye-Tracking to Analyze Collaboration in a Virtual Role Play Environment

Julia Othlinghaus-Wulhorst[1]([✉]), Anna Jedich[1], H. Ulrich Hoppe[1],
and Andreas Harrer[2]

[1] University of Duisburg-Essen, Lotharstraße 63, 47057 Duisburg, Germany
{othlinghaus,hoppe}@collide.info,
anna.jedich@stud.uni-due.de
[2] Dortmund University of Applied Sciences and Arts,
Emil-Figge-Str. 42, 44227 Dortmund, Germany
andreas.harrer@fh-dortmund.de

Abstract. The ColCoMa environment supports the training of workplace-oriented conflict management strategies through virtual role play. The role play relies on a web-based environment in which the participants interact through chat dialogues. Two of the participants (the parties in conflict) are human actors whereas the third role ("mediator") is occupied by a chatbot. Our study aims at exploring the potential of eye-tracking analyses to assess the quality of cooperation in this situation. The standard assumption is that a certain "convergence" of the visual foci of attention between cooperation partners indicates better coordination and consideration of the other party. In our scenario, this assumption has to be refined by taking into account the different roles (including the role of the chatbot) and the distribution of utterances on the chat history. The eye-tracking parameters are compared to quality criteria such as successful completion of the game or richness/mutuality of the chat interactions. There are quite strong correlations on the aggregate level (taking overall eye-tracking convergence as a global parameter), yet not in terms of synchronicity between convergent eye-tracking and chat interaction. This is possibly due to the specific distribution of roles in our virtual training environment.

Keywords: Eye-tracking · Collaboration · Role play

1 Introduction

Collaborative virtual environments are increasingly recognized as effective and powerful tools for supporting learning and training, and a multitude of contexts and pedagogical approaches have been supported by different types of collaborative virtual environments [1]. Virtual role play environments are a special form of serious games that provide mobile and repeatable settings for learners and allow them to take over roles in particular contexts and to learn from the enacted experiences [2, 3]. In a safe environment, they can act, experiment, learn and teach without risking irreversible consequences [2].

© Springer Nature Switzerland AG 2018
A. Rodrigues et al. (Eds.): CRIWG 2018, LNCS 11001, pp. 185–197, 2018.
https://doi.org/10.1007/978-3-319-99504-5_15

It is of specific interest to combine virtual role playing with the collaborative learning perspective [1]. Dillenbourg [4] identifies the following criteria as important ingredients of rich and successful computer-supported collaborative learning interactions: interactivity, synchronicity and negotiability. *Interactivity* needs to be part of any collaborative situation, while its degree is not defined by the frequency of interactions, but rather by the extent to which the partners' cognitive processes are influenced by those interactions. *Synchronicity* means that the persons involved in such a situation are waiting for messages from the others' and process them immediately after delivery, so it is less a technical parameter than a social rule. *Negotiability* refers to the structure of collaborative dialog as being more complex than hierarchical situations: a partner will (to some extent) argue for his standpoint, justify and try to convince instead of imposing his view on the sole basis of his or her authority. According to Dillenbourg, collaboration only works under certain conditions and it should be the aim of research to determine the conditions under which collaborative learning is efficient [5]. Collaborative virtual environments may help to gain a better understanding of the underlying mechanisms of collaborative interactions by enabling a detailed recording of all interactions on the one hand and a careful design of the empirical situation on the other hand [4].

Many studies of collaborative learning rely on the quantitative or qualitative analysis of dialogues (or multi-party conversations), i.e. they focus on verbal interactions. Eye-tracking, which has become more and more easily available and applicable in recent years, allows for enriching the analysis techniques towards non-verbal behavior. The possibility to track people's eye gaze can provide rich and insightful information and offer unique opportunities to understand their cognitive and perceptual processes [6]. Especially using several eye-tracking devices in parallel, combined with other types of analysis, is helpful to afford an indication of the level of gaze synchronicity of the different group members, allowing to measure to what extend one person is "with" the other, i.e. how much are persons looking at the same thing at the same time [6]. This approach of using eye-tracking and automated analysis as a complement to content analysis methods is a recent development in the field of learning analytics.

Our study provides interesting opportunities to understand collaboration using eye-tracking data by analyzing visual coordination and its relationship to collaborative learning by investigating the fundamental question if there is a correspondence between gaze synchronicity and the quality of collaboration. The usage of eye-tracking analysis within collaborative serious games is to our knowledge a novel contribution as well as the exploration of interdependencies between synchronicity of gazes and collaboration quality, which is related to the dimension interactivity mentioned above.

2 Related Work

In relation to studies on collaboration and collaborative learning, eye-gaze can serve as an analysis technique, yet mutual gaze awareness can also be used as an additional channel of interaction and not only as an analytic instrument. Both aspects have been the subject of recent studies:

Richardson and Dale investigated the coupling between a speaker's and a listener's eye movements [7]. In their observational study, one set of participants (the speakers) talked spontaneously about a television show whose characters were displayed on a screen in front of them. Later, the other set of participants (the listeners) listened to the recorded monologues while looking at the same visual scene. By using a cross-recurrence analysis, Richardson and Dale found out that a listener's eye movements most closely matched a speaker's eye movements at a delay of 2 s and the more closely a listener's eye movements were coupled with the ones of a speaker, the better the listener performed on a comprehension test. Thus, the results indicate that the coupling between the eye movements of speaker and listener reflects the success of their communication.

Cherubini et al. developed an algorithm for detecting misunderstanding in a remote collaboration, which combines a linguistic model with eye-tracking data [8]. The participants of their study had to collaborate remotely via a chat tool and a map. The algorithm was designed to detect misunderstandings between the two persons using their eye movements on the shared workspace, their utterances containing references on the plan, as well as the availability of explicit referencing. This proposal was based on the finding that participants look at the points they are talking about in their messages at above the level of chance, and that the eye movements are denser around these points compared to any other region looked at during the same time period during reading or editing messages containing references to the shared workspace. The algorithm associates the distance between the gaze of the emitter and the receiver of a message with the probability that the message was not understood by the recipient. The results of the study show that the likelihood of misunderstandings is increased, if there is more dispersion.

Jermann et al. used synchronized eye-trackers to assess how dyads of programmers worked collaboratively on a code segment [9]. They contrasted a 'good' and a 'bad' dyad, and the results of their work suggest that a productive collaboration is associated with high visual recurrence. Schlösser et al. have used both mutual gaze awareness as well as eye-tracking analysis in a study of collaborative problem solving. They found that gaze awareness had a positive effect on problem solving results. They also identified share gaze events as an indicator of collaboration quality [10].

Schneider and Pea performed an eye-tracking study on collaborative problem-solving dyads [6]. These dyads collaborated remotely via an audio channel to learn from contrasting cases involving basic concepts about how the human brain is processing visual information. While in one group, the dyads were able to see the eye gaze of their partner on the screen, in the control group, they had no access to the information on their partner's gaze. The results of the study indicate that this real-time mutual gaze perception intervention enhances collaborative learning and collaboration quality. Collaboration quality was rated using dimensions developed by Meier et al. [11], who developed a five-point scale across nine dimensions (sustaining mutual understanding, dialogue management, information pooling, reaching consensus, task division, task management, technical coordination, reciprocal interaction, and individual task orientation) for assessing collaboration.

Schneider and Pea combined joint visual attention, network analysis and machine learning to predict dimensions of productive collaboration [12] based on the dataset of their previous study [9]. They visualized the eye-tracking data as networks, where the nodes of the graph represent fixations and edges represent saccades and used network metrics to interpret the properties of the graph to find proxies for the collaboration quality of the participants. They found that different characteristics of the graphs correlated with different dimensions of collaboration quality. Those characteristics have been used to predict the collaboration quality by using a machine-learning algorithm. This way it was possible to roughly predict the participants' collaboration quality with an accuracy between 85% and 100%. Here again the rating scheme for assessing collaboration quality by Meier et al. [11] has been used.

Sharma et al. applied the so-called *extreme value theory* (EVT) to eye-tracking data collected during an online collaborative problem-solving task in order to predict the collaboration quality [13]. In the univariate mode, each pair of time episodes from participants A and B is substituted by a measure of their differences, which results in a series of single values. In the bivariate mode, they also took into account the dynamic coupling of the two-time series. A comparison between the results by EVT and traditional approaches revealed that EVT provides a better prediction of the collaboration quality.

The results of the mentioned studies support the idea that eye gaze synchronicity is crucial for effective collaboration. In our study, we attempt to explore the dependencies between gaze synchronicity that is automatically computed and collaboration quality that is measured via a rating scheme manually, thus combining these two lines of analytical methods within one study.

3 Virtual Role Play Environment: ColCoMa

For our eye-tracking based study, we used the collaborative game-like environment *ColCoMa* (Collaborative Conflict Management), which supports the training of workplace-oriented conflict management strategies through virtual role play [13]. It engages two players to participate in a chat conversation about a given fictitious conflict in a 2D virtual environment. The conversation is moderated by a chat bot acting as mediator, and follows the typical structure of mediation talks. The main goal is to come to a conflict resolution at the end of the conversation by showing appropriate and constructive behavior.

In ColCoMa, each player is assigned a predefined role in the conflict scenario: Mr. Meier is working as a member of the computer support hotline team in a software company and conscientiously takes much time for his customers. His supervisor, Mrs. Schmidt, does not embrace Mr. Meier's very long call sessions. She wants him to work more efficiently. After a negative appraisal of Mr. Meier's performance on the part of Mrs. Schmidt, the situation escalates. The scenario is intentionally kept simple and comprehensible, focusing on the main conflict and each person's feelings in order to support both immediate understanding and empathy with the assigned role.

During the mediation, each player is seeing cartoon-like representations of the other conflict party and the mediator on screen, similarly to sitting opposite to the dialog partners. The players are able to communicate with each other and the mediator via an integrated chat. The players also have the possibility to evoke facial animations through the character images by using common emoticons. Figure 1 is showing the general interface of the ColCoMa environment. Besides the chat section, it includes a notepad and a help section in order to get additional information about the scenario as well as the game controls and possible actions.

The mediation talk consists of five conversational phases: (1) framing phase, (2) topic collection, (3) working on the conflict, (4) looking for a solution (5) contract. During each phase of the mediation talk, the players are offered specific sentence openers in order to (a) provide support to the players, (b) help the chatbot to understand the general gist of each message, and (c) help the chatbot to identify the speaker. In every phase, the conversation provides the players with sentence openers indicating "affirmation", "rejection", "further inquiry", and also specific openers depending on the current phase, if needed. The players are always forced to choose one of the sentence openers, but they are able to freely finish the selected sentence.

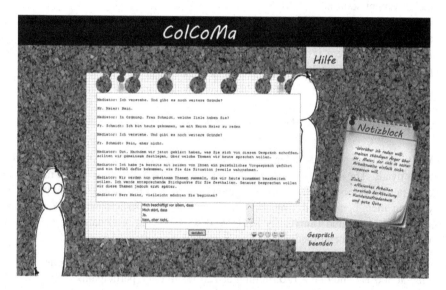

Fig. 1. Interface of the ColCoMa chat environment

The conversation can be either successfully finished in case a conflict resolution has been achieved or canceled by the mediator bot if he notices that the conversation does not advance anymore or if one of the players leaves. Irrespective of the way the mediation talk ends, the game phase is followed by a reflection phase, in which participants receive textual feedback on their overall performance during the conversation, followed by a replay session, in which the whole chat conversation is recaptured. The replay is augmented with individual feedback at certain points of interest. For example, a player will be praised for especially positive contributions or be criticized for interrupting the dialogue partner or showing inappropriate behavior. In this phase, the players are supposed to leave their role and reflect on their own behavior from an outside perspective.

4 Goals and Hypotheses

Our goal for this experiment was to investigate the question if there is a correspondence between gaze synchronicity, quality of game result (called achievement score) and the quality of the collaboration process, which can be perceived as a measurement of interactivity for this situation. How we derive these measurements is described in Sect. 6.1. for the gaze synchronicity, Sect. 6.2 for the achievement score and Sect. 6.3 for collaboration quality. We assume that the quality of collaboration as well as the successful mastering of the given task (conflict resolution) is somewhat connected to the synchronicity of the eye gaze movements. To examine the validity of this assumption, three main hypotheses were formulated:

> Hypothesis 1: There is a positive relation between the convergence of visual foci of attention (gaze synchronicity) and the successful completion of the game (achievement score).
> Hypothesis 2: There is a positive relation between the convergence of visual foci of attention (gaze synchronicity) and the quality of collaboration in the chat.
> Hypothesis 3: There is a dynamic (time-related) congruence between similar eye gaze movements (synchronicity) and the quality of collaboration in the chat.

5 Experimental Design

Population. 20 participants (average 22.8, SD = 2.84, 5 females, 15 males) have been tested in dyads. They did not know each other prior to the study and did not meet each other in person during the experiment to avoid the possibility of any first impressions influencing their behavior during the chat situation. The participants were recruited from the FH Dortmund (university of applied sciences and arts) campus, as well as through flyers and social media.

Eye-Tracking Setup. We used two desktop-based Tobii eye-trackers, one TX300 running at 300 Hz and one X120 running at 120 Hz to track participants' gaze. For the experimental setup, the recording and later the analysis of the gaze data, the software Tobii Studio has been utilized, which offers a standard procedure for eye-tracking studies and simplifies the data analysis. An in-house server was used to synchronize and capture all eye gaze data.

Procedure. The role distribution was randomized. After the briefing and the eye-tracker calibration, the participants were introduced to the scenario in the form of a picture story, each from the perspective of the respective role. During the main game session, the participants saw the representations of the two dialog partners (the other conflict party and the mediator) and were able to communicate with each other and the mediator by means of an integrated chat.

There were two possible outcomes in this scenario: Either the participants successfully completed the conversation by achieving a conflict resolution or the mediator canceled it in case he noticed that there was no more advancement or one of the participants left the conversation. The participants took as much time as they needed for completion (usually around 40 min). The session with the system was followed by answering several post-experiment questionnaires.

6 Method of Analysis

For the evaluation of the three main hypotheses mentioned above, we applied the following methods of analysis:

6.1 Eye-Tracking Data

In order to be able to compare the eye gaze movements of the two participants of each dyad, we defined six areas of interest. As shown in Fig. 2, the chat interface was subdivided into three different parts because otherwise the chat area would have been too extensive. Apart from the chat area, three additional areas of interest—the input area, the face of the mediator and the face of the game partner – were defined.

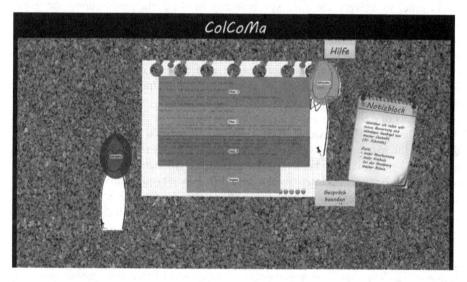

Fig. 2. Areas of Interest in the ColCoMa interface (3 sections of the chat protocol, input area, mediator face and partner face)

After the recordings, the tracking software converted the gaze movements into metric data based on these areas of interest in the form of a table. The table contains a time stamp column and six additional columns – each for one area of interest. Once a participant gazed at one of the areas of interest at a specific point of time, the respective cell was coded with a one. In contrast, a non-gazed area of interest was coded with a zero.

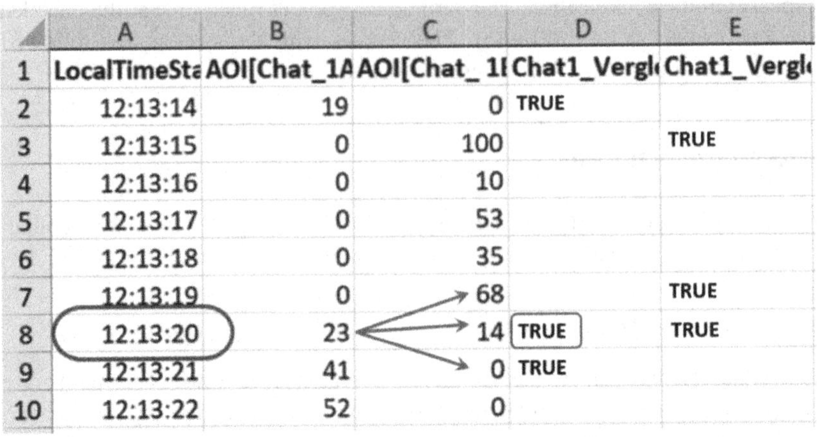

	A	B	C	D	E
1	LocalTimeSta	AOI[Chat_1A	AOI[Chat_ 1[	Chat1_Vergl	Chat1_Vergl
2	12:13:14	19	0	TRUE	
3	12:13:15	0	100		TRUE
4	12:13:16	0	10		
5	12:13:17	0	53		
6	12:13:18	0	35		
7	12:13:19	0	68		TRUE
8	12:13:20	23	14	TRUE	TRUE
9	12:13:21	41	0	TRUE	
10	12:13:22	52	0		

Fig. 3. Calculation of coincidences of areas of interest within 3 s windows

In order to analyze the gaze synchronicity of the participants during the game session, the recorded data needed to be compared. Due to the high amount of data, we used VBA (Visual Basic for Applications) to enable an automated comparison and evaluation of the tables. In a first step, the tables were formatted. The second step compared the tables of both participants of the same dyad. In doing so, the same area of interest was matched at a specific time stamp, using a timeframe of three seconds with one second back and one second ahead. The three second interval is an adaptation to the 2 s delay of gaze following within gaze sharing [7]. We assume a shared focus and thus synchronicity if the gaze of the two partners focused on the same area within less than 2 s difference. Since we did not (yet) use mutual gaze and thus do not have asymmetric gaze following behavior we compute the symmetric difference into the past and future second(s). A positive match for this time point (minimally one coincidence) was coded with "true". An example of applying this procedure is shown in Fig. 3.

At the end, the matches were summed up and divided through the total number of seconds to normalize against shorter or longer experiment duration. The calculations resulted in a percentage, which indicates to what extent the two participants have been looking at the same areas of interest in the same time interval during the course of the whole game. This aggregated percentage represents what we call "convergence of visual foci".

6.2 Rating Scheme for the Success in Game

To measure the success in the game we developed an *achievement score*. This achievement score reflects the participants' performance during the mediation talk based on three main criteria: Automated feedback provided by the system, successful completion of phase 2 (topic collection), and successful completion of phase 5 (contract).

The first criterion is based on the systems' automatically generated feedback. It appears at the end of the game and summarizes the participants' behavior during the game in terms of objectivity, aggressiveness and the relation between I- and You-messages. For each positive feedback, the participants receive one point in our rating, so three points in total. The second criterion refers to the second phase of the mediation talk (topic collection). In order to achieve the total of six points, the participants have to find three topics, which are needed to reach the next phase. When the process of finding these topics is not successful, the mediator interrupts the participants at some point and asks them again to think of an (further) issue they want to talk about. This process ends after three topics are found or after the mediator repeated his question three times. At this point, the mediator cancels the mediation talk when the participants still did not find the required number of topics. According to the mediator's count of repetitions, this amount is subtracted from the six possible points. The third criterion refers to the successful completion of the game. It is fulfilled when the dyad completes the game by verbally signing a contract between the parties, which includes the arrangements and rules the dyad worked out together with the mediator. For finishing the game, the participants receive three points. In total, a dyad can achieve 12 points.

6.3   Rating Scheme for Collaboration Quality

To assess collaboration quality in the chat situation we first needed to define a suitable method for analyzing the chat content of a dyad. Previous research has shown many possibilities to analyze such data, like counting certain words or analyzing the time sequences between each text message [14, 15]. However, the chat of the game ColCoMa is not suitable for any of the suggested methods due to a variety of reasons. First, this is a mediated chat in which the participants do not directly interact with each other but have a conversation guided by a mediator. Second, the structure of the chat is predefined, which makes it difficult to analyze any time related aspects of the conversation.

To find a suitable method, we first looked at all aspects of the chat conversations, which indicated a collaborative communication between the participants. We found that successful dyads had more suggestions for a solution and argued more with each other, compared to other (less successful) dyads. These findings are similar to the rating scheme of Meier et al. [11]. Their dimensions reaching consensus was about solution-focused communication, where the participants argued with each other in order to find a solution. Furthermore, it was clear that successful dyads referred more often to each other by using personal pronouns or the name of the chat partner than the less successful dyads. In addition, successful dyads talked more about their shared future or shared past with the other one. Based on these findings we developed a rating scheme to access the quality of collaboration. It includes five dimensions:

- *Argumentation:* participants discuss or bring forward arguments giving justifications (e.g. "…for this reason we are losing clients")
- *Agreement/disagreement:* participants explicitly endorse or dissent from one another (e.g. "…I agree", "…I don't agree")
- *Collaborative orientation:* participants refer to each other, ask questions, give feedback or act on topics brought up by another party ("…like Mr. Meier/Mrs. Schmidt said")

- *Solution orientation:* participants try to find a solution or make a proposal to find one ("...I'll try to pay more attention to this in future")
- *Shared awareness/reinforcing shared history:* participants share common knowledge, explain their situation ("...that my assessments of Mr. Meier's performance are always taken personally")

In order to assess the collaboration, every single chat message had to be analyzed and checked against the five dimensions. The more dimensions were matched, the higher the quality score. At the end, all matches were summed up for all chat messages in a session of a given dyad. The calculations resulted in a percentage indicating the overall collaboration quality of the chat conversation for this dyad.

In addition to the eye-tracking data and the textual chat analysis, we assessed the participants' perception of the chatbot, the perception of their partner, the performance of their partner and the collaboration. To gain this subjective data, we used several post-experimental questionnaires at the end of each game session. One of these measured human-like qualities of the mediator [16]. Additionally, we used a questionnaire to measure the interpersonal attraction [17] for the bots and the partner's perception. Furthermore, we used a questionnaire to measure the group awareness [18]. Finally, the participants were asked to rate the quality of their collaboration by a self-designed questionnaire.

7   Results

Referring to hypothesis 1, we found a highly significant correlation between the percentage value for convergence of visual foci of attention (aggregated) and the achievement score ($r = .589$, $p = .006$) as a measure for the success in the role playing game.

Relating to hypothesis 2, we found a highly significant correlation between the convergence of visual foci of attention (aggregated) and the quality of collaboration in the chat ($r = .774$, $p = .000$), which was assessed using the rating scheme presented in Sect. 6.3. There are also significant correlations between the convergence of visual foci of attention and single dimensions of collaboration quality, namely agreement/disagreement, solution orientation and shared awareness (Table 1). These findings correspond to our expectations and show that there is a connection between the synchronicity of the eye gaze movements and the performance of the participants in the game.

Table 1. Correlations between the convergence of visual foci of attention and dimensions of collaboration quality

Dimension	Gaze synchronicity
Argumentation	.228
Agreement/disagreement	.456*
Collaborative orientation	.386
Solution orientation	.509*
Shared awareness/reinforcing shared history	.609**

*$p < .05$; **$p < .01$

Surprisingly, hypothesis 3 could not be verified. There is no significant (time-related) congruence between similar eye gaze movements and the quality of collaboration in the chat. Possible reasons for this finding will be discussed in Sect. 8.

The post-questionnaires revealed interesting results, too. The participants reported above-average satisfaction with the collaboration (Fig. 3). Regarding the perspective, participants rated their own contribution better than the one of the partner or the conjoint contribution (Table 2).

Table 2. Perception of the collaboration (1 to 5 scale)

	Self		Partner		Conjoint	
	M	SD	M	SD	M	SD
Collaboration	3.65	1.13	3.50	1.05	3.55	1.19
Competence	3.50	1.05	3.30	.98	3.65	1.30

The results regarding the perception of the chatbot show that it is perceived as especially "polite" (M = 6.90 of 9), "thoughtful" (M = 6.55 of 9) and "engaging" (M = 6.45). The conversational skill of the bot was rated average to above-average (M = 5.25 of 9). Only the human-likeness of the bot was rated below-average (M = 3.95 of 9).

The perceived task attraction of the partner has been rated above-average (M = 6.90), while the social attraction achieved only an average level (M = 4.60). Furthermore, the group awareness was rated above-average.

8 Discussion

The results of the study confirmed hypothesis 1, i.e. we found a correspondence between the convergence of visual foci of attention and the success in the game. It is plausible that the extent of gaze synchronicity influences the outcome of the game and not vice versa. So we assume: the more similar the visual foci of attention, the better the collaborative performance of the two participants. Of course, other factors might have an influence on the performance, which have not been comprised in this study, so a causal relation cannot be verified.

We also found a positive relation between gaze synchronicity and the quality of collaboration (hypothesis 2), especially with the three dimensions of agreement/disagreement, solution orientation and shared awareness (on the aggregate level). Those three dimensions might be particularly good quality criteria. Here we do also suppose that a higher gaze synchronicity results in a higher collaboration quality. It could be argued that it is not necessarily the gaze synchronicity between the participants, which has a positive effect on the collaborative performance, but instead their 'general attention' (the extent to which the participants' gaze resides in the areas of interest in general). From our point of view, both the synchronicity of the eye movements and this general attention can serve as indicators for successful collaboration, and they complement one another instead of contradict.

However, hypothesis 3 could not be verified. We expected to find also a congruence between the gaze synchronicity and the quality of collaboration during the course of the game, but we found only strong correlations on the aggregate level (taking overall eye-tracking convergence as a global parameter), yet not in terms of synchronicity between convergent eye-tracking and chat interaction. We assume, that the specific nature of the chat in ColCoMa might be a reason for these results, since there are three persons involved and the two human dialog partners do not directly communicate with each other. They do always talk to the mediator and reply to his questions, and never really have the chance to react on the messages of the other conflict party immediately. Thus, the structure of the chat conversation is predefined to a certain extent and the time interval between the utterances of the different dialog partners is rather high due to the fact, that there is always the mediator writing in-between.

9 Conclusion and Future Work

The results of our study provide strong indication of that a certain convergence of the visual foci of attention between cooperation partners indicates higher success and quality of collaboration, although not all three hypotheses have been confirmed. There are quite strong correlations on the aggregate level (taking overall eye-tracking convergence as a global parameter), yet not in terms of synchronicity between convergent eye-tracking and chat interaction. This is possibly due to the specific distribution of roles in our virtual training environment. The novelty of our approach lies in the combination of this eye-tracking method with virtual role play, especially considering a scenario with two human players and a chatbot.

Due to the relatively small amount of participants, no generalization should be made here, but the results are promising and should be elaborated on in larger studies. Further studies should be conducted to re-check synchronicity between convergent eye-tracking and collaboration quality with a modified chat environment which allows direct communication between the cooperation partners.

Future work could also include chat awareness tools, which e.g. indicate if a chat message has been read or even visualize the eye gaze of the chat partner. Recent studies indicate that real-time mutual gaze perception via awareness visualisations enhances collaborative learning and collaboration quality [19]. Finally, further studies are needed to identify more factors, which are influencing the quality of collaboration in order to improve collaborative processes.

References

1. Whitton, N., Hollins, P.: Collaborative virtual gaming worlds in higher education. ALT-J, Res. Learn. Technol. **16**(3), 221–229 (2008)
2. Greco, M.: The use of role-playing in learning. In: Connolly, T., Stansfield, M., Boyle, L. (eds.) Games-Based Learning Advancements for Multi-Sensory Human Computer Interfaces, pp. 158–173. Information Science Reference, New York (2009)

3. Slator, B.M., Chaput, H.: Learning by learning roles: a virtual role-playing environment for tutoring. In: Frasson, C., Gauthier, G., Lesgold, A. (eds.) ITS 1996. LNCS, vol. 1086, pp. 668–676. Springer, Heidelberg (1996). https://doi.org/10.1007/3-540-61327-7_167

4. Dillenbourg, P.: What do you mean by collaborative learning? In: Dillenbourg, P. (ed.) Collaborative-Learning: Cognitive and Computational Approaches, pp. 1–19. Elsevier, Oxford (1999)

5. Dillenbourg, P., Baker, M., Blaye, A., O'Malley, C.: The evolution of research on collaborative learning. In: Reimann, P., Spada, H. (eds.) Learning in Humans and Machine: Towards an Interdisciplinary Learning Science, pp. 189–211. Elsevier, Oxford (1996)

6. Schneider, B., Pea, R.: Real-time mutual gaze perception enhances collaborative learning and collaboration quality. Int. J. Comput.-Support. Collab. Learn. 8(4), 375–397 (2013)

7. Richardson, D.C., Dale, R.: Looking to understand: the coupling between speakers' and listeners' eye movements and its relationship to discourse comprehension. Cogn. Sci. 29(6), 1045–1060 (2005)

8. Cherubini, M., Nuessli, M., Dillenbourg, P.: Deixis ad gaze in collaborative work at a distance (over a shared map): a computational model to detect misunderstandings. In: Proceedings of the 2008 Symposium on Eye Tracking Research & Applications, pp. 173–180. ACM, New York (2008)

9. Jermann, P., Mullins, D., Nuessli, M.-A., Dillenbourg, P.: Collaborative gaze footprints: correlates of interaction quality. In: CSCL 2011 Conference Proceedings, Long Papers, vol. 1, pp. 184–191. International Society of the Learning Science, Hong Kong (2011)

10. Schlösser, C., Schlieker-Steens, P., Kienle, A., Harrer, A.: Using real-time gaze based awareness methods to enhance collaboration. In: Baloian, N., Zorian, Y., Taslakian, P., Shoukouryan, S. (eds.) CRIWG 2015. LNCS, vol. 9334, pp. 19–27. Springer, Cham (2015). https://doi.org/10.1007/978-3-319-22747-4_2

11. Meier, A., Spada, H., Rummel, N.: A rating scheme for assessing the quality of computer-supported collaboration processes. Int. J. Comput.-Support. Collab. Learn. 2(1), 63–86 (2007)

12. Schneider, B., Pae, R.: Toward collaboration sensing. Int. J. Comput.-Support. Collab. Learn. 9(4), 371–395 (2014)

13. Sharma, K., Chavez-Demoulin, V., Dillenbourg, P.: An application of extreme value theory to learning analytics: predicting collaboration outcome from eye-tracking data. J. Learn. Anal. 4(3), 140–164 (2017)

14. Bratitsis, T., Dimitracopoulou, A., Martínez-Monés, A., Marcos, J.A., Dimitriadis, Y.: Supporting members of a learning community using Interaction Analysis tools: the example of the Kaleidoscope NoE scientific network. In: 8th IEEE International Conference on Advanced Learning Technologies (ICALT 2008). IEEE Computer Society, Santander (2008)

15. Kahrimanis, G., Chounta, I.-A., Avouris, N.: Study of correlations between logfile based metrics of interaction and the quality of synchronous collaboration. Int. Reports Socio-Inform. 7(1), 24 (2010)

16. Holtgraves, T.M., Ross, S.J., Weywadt, C.R., Han, T.L.: Perceiving artificial social agents. Comput. Hum. Behav. 23, 2163–2174 (2007)

17. McCroskey, J.C., McCain, T.A.: The measurement of interpersonal attraction. Speech Monogr. 41, 261–266 (1974)

18. Mock, A.: Open (ed) classroom–who cares? MedienPädagogik: Zeitschrift für Theorie und Praxis der Medienbildung 28, 57–65 (2017)

19. Schlösser, C., Cedli, L., Schröder, B., Kienle, A.: Beyond gaze cursor - exploring information-based gaze sharing in chat. In: Workshop on Communication by Gaze Interaction, COGAIN 2018, Warsaw, Poland. ACM, New York (2018)

Is Group-Awareness Context-Awareness?

Manuele Kirsch Pinheiro$^{(\boxtimes)}$ and Carine Souveyet

Centre de Recherche en Informatique, Université Paris 1 Panthéon Sorbonne,
Paris, France
{Manuele.Kirsch-Pinheiro,
Carine.Souveyet}@univ-paris1.fr

Abstract. Group awareness correspond to an important concept on Groupware applications, allowing individual users to be kept aware of group's activities and status. Similarly, on Pervasive Computing, context is defined as any relevant information that can be used to characterize the situation of an entity [7]. In this position paper, we advocate that group awareness information should be considered as context information and handled as such. Group awareness information is often employed for decision making, contributing to users' activities and decisions. It represents also an important clue about user's context, characterizing individual's actions regarding the group. As such, group awareness may be used for adaptation purposes, adapting the system behavior, the supplied content or its services. To illustrate this point, we discuss the use of a context distribution system as a group awareness distribution mechanism.

Keywords: Group awareness · Context-awareness · Groupware applications
Context-aware applications · Context distribution
Pervasive Information Systems

1 Introduction

Group awareness is a well-known concept from Groupware Systems. It refers to the knowledge group members have about the group and its activities (past, present and future activities) [8, 12]. This information is commonly used for helping decision making, since it promises to group members a common context for their own activities inside the group. Presenting this information offers an important knowledge about the current status of the group, allowing group members to better evaluate the relevance of their own activities for the group and its goals.

A similar concept exists on Pervasive Computing: the notion of context, which is defined as any information capable of characterizing the situation of an entity [7]. This information, that often refers to physical and execution environment (e.g. user's location, device available memory, network connection, etc.), is traditionally applied for adaptation purposes. Context-Aware Systems [1, 7] observe it in order to adapt accordingly their own behavior. They perform adaptation tasks in the behalf of the user in order to propose her/him the most appropriate service or content.

Both notions can be seen as an information capable of characterizing user's interactions, individually or as a group member, but their treatment is not the same. For group awareness, the focus is on delivering this information to the user, while on

A. Rodrigues et al. (Eds.): CRIWG 2018, LNCS 11001, pp. 198–206, 2018.
https://doi.org/10.1007/978-3-319-99504-5_16

context awareness the focus is on adapting the system behavior in a transparent way. Even on mobile Groupware Systems (e.g. [11, 21]), these notions are distinguished and handled separately: the first is delivered to the user, while the latter is used for adaptation purposes. However, group awareness information offers an important clue about user's context, characterizing individual's actions with regard to the group and its status.

In this position paper, we advocate that group awareness information should be considered as context information and handled as such. By considering group awareness as context information and giving it a similar treatment, we may reach a more dynamic and proactive behavior on groupware systems, offering applications that may adapt their behavior (content and services) to current usages and technologies, as well as to the group and its activities. To illustrated this point, we discuss the use of a context distribution mechanism for distributing both group awareness and context information among group members according their current context.

This position paper is organized as follows: Sect. 2 discusses the notion of group awareness and its treatment on Groupware Systems, while Sect. 3 introduces the notion of context and its application on context-aware applications. In Sect. 4, we discuss similarities and dissimilarities between both concepts. In Sect. 5, we illustrate this discussion with a context distribution mechanism, before concluding in Sect. 6.

2   Group Awareness on Groupware Systems

The term group awareness refers to actors' taking heed of the context of their joint effort, to a person being or becoming aware of something [19]. It is defined as an understanding of others' activities, which provides a context for our own activity on a group, allowing evaluating individual actions with respect to group goals and progress, and assuring that individual contributions are relevant to the group's activity [8]. This relevant concept of Groupware Systems allows to transform irregular interactions of group members into a consistent and perceptive performance over time [18].

Group awareness information is mainly considered from a 'knowledge management' perspective. It represents a knowledge that has to be externalized and made visible to group members, offering a common basis in which members' individual actions take place and gain a meaning. This knowledge is necessary for a better understanding of the individual's activities and group status. Through this knowledge, group members dispose of a better perspective for their own activities, being able to evaluate their relevance for the group itself. As a result, group awareness mechanisms may contribute to reduce common coordination problems, preventing problems due to a lack of knowledge about group activities (e.g. double work, unfinished or delayed tasks, etc.). This knowledge is used for decision making, allowing each group member to place her/his own contribution on the context of the group.

Literature proposes different group awareness mechanisms [3, 11, 12]. Works, such as [9], point out the contribution of these mechanisms to successful group work. They also demonstrate that inappropriate mechanisms may have a disruptive effect on group work, disturbing users on their working tasks. A challenge is then to propose group awareness information while preventing the risk of an information overload. Since this information is directly proposed to the users, this risk increases with the volume of available information, leading group members to spend more time assimilating it than performing their working tasks. Several mechanisms tackle this issue through filtering or appropriate user interfaces [3, 12]. Whatever mechanism is adopted, the main ambition remains: to make available to group members information about the group itself, its activities (current, past or future) and its status, in order to help these members to better coordinate their own actions considering group goals and situation.

3   Context Information on Pervasive Computing

Similar to group awareness, the notion of context denotes a large concept. It is often defined as any information that can be used to characterize the situation of an entity (a person, place, or object) that is considered relevant to the interaction between a user and a system [7]. Multiple elements can be considered as context information, even if this definition delimits those to the boundary of a computing system. Defining what elements could be considered as context on a given system implies identifying the entities that can be observed and the relevant information about these. Different elements are cited in the literature [13], including information about the physical and the execution environment (e.g. user's location, device memory and network connection).

Independently of these elements, the purpose of observing context information remains the same. Context-aware applications consider it in order to adapt their behavior according to context changes, aiming at increasing their usability and effectiveness [1, 7]. The final goal is to improve the user's satisfaction in a transparent way, offering her/him the most appropriate service (or content) according to changes on the observed context. The user does not necessarily need to be aware of any adaptation performed by the system. It is up to this later to adapt itself to the user and her/his context, without an active intervention from this user.

This transparency is a key element of context-aware systems, for obtaining more adapted and proactive software applications. Thanks to different adaptation mechanisms, these systems may apply context information for adapting content [11], services [16], internal composition [10] or deployment [5]; they may even anticipate user's requests, offering a proactive behavior [16]. Nevertheless, the success of such adaptation mechanisms depends on the context information that guides them. The richer is the observed context information, the richer these mechanisms might be.

4   Common Aspects and Divergences

Dourish [8] defined group awareness as "an understanding of the activities of others, which provides a *context* for your own activity. This context is used to ensure that individual contributions are relevant to the group's activity as a whole and to evaluate individual actions with respect to the group goals and progress". Supplying group awareness information may offer users the necessary knowledge for creating an implicit coordination mechanism, by improving understanding about the relevance of their own activities to the group. We may thus expect better results for the group as a whole since each member is aware of the group overall situation.

Group awareness offers then a *shared context* for the group and for our own individual activities on it. Since its definition, group awareness can be seen as context information. It represents a knowledge referring to the organizational context in which the cooperative work takes place [11]. It participates on the user's context, by placing the individual as part of a group.

Inversely Kirsh [14] points out that "context is a highly structured amalgam of informational, physical, and conceptual resources that go beyond the simple facts of who or what is where and when to include the state of digital resources, people's concepts and mental state, *task state*, *social relations*, and the *local work culture*". In other terms, context information could (or should) include collaborative elements, describing the social environment in which user's actions take place. This notion is not limited to physical and execution elements as often on Pervasive Computing. Authors such as [11, 15] have considered organizational elements, such as the notion of group or role, on their context models. By considering those, they enlarge the notion of context usually adopted on Pervasive Computing, considering users as part of a group.

Both definitions (group awareness and context information) point towards the notion of context, since both can be used to characterize user's actions when interacting with a given system. Because a user is not anymore considered as an isolated individual, and that the interaction between this user and her/his group is mediated by a system, group awareness information becomes context information, since it becomes relevant for the interaction between this user and the system. Information about the group and its status (i.e. group awareness information) may affect user's needs considering the system and then influence the way this user might interact with the system.

Nevertheless, group awareness information is not handled as context information on Groupware Systems, and inversely, Context-Aware Systems often ignore collaborative aspects involving the user. Even if the first have evolved and are now confronted to pervasive environments, the treatment of group awareness information has not fundamentally changed. Conversely, the later, as noted by [6], have focused mostly on the context of a single user, so the context of multiple users involved in a common endeavor remains unexplored. These systems, in their majority, consider users as individuals, ignoring the effects of the group on the individual's activities.

Works on mobile Groupware System often distinguish group awareness from context information, the latter being used for adaptation purposes, while the former is somehow proposed to the user. On [11] authors proposed to filter group awareness information according the user's context. Even if concepts from group awareness (e.g. group, activities and role) are considered as context information, group awareness information is handled separately. On [21], even if execution context is considered for proposing group awareness widgets, authors discard a pure automatic adaptation, such as in context-aware applications. On [15], context information includes group related information, but it is used for deriving process adaptation, and not proposed to users. Similarly, on [4], traditional group awareness information is analyzed as context information, but the purpose remains making it explicit and guiding the design process, without yet considering physical and environmental influences. Authors on [6] consider the notion of group when conceptualizing the notion of context of use for adaptation purposes. Unfortunately, this conceptualization is not clearly associated with group awareness supply, leaving it to its traditional purposes of helping user's decision making. Even if conceptually some authors are relating context and group awareness concepts [4, 6, 15], these approaches are often limited to modeling issues. Advances on context management and context-aware systems architecture (e.g. [1, 5, 10, 13]) do not seem yet to benefit Groupware Systems architecture. Those remain dealing with both separately: acquisition, modeling, storage and treatment of both are separate, complexifying an architecture that is already enough complex.

Another aspect distinguishes the treatment of context and group awareness information: their dynamicity. Context information is characterized by its dynamicity, evolving with environment changes and user's movements [20]. When managing context information, a system must consider it as something that will evolve potentially quickly [13]. Such dynamicity also affects collaborative aspects of the user's context [15, 17]. As pointed by [17], context in a design work process has a dynamic nature, new events appear and new decisions are taken, modifying its flow. Dynamicity is then part of the notion of context as a whole. However, when considering group awareness mechanisms, this concern is not necessarily a priority, except for mechanisms dealing with workspace awareness (e.g. [3]). These mechanisms use to deal with real time interactions, making the dynamicity of the observed information a key aspect for their success. For other mechanisms, the dynamicity of group awareness information is not a priority. Evolution and dynamicity of group awareness information do not receive the same attention that changes on the execution context.

For us, clearly associating group awareness and context information is assuming that both can be used for decision making and for adaptation purposes. It is assuming that Groupware systems may adapt their behavior according to group awareness and context information in a transparent way (i.e. without an active intervention of the user), and that any context-aware system may consider users not only as individuals. Considering group awareness information as context information is also assuming its dynamicity, assuming that groups and their situation may evolve according members' activities and that dynamicity is a 'first class' characteristic of group awareness information too.

5   Illustration: Distributing Group Awareness Information

In order to illustrate the feasibility of judging group awareness information as context information, let us consider the case of the context distribution, which is defined as the capability to gather and deliver context information to interested entities [2]. Context distribution mechanisms are necessary to organize the distribution of context information, since the success of a context-aware system depends on the availability of this information, often disseminated over the network [20]. Similarly, Groupware systems must also consider the distribution of group awareness information over the network, making it available on each node used by a group member. Considering group awareness as context information allows considering a single distribution mechanism for both, which contributes to reduce the complexity of Groupware systems, notably mobile and context-aware ones, which are confronted to the complexity of collaborative aspects and of context management tasks.

Let us consider the context distribution mechanism proposed by [20]. This context-based grouping mechanism organizes groups of peers based on a criteria set and a dissemination set (i.e. which information can be shared in the group). A context group G_D is defined as follows [20]:

$$G_D = <C_D, I_D>,$$

where C_D is the criteria set, i.e. set of context elements determining the group, represented in a query according the context model; and I_D is the dissemination set, representing the context information to be shared among group members.

These groups can be statically predefined or discovered based on contextual characteristics shared among members of the group [20]. The group definition, called template, remains stable over the time. However, since it relies on context information, it is naturally dynamic. This template is used to instantiate a group: the query representing the group criteria is processed with the current values of the corresponding context elements forming a concrete contextual group. As context changes, values corresponding to the group criteria are updated, changing the group composition since members may leave the group instance and integrate another one. Moreover, each group member constantly updates other members about new values on its dissemination set, keeping them updated about context changes on this set.

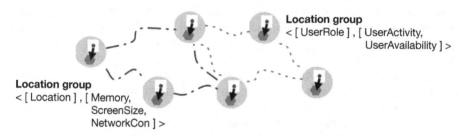

Fig. 1. Example of two group templates for context distribution inspired by [20].

The group can be seen as a neighborhood [20] that is semantically defined by the application: nodes in the same network, nodes in the same location, nodes executing over similar devices, nodes acting on behalf of users playing a given role, etc. For instance, on Fig. 1, two groups are defined, one based on the location (devices sharing the same location), and another based on the notion of role (users sharing the same role). On the first group, information concerning the execution context is shared among group members, while on the second, information about the user's activities is shared. The first group can be used in GDSS, such as [21], for adapting application deployment, using nodes with better interaction conditions (more available memory, better screen size and network connection). The second concerns availability awareness, informing users about the availability and the activity of nearby colleagues playing a similar role. This offers interesting clues for opportunistic interaction among group members, useful, for instance, on supporting maintenance tasks, such as mentioned on [15].

By considering group awareness information as context information, this first may benefit from context management. Group awareness information contributes to context data, as any other source of context information, and is distributed using the same context distribution mechanism. No extra mechanism for distributing group awareness information is needed. Moreover, the same information can be used for adaptation purposes or for helping decision making, in a very homogenous way.

6 Conclusions and Perspectives

On this position paper, we advocated that group awareness information should be considered as context information and handled using similar mechanisms. We discussed similarities between these concepts, which lead us to consider that group awareness as context information about the group and its status. We also discussed the differences on their treatment and illustrated this idea through a single context distribution mechanism distributing both for different purposes (adaptation as well as decision making).

In our opinion, the convergence between group awareness and context information is needed for better supporting Information Systems (IS) of tomorrow. With the growing evolution of information technologies such as smartphones, network connections or IoT, Information Systems are not anymore limited to the boundaries of their organization, integrating the actors' mobility and the physical environment. They are evolving into Pervasive Information Systems (PIS) [16], in which context-aware applications and groupware systems will play a key role. More than never collaboration should be supported appropriately, considering moving and dynamic environments. Adaptation to this changing environment and supporting group activities are essential for tomorrow's organizations. Information Systems themselves should become more proactive and adapted to its users and their needs. For successful Pervasive Information Systems, context-awareness is necessary, and in particular context-aware groupware applications, capable of adapting their behavior to any changes on the user or group context. This means applications that are able to consider group awareness information as part the user's context. Actors on any modern organization cannot be considered anymore only as individuals, they must be considered as part of the organization. Integrating the concepts of group awareness and context information as a single concept that must be handled transparently and homogeneously on any Information Systems is a key aspect for successfully transforming these systems on Pervasive Information Systems.

References

1. Baldaulf, M., Dustdar, S., Rosenberg, S.: A survey on context-aware systems. Int. J. Ad Hoc Ubiquit. Comput. **2**(4), 263–277 (2007). (91-S46)
2. Bellavista, P., Corradi, A., Fanelli, M., Foschini, L.: A survey of context data distribution for mobile ubiquitous systems. ACM Comput. Surv. **45**, 1–49 (2013)
3. Blichmann, G., Meißner, K.: Customizing workspace awareness by non-programmers. In: ACM SIGCHI Symposium on Engineering Interactive Computing Systems, pp. 123–128 (2017)
4. Borges, M.R.S., Brézillon, P., Pino, J.A., Pomerol, J.C.: Groupware system design and the context concept. In: Shen, W., Lin, Z., Barthès, J.-P.A., Li, T. (eds.) CSCWD 2004. LNCS, vol. 3168, pp. 45–54. Springer, Heidelberg (2005). https://doi.org/10.1007/11568421_5
5. Da, K., Roose, P., Dalmau, M., Nevado, J., Karchoud, R.: Kali2Much: a context middleware for autonomic adaptation-driven platform. In: 1st Workshop on Middleware for Context-Aware Applications in the IoT (M4IoT@Middleware 2014), pp. 25–30 (2014)
6. Decouchant, D., Mendoza, S., Sanchez, G., Rodrigues, J.: Adapting groupware systems to changes in the collaborator's context of use. Expert Syst. App. **40**, 4446–4462 (2013)
7. Dey, A.: Understanding and using context. Pers. Ubiquit. Comput. **5**(1), 4–7 (2001)
8. Dourish, P., Bellotti, V.: Awareness and coordination in shared workspaces. In: ACM Conference on Computer-Supported Cooperative Work, pp. 107–114 (1992)
9. Espinosa, A., Cadiz, J., Rico-Gutierrez, L., Kraut, R., Scherlis, W., Lautenbacher, G.: Coming to the wrong decision quickly: why awareness tools must be matched with appropriate tasks. In: CHI Letters, CHI 2000, vol. 2, no. 1, pp. 392–399 (2000)
10. Floch, J., et al.: Playing MUSIC: building context-aware and self-adaptive mobile applications. Softw. Pract. Exp. **43**(3), 359–388 (2013)
11. Kirsch-Pinheiro, M., Gensel, J., Martin, H.: Representing context for an adaptative awareness mechanism. In: de Vreede, G.-J., Guerrero, L.A., Marín Raventós, G. (eds.) CRIWG 2004. LNCS, vol. 3198, pp. 339–348. Springer, Heidelberg (2004). https://doi.org/10.1007/978-3-540-30112-7_28
12. Kirsch-Pinheiro, M., Lima, J., Borges, M.: A framework for awareness support in groupware systems. Comput. Ind. **52**(1), 47–57 (2003)
13. Kirsch-Pinheiro, M., Souveyet, C.: Supporting context on software applications: a survey on context engineering. Modeling and Using Context, ISTE Openscience (2018)
14. Kirsh, D.: The context of work. Hum. Comput. Interact. **13**(2–4), 305–322 (2001)
15. Knoll, S.W., Lukosch, S.G.: Context and collaborative work: a context-sensitive intervention approach for collaboration in dynamic environment. In: Brézillon, P., Gonzalez, A.J. (eds.) Context in Computing, pp. 327–341. Springer, New York (2014). https://doi.org/10.1007/978-1-4939-1887-4_21
16. Najar, S., Kirsch-Pinheiro, M., Souveyet, C.: Service discovery and prediction on pervasive information system. J. Ambient Intell. Hum. Comput. **6**(4), 407–423 (2015)
17. Nunes, V.T., Santoro, F.M., Borges, M.: Capturing context about group design processes. In: Proceedings of the 11th International Conference on Computer Supported Cooperative Work in Design, CSCWD 2007, Melbourne, Australia, 26–28 April 2007
18. Preguiça, N., Martins, J.L., Domingues, H., Duarte, S.: Data management support for asynchronous groupware. In: ACM Conference on Computer-Supported Cooperative Work, pp. 69–78 (2000)
19. Schmidt, K.: The problem with 'awareness': introductory remarks on 'awareness in CSCW'. Comput. Support. Coop. Work **11**(3–4), 285–298 (2002)

20. Vanrompay, Y., Pinheiro, M.K., Mustapha, N.B., Aufaure, M.-A.: Context-based group-ing and recommendation in MANETs. In: Kolomvatsos, K., Anagnostopoulos, C., Hadjiefthymiades, S. (eds.) Intelligent Technologies and Techniques for Pervasive Computing, pp. 157–178. IGI Global (2013)

21. Wang, W., Reani, M.: The rise of mobile computing for group decision support systems: a comparative evaluation of mobile and desktop. Int. J. Hum. Comput. Stud. **104**, 16–35 (2017)

Relations Between Actions Performed by Users and Their Engagement

Ana Paula O. Bertholdo[1]([⊠]), Claudia de O. Melo[2],
Artur S. Rozestraten[3], and Marco Aurelio Gerosa[1,4]

[1] Department of Computer Science, University of Sao Paulo,
São Paulo, Brazil
`ana@ime.usp.br, Marco.Gerosa@nau.edu`
[2] Department of Computer Science, University of Brasilia, Brasília, Brazil
`claudiam@unb.br`
[3] Faculty of Architecture and Urbanism, University of Sao Paulo,
São Paulo, Brazil
`artur.rozestraten@usp.br`
[4] Northern Arizona University, Flagstaff, USA

Abstract. Although Galleries, Libraries, Archives, and Museums (GLAMs) increasingly encourage users to assist in the curation of online collections through open collaboration systems, measuring users' engagement in these systems is a dynamic and complex challenge. We analyzed 18 user's actions over 20 days according to the User Engagement Scale (UES) and based on Maximal Repeating Patterns (MRPs) and correlations between user interaction elements and dimensions of user engagement (focused attention, perceived usability, aesthetics, and reward). Our results show differences in usage tactics for users with high, medium, and low scores from UES, and monotonically increasing moderate correlations between perceived usability scores and game design elements. Additionally, we found that the longer the mean time interval between two consecutive user actions during a usage period lasted, the higher the UES score was. These results help to understand what influences user engagement, isolating the effects of user interaction elements.

Keywords: User engagement · User action · User interaction element
Gamification · UES · MRP · Open collaboration community · GLAM

1 Introduction

Galleries, Libraries, Archives, and Museums (or GLAMs) have been struggling to engage users in the selection, cataloging, contextualization, and curation of collections [20, 26] through crowdsourcing in open collaboration systems [26]. This new mode of interaction surpasses passive access and can lead to a deeper level of engagement with collections [15, 26].[1] Since user participation is key to success in this context [26], GLAMs need to create and maintain an open collaboration system that fosters a sense

---

[1] This research is part of the INCT of the Future Internet for Smart Cities funded by CNPq, proc. 465446/2014-0, CAPES proc. 88887.136422/2017-00, and FAPESP, proc. 2014/50937-1.

A. Rodrigues et al. (Eds.): CRIWG 2018, LNCS 11001, pp. 207–222, 2018.
https://doi.org/10.1007/978-3-319-99504-5_17

of community around artifacts [25]. Put simply, communities that support open collaboration [9] must engage people [17]. As users become engaged, certain behaviors should increase, such as click frequency [7]. However, with search actions, which are common in GLAMs, there is evidence that the most engaged users have the least amount of search interaction [24] and exhibit more search behaviors when they are frustrated [7, 8, 24]. It is necessary to distinguish users' recurring actions in terms of whether they cause engagement or frustration. Furthermore, Lalmas *et al.* [19] report that in user engagement measurement there is "less emphasis on the role of the task (i.e., what the user is doing), device (desktop versus mobile), and context (e.g., quickly checking something or browsing leisurely), (...) and more work is needed to see how measures from one type of approaches align with that of another one."

Our goal is to analyze the relation between users' recurring actions, based on Maximal Repeating Patterns (MRPs) and the User Engagement Scale (UES), to understand whether recurring actions are related to higher engagement in an online open collaboration community in the context of GLAMs. We begin by introducing background about UES and theories about user attention and task reaction time. Next, we present related work in the context of MRPs and describe the context of the current study, the research questions, and the method. Lastly, we show our results, summarize our findings, and discuss the limitations and implications of this work.

2 Background and Related Work

User engagement is "a quality of user experience characterized by the depth of an actor's investment when interacting with a digital system" [27]. O'Brien and Toms [25] consider engagement as a process with four distinct stages: point of engagement, period of sustained engagement, disengagement, and reengagement. This process is characterized by attributes of engagement from the user, system, and user-system interaction.

O'Brien *et al.* define the **User Engagement Scale (UES)** [25, 28] as a tool to measure user engagement. The original UES consists of 31-items to measure six dimensions of engagement. Recent research from O'Brien *et al.* [28] proposed a shorter version with 12 items to measure a four-factor structure: focused attention (FA), perceived usability (PU), aesthetic appeal (AE), and reward (RW). UES can be analyzed by subscales or dimensions or aggregated as an overall engagement score.

Participants' scores on each of the UES subscales can be calculated by summing individual responses to items within each subscale and dividing this total by the number of items. Total scores for the UES are calculated by adding the averages of each subscale and dividing by the number of subscales. The scores can be then divided according to percentiles to create three groups (low, medium, and high) based on the median [24]. Table 1 summarizes the self-reported engagement metrics according to the shorter version of the UES [28].

User actions relate to user interaction elements. Categorizing user actions according to accessed user interaction elements can help us to understand user engagement. According to Harnad [12], "cognition is categorization;" consequently, "assigning terms to categories plays a major role in communication" [38]. There are many user interaction elements according to the domain of a software system. We focus on user

Table 1. Self-reported engagement metrics from the shorter version of the UES [28].

Engagement metric	Description
Focused attention (FA)	Refers to feelings absorbed in the interaction and losing track of time
Perceived usability (PU)	Refers to negative effect experienced as a result of the interaction and the degree of control and effort expended
Aesthetic appeal (AE)	Refers to the attractiveness and visual appeal of the interface
Reward (RW)	Refers to endurability (or the overall success of the interaction), novelty, and felt involvement
UES total score	Overall self-reported engagement score

interaction elements related to online open collaboration communities, specifically collaborative and functional elements. Since gamification - the use of game design elements in non-game contexts [5] - has been defined as a way to foster greater user engagement in online communities [2], our study analyzes game design elements [5]. Table 2 provides a summary of the definition of each user interaction element we address in this study.

Table 2. Definition of each user interaction element addressed in this study.

User interaction elements	Definition
Game design elements (gamification)	Elements that belongs to one of the five levels of the game design elements [5]
Collaborative elements (collaboration)	Elements that give support for collaboration [10, 11]
Functional elements	Elements related to functional requirements [29]

As defined by Deterding *et al.* [5], game design elements consider: (1) game interface design patterns, (2) game design patterns and mechanics, (3) game design principles and heuristics, (4) game models, and (5) game design methods. As argued by Fuks *et al.* [10], collaborative elements can be related to one of the following dimensions: (1) communication, (2) coordination, and (3) cooperation (3C collaboration Model). Finally, a functional requirement specifies functions that systems must be able to perform [29]. In our study, game design and collaborative elements are not defined by functional elements, although they have functional requirements. For game design elements, this study only considers elements from "game interface design patterns."

2.1 User Attention, Reaction Time to Tasks, and Usage Tactics

According to Manly and Robertson [21], "action doesn't necessarily stop when our mind is elsewhere." Theorists have investigated people's attentional lapse over decades

[21, 22, 30]. The Sustained Attention to Response Test (SART) [21] was designed to measure attentional lapses; it is a laboratory test in which participants view a computer monitor and are tasked to press a response key after each presentation, except for a "no-go digit," to which no response should be performed. Performance on SART was predictive of action slips and everyday attentional failures in participants [21].

Smallwood *et al.* [33] reported task engagement and disengagement during the SART. They performed experiments to investigate the relationship between subjective experience and attention lapses. The results suggest that during sustained attention people experience task unrelated thought (TUT), which corresponds to an absent-minded disengagement from the task [33, 34]. TUT [34] and attentional lapses are attributed to situations of boredom and worry [30, 33]. In the context of SART and under conditions of low target probability, shorter reaction times were related to more significant distraction and insensitivity to the task. Robertson *et al.* [30] support this claim when reporting that the "oops" phe- nomenon associated with errors suggests that error detection tends to redirect attention towards the task, resulting in slower emer- gence of the alternative or correct answer.

On a task that is repetitive in nature, an engaged user's thinking usually strays from information visible in the current environment, and in this con- text, the user's attention becomes more focused on the task [33]. Performance is crucially determined by the duration of time over which attention must be maintained on one's actions [22]. Maximal Repeating Patterns (MRPs) are used to extract recurring user action patterns (or usage tactics) from a user session transcript [13]. MRPs identify the longest string of actions that is repeated at least once in the entire data set [32]. According to Siochi [32], a repeating pattern is a substring that occurs at more than one position in a string. Substrings of longer patterns are also considered MRPs if they occur independently. MRPs may also overlap, as in "abcabcabc," where "abcabc" is the MRP.

In the context of a video retrieval system, Wildemuth *et al.* [37] collected users' search tactics to understand how people search databases for videos, and how the medium of the object can influence the search behaviors. Each search move was coded, and the data was examined for MRPs. Tactics were mainly characterized by the addition of concepts, and frequent display and browsing of the search results. A pre- vious study by Wildemuth [36] found that the search tactics changed over time as the participants' domain knowledge changed. Edwards and Kelly [7] examined the dif- ferences in the search behaviors and physiological characteristics of people who were engaged or frustrated during searches. Users engaged more with search results for tasks they found interesting. Their results support the idea that task interest is an important component of engagement. The authors demonstrated that increased search behavior was a stronger indicator of frustration than interest.

In the context of usability evaluations, analyzing maximum repeating pat- terns might reveal interesting information on user interface usability [13]. Several researchers have used MRPs in the context of search tactics [3, 36, 37]. A search tactic comprises several individual moves, where a move is a single step in executing a search tactic, such as "deleting a concept to increase the size of the result set" [37]. In this study, we applied MRPs to examine users' usage tactics. Compared to search tactics, **usage tactics** comprise one or more individual moves, which involve **user recurring**

actions in general. Additionally, we analyzed correlations between user actions and user engagement collected through users' self-reports according to the UES scale.

3   Research Method

This study was conducted in the context of the Arquigrafia online community. Arquigrafia is a public, nonprofit digital collaborative community dedicated to disseminating architectural images, with special attention to Brazilian architecture (www. arquigrafia.org.br). The main objective of the community is to contribute to the teaching, research, and diffusion of architectural and urban culture by promoting collaborative interactions among people and institutions. Arquigrafia is still small and needs to foster a community around architecture images and information. Participants include professional architects, architecture and urbanism students, architecture and urbanism professors, librarians, library science students, and professional photographers; whose ages range between 20–68 years old; and of which 61.11% are male (11 out of 18).

We designed this study as a correlational research, which aims to discover the existence of a relationship, association, or interdependence between two or more aspects of a situation [18]. This study comprises an analysis from another point of view for an experiment described in [1]. In the current study, our goal was to understand the relationship between users' actions and their engagement for 18 users that used the system for 20 days (November 16, 2017 to December 5, 2017) and answered an online questionnaire based on the **User Engagement Scale (UES)** [25, 28], described in Sect. 2.

The online questionnaire was applied according to a UES-translated version for Portuguese. Users actions were collected from logs inserted in the system or user session transcripts, which represent the time-ordered sequence of actions users performed [32]. We then investigated what user actions and usage tactics - one or more user recurring actions - contributed to high, medium, and low user engagement, as defined in Sect. 2. We also analyzed whether there are correlations between the actions performed by each group and their score in the UES scale. We decomposed user actions according to user interaction elements, defined in Sect. 2.

Therefore, each user action was classified by the number of collaborative, functional, and game design elements accessed by 18 users when performing the actions. This number was correlated to UES. We analyzed reaction time [22, 30, 33] in the context of Arquigrafia as the interval between two consecutive actions, since the user performed an action, received a response from the system, and performed another action as a reaction to system response. In this context, we answer the following research questions:

RQI. How do different usage tactics relate to high, medium, and low user engagement?
RQII. How do users' level of engagement relate to their reaction times?
RQIII. Are the user interaction elements correlated to users' engagement?

3.1   Data Preparation and Analysis

To evaluate the reliability of the UES, we calculated Cronbach's alpha. The goal was to examine the internal consistency of subscales based on DeVellis's guidelines (0.7–0.9 is optimal) [6]. As shown in Table 3, the UES was highly reliable. Initially, 12 items were considered in the UES. After the analysis of Cronbach's alpha, one item was dismissed to improve the value of Cronbach's alpha for the AE (from 0.65 to 0.84) subscale.

Table 3. Cronbach's alpha and descriptive statistics of UES.

UES subscales	N items	Mean	Std.	Alpha
Focused attention (FA)	3	2.7	1.2	0.95
Perceived usability (PU)	3	3.7	0.89	0.86
Aesthetic appeal (AE)	2	3.6	0.61	0.84
Reward (RW)	3	4	0.83	0.91
Total Engagement	11	3.5	0.74	0.92

Table 4 presents users' actions classified according to functional, game design, and collaborative elements. The research was applied in a naturalistic setting. Although there are other user interaction elements available in the system, the focus was on the elements accessed by users. Therefore, the number of each element described in Table 4 refers to how many user interaction elements of each type were effectively involved in user interaction with the system. The number of collaborative and game design elements accessed was much smaller than the number of functional elements accessed, which demonstrates the challenge of engaging users to collaborate in GLAMs, in which users consume information rather than collaborate to produce it.

Table 4. Users actions classified by the user interaction element (functional, game design, or collaborative).

User interaction elements	Action	High n	Medium n	Low n
Functional elements	Home page	7	18	33
	Image searching	27	80	6
	Download	82	36	0
	User selection	4	5	5
	User edition	1	1	1
	Access to similar evaluations	0	0	2
	Image selection (institution)	126	62	6
	Image selection (no progress bar)	0	1	15
	Logout	1	4	4

(continued)

Table 4. (*continued*)

User interaction elements	Action	High n	Medium n	Low n
Collaborative elements	Image evaluation	0	0	2
	User following	0	1	1
	Chat	0	1	0
	Access to upload	1	0	0
	Access to chat page	0	0	1
	Access to public albuns creation	0	1	0
	Sharing by Facebook	0	0	1
	Sharing by Google+	3	0	0
	Access to data review (no points)	0	0	3
	Completed data review	0	0	1
Game design elements	Image selection (progress bar view)	4	1	5
	Access to data review (points view)	0	0	1
Total	Functional elements	248 (96.88%)	207 (98.1%)	72 (82.76%)
	Collaborative elements	4 (1.56%)	3 (1.42%)	9 (10.34%)
	Game design elements	4 (1.56%)	1 (0.47%)	6 (6.9%)
	All user interaction elements accessed	256	211	87

The analysis of MRPs was performed by manually looking for the MRPs in each group of users according to UES scores (low, medium, and high), and by comparing usage tactics based on MRPs from different user groups. The Shapiro-Wilk normality test rejected the hypothesis that UES scores and amount of user interaction elements for each user come from a normal population. Therefore, we used the Spearman's rank correlation coefficient to measure the strength of the relationship between the number of each user interaction element and each one of 4 subscales, as well as the overall score from UES; the Kruskal-Wallis rank sum test was used to compare user interaction elements from high-UES-score, medium-UES-score, and low-UES-score groups. To define an effect size for this comparison, the Epsilon-squared was measured. We used guidelines to interpret Spearman's correlation coefficient [14, 23] and effect sizes [4, 16].

4   Results

4.1   How Do Different Usage Tactics Relate to High, Medium, and Low User Engagement? (RQI)

Out of the 18 participants, 6, 7, and 5 participants are in low-UES-score, medium-UES-score, and high-UES-score groups, respectively. High-UES-score users had scores above 4.02; medium-UES-score users had scores between 3.27 and 4.02, and low-

UES-score users had scores below 3.27. The minimum overall UES score was 1.72, and the maximum score was 4.45. The 5-item Likert-scale score was used, so the highest overall score for any subscale was 5. Figure 1 presents the main usage tactics based on MRPs during the analyzed period for each group.

User recurring actions were represented by action name multiplied by (*) the number of consecutive invocations. The number of MRPs for each group was represented by n(High), n(Medium), and n(Low). For example, the MRP "A" comprises three consecutive invocations of the action download, (i.e., download * 3), and the number of MRPs "A" found for high-UES-score users is 21, and for medium and low UES-score users, the MRP "A" was not found.

For high score users, there was a predominance of single recurring actions, especially actions of image selection and download from the institutional col- lection. This behavior occurred because users first selected images and then downloaded them. For medium score users, there was a predominance of the usage tactic of image search, image selection from the institutional collection, and download, and single recurring actions of image search and image selection that were not followed by downloading. For low score users, the usage tactics of accessing the homepage and selecting an image from the institutional collection were most recurrent.

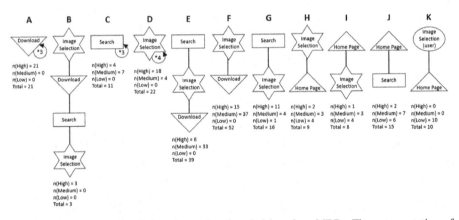

Fig. 1. Main usage tactics during the analyzed period based on MRPs. The representation of tactics is based on Wildemuth *et al.* [37].

Figure 1 distinguishes image selection and image selection (user); the first is the image selection from the institutional collection, and the second is the image selection from private users' collections. The last can be presented with or without progress bar view. The progress bar is a game design element intended to help users check the completeness of the image data, according to a previous experiment described in [1]. For low-UES-score users, the action of image selection (without progress bar view) was the second most accessed, after only access to the homepage. These actions are presented in usage tactic K. In summary, usage tactics differed among groups of users with high, medium, and low user engagement, but involved the same group of actions: accessing the homepage, image searching, downloading, and image selecting. These actions are related to functional elements.

4.2 How Do Users' Level of Engagement Relate to Their Reaction Time? (RQII)

Consecutive actions from low-UES-score users occurred in an interval between 0 and 49 s, with one user (outlier) reaching 8 min and 17 s. The mean was 28 s with a standard deviation of 35 s. For medium-UES-score users, consecutive actions occurred in an interval between 0 and 6 min and 49 s, with one user reaching 8 min. The mean was 1 min and 15 s with a standard deviation of 2 min and 06 s. For high-UES-score users, consecutive actions occurred in an interval between 0 and 37 min and 18 s. The mean was 7 min and 37 s with a standard deviation of 12 min and 58 s. Therefore, in this study with 18 users, the longer the mean time interval between two consecutive actions (i.e., user reaction time) during a usage period, the higher the user's UES score.

4.3 Are the User Interaction Elements Correlated to Users' Engagement? (RQIII)

Table 5 presents the correlation between the number of user interaction elements accessed by 18 users and the user's engagement according to Spearman's rank correlation rho. Table 6 presents the same correlation classified by high, medium, and low scores based on UES. The main results can be summarized as follows:

1. **A monotonically increasing moderate correlation between the number of game design elements in general and the perceived usability (PU) score** (see Table 5). The PU scores varied between 1.66 and 5 for users who have not accessed game design elements (mean 3.48, sd 0.49); whereas PU scores varied between 3.66 and 5 for users who accessed game design elements (mean 4.39, sd 0.88). Ten actions (90.9%) were related to the progress bar element, and only one action was related to the points view.

Table 5. Correlations between user interaction elements and the user's engagement (Spearman's rank correlation rho).

UES score	Functional - rho (p)	Collaborative - rho (p)	Game design - rho	(p)
Overall	0.17 (0.4993)	−0.02 (0.9185)	0.28 (0.2581)	
FA	0.20 (0.403)	−0.16 (0.5024)	0.18 (0.4531)	
PU	−0.009 (0.9687)	0.30 (0.2125)	**0.55 (0.01733)**	
AE	−0.025 (0.9203)	0.28 (0.2494)	0.016 (0.9483)	
RW	0.29 (0.234)	0.15 (0.526)	0.37 (0.1199)	

Table 6. Correlations between user interaction elements and the user's engagement classified by High, Medium, and Low scores (Spearman's rank correlation rho).

User interaction elements	Score	UES rho (p)	FA rho (p)	PU rho (p)	AE rho (p)	RW rho (p)
Functional	High	0.44 (0.4502)	0.3 (0.6833)	−0.66 (0.2189)	0.35 (0.5594)	0 (1)
	Medium	−0.19 (0.6701)	0.13 (0.7752)	−0.30 (0.5007)	**−0.79** **(0.03432)**	0.31 (0.4869)
	Low	0.04 (0.9339)	−0.12 (0.8131)	0.08 (0.8699)	−0.31 (0.5452)	0.36 (0.4734)
Collaborative	High	0.12 (0.8413)	−0.44 (0.4502)	0.34 (0.5707)	0.39 (0.5101)	0.39 (0.5101)
	Medium	−0.15 (0.7362)	0 (1)	−0.09 (0.8374)	0.39 (0.3813)	−0.42 (0.3481)
	Low	0.73 (0.09312)	0.09 (0.8529)	0.75 (0.08014)	0.37 (0.4636)	**0.95** **(0.00301)**
Game Design	High	0.17 (0.7761)	0.21 (0.7336)	0.10 (0.8626)	−0.18 (0.7641)	−0.18 (0.7641)
	Medium	−0.61 (0.1392)	**−0.76** **(0.04566)**	0 (1)	−0.64 (0.1174)	0 (1)
	Low	0.53 (0.278)	−0.42 (0.4018)	0.65 (0.1583)	0.53 (0.2694)	0.39 (0.4339)

2. **A monotonically decreasing strong correlation between the number of Functional elements from medium score users and the aesthetic appeal (AE) score** (see Table 6). From 7 users with medium scores from overall UES, 5 users who accessed few functional elements (at most n = 9) classified with 4 as their AE score; and 2 users that accessed 48 and 134 functional elements, respectively, classified with 3.5 as their AE score. For both users, there were few downloads when compared to the number of image searches and selections. This result indicates that search results were unsatisfactory or that they faced difficulties with the search process.

3. **A monotonically increasing very strong correlation between the number of collaborative elements from low score users and the reward (RW) score** (see Table 6). From 6 users with low score from overall UES, highest RW scores users accessed collaborative elements (with RW scores of 3.33, 4, and 4.33). For users who did not access collaborative elements, scores varied between 2 and 3.

4. **A monotonically decreasing strong correlation between the number of game design elements from medium score users and the focused attention (FA) score** (see Table 6). Out of the 7 users with medium score from overall UES, the only user who accessed game design elements was the one with the lower score for FA (2.33).

Figure 2 presents results for the Kruskal Test among functional, collaborative, and game design elements, respectively, classified by high, low, and medium scores from overall UES. Although Fig. 2 does not present statistically significant results, it helps to understand that the number of users who accessed each user interaction element differed between groups.

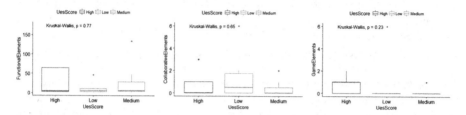

Fig. 2. Kruskal test for functional, collaborative, and game design elements, comparing high, medium, and low scores from UES.

Table 7. Effect sizes for functional, collaborative, and game design elements compared according to high, medium, and low scores from UES.

User interaction elements	Kruskal-Wallis chi-squared	Epsilon-squared
Functional	0.51182 (p = 0.77)	0.0301
Collaborative	0.84853 (p = 0.65)	0.0499
Game design	2.9423 (p = 0.23)	0.173

Table 7 presents Epsilon-squared effect sizes for the Kruskal Test with high, medium, and low scores from overall UES for each user interaction element. Epsilon-squared presented relations of 0.03, 0.04, and 0.17 in the UES overall score for functional, collaborative, and game design elements, respectively. Only game design elements present large effect sizes, according to the guidelines [4, 16]. Functional and collaborative elements show small effect sizes. However, the Kruskal Test did not present statistically significant results, which indicates the need to analyze a higher sample size because there are indications of strong effects between the most-accessed game design element (Progress Bar) and the user's UES score.

5 Discussion

5.1 Main MRPs, Reaction Times and Their Meanings

Siochi [32] classified Type 1 MRPs, i.e., consecutive invocations of the same command, as a behavior that may indicate that a user needs to perform the same command on several objects, or that the user is "fine-tuning" a single object. In line with Siochi's studies, we found MRPs consisting of consecutive invocations of the same action or Type 1 MRP. Main consecutive actions were: image searching, downloading, and image selection from the institutional collection. Information consumption behavior (passive participation) is the most common behavior in the context of GLAMs.

A sequence of image searches indicates that users reformulated their keywords several times before a relevant result appeared. A series of downloads that occurred after a sequence of actions of image selection from the institutional collection indicates that users opened many tabs, one for each selected image, and then returned to each image for their analyses and the decision to download images. Only for high-UES-score users were there consecutive sequences of actions of download after actions of image selection from the institutional collection.

However, a sequence of image searches occurred for high and medium-UES-score users, or a possible difficulty to find an object. Finding an interesting image to download after fine-tuning produced a positive impression, which is presented by users for high-UES-score. The opposite occurred with medium-UES-score users, for whom fine-tuning resulted in downloading few of the selected images. This result aligns with previous studies [7], wherein participants presented with poor result quality submitted more queries and saved fewer documents.

Edwards and Kelly [7] reported a number of significant differences in participant search behaviors based on the quality of search results. Studies from Smallwood *et al.* [33], described in Sect. 2.1, can explain why Type 1 MRPs were not found for low-UES-score users. Consecutive invocations of the same MRP represent a level of attention from users to maintain the same response.

Additionally, most MRPs from low-UES-score users involved accessing the homepage. This behavior can indicate that: (1) users in this group did not understand how the system worked, (2) they were exploring the system without a specific goal, or (3) they were concurrently executing other tasks. The first case can indicate a usability problem, while the second can indicate a lack of prior motivation to use the system, in which users tried to understand what value the system might have for them. The third case can indicate Task Unrelated Thought (TUT) [34]. TUT and attentional lapses are attributed to situations of boredom and worry [30, 33]. This may be why low-UES-score users self-reported their engagement as low and why users in this group over-looked other options for executing actions, which led them to return to the homepage.

The mean time between two consecutive actions differed among groups. Although there were users in all groups with similar time intervals between successive actions (i.e., reaction time), significant differences appeared in the mean time between actions. We found as the mean time interval between two consecutive actions during a usage period increased, so did the higher the user's score in the UES. This behavior is in accordance to the literature [30, 33].

In the context of Arquigrafia, we did not find periods of high search activity for low-UES-score users. This behavior was found only for high and medium-UES-score users. Between these two, high-UES-score users presented the lowest browsing times when compared to medium-UES-score users. However, the time of each user session and the reaction time were higher for high-UES-score users. This behavior was in line with results from the literature [22, 33].

5.2   Relations Among User Interaction Element and the UES

Spearman's rank correlation presented statistically significant results, varying from moderate to very strong correlations. By decomposing the accessed user interaction elements and correlating them with UES, there is a statistically significant positive relationship between PU and the number of game elements accessed. This behavior may have occurred because the progress bar only presents the information and does not allow the user to perform an active action. Therefore, it is worth distinguishing between elements that can passively influence users' actions and those that allow them to act.

The monotonically decreasing strong correlation between the number of functional elements from Medium score users and the AE score could be explained by the frustration in locating images in the desired subject, which may have led the user to have a lower aesthetic quality impression in this group. The monotonically increasing very strong correlation between the number of collaborative elements from low score users and the RW score could indicate that collaborative elements did not influence the lowest UES score.

5.3   Limitations

The limitations of this study derive from the number of users (n = 18) who answered the questionnaire, which resulted in 5 High-UES-Score users, 7 Medium-UES-Score users, and 6 Low-UES-Score users. However, the study was performed in a naturalistic configuration in a system with engagement problems, allowing for evaluation of actual use rather than a simulated laboratory environment. The study was short-term and one-off in nature [31]. One-off studies need to be replicated and comparative and longitudinal designs employed to draw stronger, more generalizable conclusions.

5.4   Implications for Future Studies

To understand the effects of a system intervention, it is necessary to evaluate which actions users accessed and how they correlate with subjective and objective engagement measures. The effects of one user interaction element can be compared to the effects of others. It is necessary to compare effects obtained during access to a given element and to a set of elements to evaluate whether the element alone or the interaction of a set of elements produced greater engagement. In this case, what are the involved user interaction elements?

By classifying user interaction elements as game design or collaborative elements, we intended to evaluate, respectively, the effect of gamification or collaboration on user engagement. In future studies, the analysis of user actions can be decomposed, for example, by correlating between characteristics from collaboration - or user interaction elements related to communication, coordination, and cooperation - and each dimension of user engagement. The same behavior can be performed for game design elements and functional elements, i.e., decomposing them to specific characteristics of each user interaction element. The benefit of this decomposition is that it isolates the effects of a system intervention.

Frustration is a function not only of the current interaction but of the previous state of frustration [8]. This behavior may imply that users who experienced frustration in a system during previous access are prone to a frustrating experience in new accesses. Future studies can analyze the correlation between each user action and each dimension of engagement, distinguishing actions from newcomers and existing users. For the latter, researchers can compare actions from previous access to current access to better understand users' reported engagement or frustration. From these results, researchers can design appropriate support for newcomers [35].

6 Conclusions

Our findings revealed that the recurring user actions set combined with the mean reaction time can inform user engagement more than the frequency of actions alone. User actions can be active, such as performing image evaluations or uploads, or passive, such as performing searches or downloads. Engaged users contribute to the system community (active access) and/or to meeting their own goals (passive access). Both are guided by a specific goal that implies a pre-existing motivation, reinforcing the idea that goal-oriented motivation guides engagement more than the exploitation of the system without specific goals, which may explain why a high amount of repeated actions do not indicate that the users were engaged when they performed them.

Additionally, results show differences in usage tactics and in the distribution of access to each user interaction element for users with high, medium, and low UES scores. Functional elements contributed to greater engagement for users with high UES scores, and monotonically increasing moderate correlations were found between perceived usability score and game design elements.

Our results are useful for further analyses of user actions to better understand what determines user engagement and to isolate the effects of each user interaction element.

Acknowledgments. We would like to thank to Dr. Heather L. OBrien from iSchool, University of British Columbia, for her valuable inputs on this study.

References

1. Bertholdo, A.P.O., Melo, C.D.O., Rozestraten, A.S., Gerosa, M.A., O'Brien, H.L.: User engagement in an open collaboration community after the insertion of a game design element: an online field experiment. In: Proceeding of the 24th Americas Conference on Information Systems (AMCIS 2018) (2018)
2. Bista, S.K., Nepal, S., Colineau, N., Paris, C.: Using gamification in an online community. In: 2012 8th International Conference on Collaborative Computing: Networking, Applications and Worksharing (CollaborateCom), pp. 611–618. IEEE (2012)
3. Bron, M., Van Gorp, J., Nack, F., de Rijke, M., Vishneuski, A., de Leeuw, S.: A subjunctive exploratory search interface to support media studies researchers. In: Proceedings of the 35th International ACM SIGIR Conference on Research and Development in Information Retrieval, pp. 425–434. ACM (2012)
4. Cohen, J.: Statistical Power Analysis for the Behavioral Sciences, 2nd edn. Academic Press, New york (1988)
5. Deterding, S., Dixon, D., Khaled, R., Nacke, L.: From game design elements to gamefulness: defining gamification. In: Proceedings of the 15th International Academic MindTrek Conference: Envisioning Future Media Environments, pp. 9–15. ACM (2011)

6. DeVellis, R.F.: Scale Development: Theory and Applications. Sage publications, London (2003)
7. Edwards, A., Kelly, D.: Engaged or frustrated? Disambiguating emotional state in search. In: Proceedings of the 40th International ACM SIGIR Conference on Research and Development in Information Retrieval, pp. 125–134. ACM (2017)
8. Feild, H., Allan, J.: Modeling searcher frustration. In: Proceedings from HCIR (2009)
9. Forte, A., Lampe, C.: Defining, understanding, and supporting open collaboration: lessons from the literature. Am. Behav. Sci. **57**(5, SI), 535–547 (2013)
10. Fuks, H., Raposo, A., Gerosa, M.A., et al.: The 3C collaboration model. In: Encyclopedia of E-Collaboration, pp. 637–644. IGI Global (2008)
11. Gerosa, M.A., Fuks, H., Lucena, C.: Analysis and design of awareness elements in collaborative digital environments: a case study in the aulanet learning environ- ment. J. Interact. Learn. Res. **14**(3), 315 (2003)
12. Harnad, S.: To cognize is to categorize: cognition is categorization. In: Handbook of Categorization in Cognitive Science, 2nd edn, pp. 21–54. Elsevier (2017)
13. Hilbert, D.M., Redmiles, D.F.: Extracting usability information from user interface events. ACM Comput. Surv.(CSUR) **32**(4), 384–421 (2000)
14. Hinkle, D.E., Wiersma, W., Jurs, S.G.: Applied Statistics for the Behavioral Sciences, vol. 663. Houghton Mifflin College Division, Boston (2003)
15. Huvila, I.: Participatory archive: towards decentralised curation, radical user orientation, and broader contextualisation of records management. Arch. Sci. **8**(1), 15–36 (2008)
16. Keppel, G., Wickens, T.: Effect size, power, and sample size. In: Design and Analysis. A Researchers Handbook, 4th edn, pp. 159–801 (2004)
17. Kraut, R.E., Resnick, P.: Encouraging contribution to online communities. In: Building Successful Online Communities: Evidence-Based Social Design, pp. 21–76 (2011)
18. Kumar, R.: Research Methodologies: A Step-by-Step Guide for Beginners, 3rd edn. Sage Publications, London (2011)
19. Lalmas, M., O'Brien, H., Yom-Tov, E.: Measuring user engagement. Synth. Lect. Inf. Concepts Retr. Serv. **6**(4), 1–132 (2014)
20. Lankes, R.D., Silverstein, J., Nicholson, S.: Participatory networks: the library as conversation. Inf. Technol. Libr. **26**(4), 17 (2007)
21. Manly, T., Robertson, I.H.: The sustained attention to response test (SART). In: Neurobiology of Attention, pp. 337–338. Elsevier (2005)
22. Manly, T., Robertson, I.H., Galloway, M., Hawkins, K.: The absent mind: further investigations of sustained attention to response. Neuropsychologia **37**(6), 661–670 (1999)
23. Mukaka, M.M.: A guide to appropriate use of correlation coefficient in medical research. Malawi Med. J. **24**(3), 69–71 (2012)
24. O'Brien, H.L., Lebow, M.: Mixed-methods approach to measuring user experience in online news interactions. J. Assoc. Inf. Sci. Technol. **64**(8), 1543–1556 (2013)
25. O'Brien, H.L., Toms, E.G.: What is user engagement? A conceptual framework for defining user engagement with technology. J. Am. Soc. Inf. Sci. Technol. **59**(6), 938–955 (2008)
26. Oomen, J., Aroyo, L.: Crowdsourcing in the cultural heritage domain: opportunities and challenges. In: Proceedings of the 5th International Conference on Communities and Technologies, pp. 138–149. ACM (2011)
27. O'Brien, H.: Theoretical perspectives on user engagement. In: O'Brien, H., Cairns, P. (eds.) Why Engagement Matters, pp. 1–26. Springer, Cham (2016). https://doi.org/10.1007/978-3-319-27446-1_1
28. O'Brien, H., Cairns, P., Hall, M.: A practical approach to measuring user engagement with the refined user engagement scale (UES) and new UES short form. Int. J. Hum.-Comput. Stud. **112**, 28–39 (2018)

29. Radatz, J., Geraci, A., Katki, F.: IEEE standard glossary of software engineering terminology. IEEE Std **610121990**(121990), 3 (1990)

30. Robertson, I.H., Manly, T., Andrade, J., Baddeley, B.T., Yiend, J.: Oops!': performance correlates of everyday attentional failures in traumatic brain injured and normal subjects. Neuropsychologia **35**(6), 747–758 (1997)

31. Seaborn, K., Fels, D.I.: Gamification in theory and action: a survey. Int. J. Hum.-Comput. Stud. **74**, 14–31 (2015)

32. Siochi, A.C., Ehrich, R.W.: Computer analysis of user interfaces based on repetition in transcripts of user sessions. ACM Trans. Inf. Syst. (TOIS) **9**(4), 309–335 (1991)

33. Smallwood, J., et al.: Subjective experience and the attentional lapse: task engagement and disengagement during sustained attention. Conscious. Cogn. **13**(4), 657–690 (2004)

34. Smallwood, J., Obonsawin, M., Heim, D.: Task unrelated thought: the role of distributed processing. Conscious. Cogn. **12**(2), 169–189 (2003)

35. Steinmacher, I., Conte, T.U., Treude, C., Gerosa, M.A.: Overcoming open source project entry barriers with a portal for newcomers. In: Proceedings of the 38th International Conference on Software Engineering, pp. 273–284. ACM (2016)

36. Wildemuth, B.M.: The effects of domain knowledge on search tactic formulation. J. Assoc. Inf. Sci. Technol. **55**(3), 246–258 (2004)

37. Wildemuth, B.M., Oh, J.S., Marchionini, G.: Tactics used when searching for digital video. In: Proceedings of the Third Symposium on Information Interaction in Context, pp. 255–264. ACM (2010)

38. Ye, M., Janowicz, K., Mülligann, C., Lee, W.C.: What you are is when you are: the temporal dimension of feature types in location-based social networks. In: Proceedings of the 19th ACM SIGSPATIAL International Conference on Advances in Geographic Information Systems, pp. 102–111. ACM (2011)

Author Index

Printed in the United States
By Bookmasters